WORLD
MINDFULNESS

FROM THE
FOUNDING FATHERS,
EMERSON, AND THOREAU
TO YOUR
PERSONAL PRACTICE

Donald McCown
Marc S. Micozzi, M.D., Ph.D.

D1040891

Healing Arts Press
Rochester, Vermont • Toronto, Canada

Healing Arts Press
One Park Street
Rochester, Vermont 05767
www.HealingArtsPress.com

Text stock is SFI certified

Healing Arts Press is a division of Inner Traditions International

Note to Reader: *This book is intended as an informational guide. The remedies, approaches, and techniques described herein are meant to supplement, and not to be a substitute for, professional medical care or treatment. They should not be used to treat a serious ailment without prior consultation with a qualified health care professional.*

Library of Congress Cataloging-in-Publication Data
McCown, Donald.
  New World mindfulness : from the founding fathers, Emerson, and Thoreau to your personal practice / Donald McCown, Marc S. Micozzi.
      p. cm.
  Summary: "Techniques to fit mindfulness into the demands and pace of real life"—Provided by publisher.
  Includes bibliographical references (p.   ) and index.
  ISBN 978-1-59477-424-9 (pbk.) — ISBN 978-1-59477-800-1 (e-book)
  1. Meditation. 2. Attention—Religious aspects. I. Micozzi, Marc S., 1953– II. Title.
  BL624.2.M383 2012
  204'.4—dc23
                                                                    2011042583

Printed and bound in the United States by Lake Book Manufacturing
The text stock is SFI certified. The Sustainable Forestry Initiative® program promotes sustainable forest management.

10   9   8   7   6   5   4   3   2   1

Text design by Jon Desautels; text layout by Virginia Scott Bowman
This book was typeset in Garamond Premier Pro, Gill Sans, and Myriad Pro with Caslon, Helios, and Helvetica used as display typefaces

To send correspondence to the authors of this book, mail a first-class letter to the authors c/o Inner Traditions • Bear & Company, One Park Street, Rochester, VT 05767, and we will forward the communication, or contact **Don McCown** directly at **www.teachingmindfulness.com** and **Marc Micozzi** at **marcmicozzi@aol.com**.

CONTENTS

—————————— PART 3 ——————————

PUTTING DOWN THE GUIDEBOOK

FOREWORD

By Richard Lowe

This wonderful, rich, and much-needed book about mindfulness helps to expand our understanding far beyond an esoteric practice of Eastern origin. Just as the practice of mindfulness helps ground us in the reality of the here and now, this book helps ground us in the development of mindfulness itself. Weaving a fascinating history of various influences and personalities, both Eastern and Western, with current research and clinical practice, the authors document how interest in this state of consciousness has been an influential force in both cultures as well as in the current leading edge of psychotherapy.

As human beings we are often trapped in the limitations of our words. Words, after all, are merely imperfect indications of what we mean. So is the case with the word *mindfulness,* a term that is in many ways problematic. For starters there's the long-held Western belief that the mind is somehow separate from the body. What, after all, do we mean by the mind? And where is it? Is it only in the brain? How about in the belly? How about in the heart? Where does the mind actually end and the body begin? Are they actually separate? Recent fascinating research is helping us reassess this long-perceived separation and is giving us new insights about the interwoven nature of what we call mind and body.

Since the word *mind* is contained within the word *mindfulness,* it could be assumed that it involves some special way of thinking, some kind of mental "doing" instead of merely just "being." Such doing, of course, would only get one more entangled within the habitual endless chatter and web of thought. As Eckhart Tolle states this dilemma, "The problems of the mind cannot be solved on the level of the mind."[1]

Another common trap can arise from associations with certain Eastern meditative practices, particularly Buddhist practices, which may suggest that to be a good mindfulness practitioner, one must sit in a certain posture, breathe in a certain way, or follow a certain dogma. Such misconceptions can lead those attempting to explore mindfulness in this fashion to end up feeling somewhat artificial, stiff, and dissociated.

Assumptions like these create misunderstandings about the true nature of mindfulness and alienate many people who could greatly benefit from what it has to offer. It may be that "somatic mindfulness" or some other alternative wording would be more fitting, but since we are dealing with such a subtle nonverbal experience that is difficult to put into words, I suspect "mindfulness" will do.

As a psychotherapist I use somatic-based mindfulness interventions in my practice. These have grown out of my experience as a student of Sensory Awareness (which the authors mention in this book), a valuable and rich mindfulness-enhancing practice developed in the West.

Sensory Awareness offers a down-to-earth, immediate way to explore and deepen one's consciousness of the present moment. Its experiential approach involves rediscovering and deepening our innate ability to be more physically and wholeheartedly present in the moment. That is, it helps us reawaken our natural capacity for more fully embodied sensitivity and consciousness.

Charlotte Selver, who brought this work to the United States from Germany, where it was originally developed, often avoided the words *body* and *mind,* feeling that they actually undermine our sense of wholeness. Instead she preferred to use the word *organism* to speak about what it is that is conscious. As she once put it,

> Even when you go to the bathroom you can be fully present for what is happening. Each of your cells could be participating in what you happen to do or whom you happen to meet in the moment, if

you really understand the organism as a living entity that is you, if you understand that every cell has mind. Every cell is sensitive. You could say you are all mind . . . you are all intelligent.[2]

There is much affinity between this Western approach and Zen. Many years ago Suzuki Roshi, the founder of the San Francisco Zen Center, invited Charlotte to offer classes to the Zen students there to help them loosen up and become more grounded in the present moment. He was concerned that they were trying too hard to *do* Zen and in their doing were missing out on the experience of just *being*.

The study of Sensory Awareness aims to cultivate not just our ability to be more conscious of what is happening, as is common with other mindfulness practices, but also to reawaken our capacity to be more actively present and responsive to what we meet. That is, not just to be passively observant, but to be more response-able, to be more fully in a living relationship to what we meet and more embodied as the human organism that we are.

As offered in classes and in private sessions, this experiential approach leads students in attentively sensing what is happening moment to moment. Let's take an example. If you are sitting right now, is it possible to be more mindful of what you are sitting on? Just see if you can take a few moments to try out experimenting with this.

Please take your time and allow yourself to settle. Is it possible to be a little more "friendly" with what you're sitting on? What can you feel of the quality of your contact where you are sitting? Can you sense what needs to wake up in you so you can feel more connected to what is supporting you? What changes do you notice when you feel more sensitively connected to what you are sitting on? Notice if anything changes in your breathing or your posture when you sense more connection with how you are being supported. What is it to simply just *be* more fully with what you are sitting on right now? Can you allow it? And finally, what is it to be a little more mindfully awake in your bottom? Such are the ways this approach invites us to become more actively and consciously present. Not just in what we assume is mind, but all over, everywhere.

As a psychotherapist I sometimes invite clients to try out sensing experiments such as this in session with me and frequently also to explore them between sessions as "homework." Usually such experiments are designed to relate to some current issue in the therapy. My hope is that any such experimenting will help motivate clients to use mindfulness practice as an important resource for their daily lives. When clients try out experiments on their own, they usually feel more empowered to explore greater awareness and vitality in their everyday living.

I find it much more potent when the client collaborates in some way in the creation of any such experiments. I also find that an important factor in helping clients develop motivation to explore further on their own usually grows out of their experiences being led in sensing explorations in our sessions and then verbally sharing what they experience with me.

Rather than emphasizing authority or form, this way of working encourages individuals to sensitively explore their felt experiences in the now and to mindfully distinguish what is habitual from what is spontaneous. Often in the course of such explorations one may encounter parts of oneself that are rigid, numb, or flabby. Our habitually held emotions, defenses, and other attitudes live in our tissues physically, as what the followers of Wilhelm Reich call "character body armor." Such armoring as well as other unconscious dynamics can be brought into more tangible awareness through the mindfulness of sensing work, and thus can provide very important "grist for the mill," which can help the therapy to deepen.

Mindfulness itself offers a positive, self-empowering, and promising new direction for psychotherapy. It helps us realize an innate source of wisdom and sanity that lies inside each one of us. Like a compass, mindfulness offers a helpful tool to help us navigate more effectively through the many challenges that life serves up. Rather than the old psychological models based on disease and the authority of various accepted experts, it shows us that through a practice of deepening our awareness and sensitivity, we can reduce many of our bad habits and dysfunctional attitudes and enjoy a healthier life more fully grounded in the present.

The more we can sense what is happening in the here and now, the more each moment becomes more freshly alive and the more we can become our more authentic selves. Through continued practice in this way, our many neurotic, ego-driven insecurities and vanities can fall away and we can rediscover our own true nature waiting to unfold. For psychotherapists and others in the healing professions, such practice is essential. Often as therapists what is most needed is for us to be more simply grounded in the reality of being. As Sogyal Rimpoche has so wisely put it, *"Only when we have removed the harm in ourselves do we become truly useful to others."*[3]

This book helps to point the way.

RICHARD LOWE is currently the executive director of the Sensory Awareness Foundation and was the first president of the Sensory Awareness Leaders' Guild. As a student of this approach for many years with Charlotte Selver and her husband Charles Brooks, he was approved by Ms. Selver to offer this work and alternated in leading classes with her and her husband in San Francisco during the 1980s. He is coeditor of *Reclaiming Vitality and Presence,* a book about the teachings of Sensory Awareness. For more than twenty years he has been a practicing psychotherapist in the San Francisco Bay Area working with adults, couples, and children.

ACKNOWLEDGMENTS

I am grateful for all the embodied voices of teachers and colleagues that inform the practices in this book. They are responsible for all the best and I alone for all the less. Teachers Jon Kabat-Zinn, Saki Santorelli, Melissa Blacker and Florence Meleo-Meyer of the Center for Mindfulness at UMASS Medical School; Stephen Batchelor and Charles Genoud whose critical, postmodern outlook feels so right; and especially Louise Boedeker, Sensory Awareness Leader, whose voice was in my ear so often as I sat alone writing. I also thank colleagues Diane Reibel and Marc Micozzi, who helped in their own ways to shape my language and thought. And as always my wonderful spouse, Gail. My work on this book is dedicated to the memory of my mother, Patricia K. McCown.

—DON McCOWN

I dedicate this book to Don McCown and Diane Reibel of the Mindfulness Based Stress Reduction Program at the Center for Integrative Medicine at Thomas Jefferson University Hospital in Philadelphia, where I was executive director from 2002 to 2005. Our work together reflected the best and most lasting part of my tenure there.

—MARC MICOZZI

PREFACE

This is a mindfulness book for skeptics, for those who think mindfulness is an exotic Asian fad, and for those who have decided, "I just don't have the time or patience to really practice." We hope not only to change your opinion, but also to change your mind.

The book presents a case for a way of practicing mindfulness that you can understand, connect to, and stick with. We approach it in three parts.

First, we offer a short retelling of the very long story of the influence of Asian spiritual thought and practice on the everyday intellectual and bodily life in Europe and America. We look at the main streams of influence from all across Asia, particularly Hinduism, Buddhism, and Taoism. We consider the personalities involved in bringing meditative and contemplative practices into Western culture and the personalities who received the practices and made them their own. In a sense, these Westerners become main characters—even heroes—in the book. We refer again and again to such major shapers of American culture as Ralph Waldo Emerson, Henry David Thoreau, and William James. They are not in the book to represent transcendentalism or pragmatism, and we're not offering philosophical scholarship or commentary. Rather, they are here as embodied presences, to be whatever help they can be as other human beings who responded to and cared deeply about their experience in the world—and articulated it with poignancy and grace. We also consider the rising heroes of the science of meditation, giving you an overview of the dramatic (and persuasive) data on the value and benefits of mindfulness practice.

Second, we take a deep look at the most basic factors of life in the body, the mind, and the everyday world. We contemplate our often-overlooked relationship to gravity, the way the earth holds us close in a wonderful and inexorable way. We ponder the breath, as the animating force of the world and as a stabilizing power in the turmoil and flux of our inner and outer lives. And we consider the inner and outer attitudes we assume as we meet our experience in each arising moment. These explorations are meant to connect you with the potential central objects of attention in formal meditation and in all the moments after—and before.

Finally, we present a simple, ancient, and highly relevant scheme for working with your awareness in the present moment in any posture in which you find yourself. The experience of the body in any of the "four dignities" of reclining, sitting, standing, and walking can act as a catalyst for investigating and knowing "how it is" for you in the now, which is one definition of mindfulness practice. We offer instructions for formal meditations in each of the four postures, as well as suggestions for translating those practices into ongoing investigations in everyday life.

And that's it. It's in the everyday-ness of your life that you will realize the benefits of mindfulness. As you find the capacity to respond, rather than react, in the situations that challenge you. As you learn to allow the things you cannot change to simply "be there"—an ongoing element of your experience. And as you find the insights and the energy that help you make the changes that you wish to make. Everyday mindfulness is not exotic, it's not time-consuming, and it really works—as we hope you'll discover for yourself.

NOTE TO READERS ON CITATIONS AND LANGUAGE

We quote the words of Emerson, Thoreau, and William James quite often, as they are major characters and sources of inspiration for the unfolding story and the way of practicing that we offer here. Their works are deeply ingrained in American thought and common place on Americans' bookshelves as well. You may very well own many of these writings. Many have been made available over the years in editions ranging from expensive presentation bindings to economical paperbacks. They are available, as well, on free sites on the Internet. To help you make instant use of the editions you may have on hand (or may search for instantly), the references to quotations are given by chapter and/or line or paragraph number (in the Notes section). We hope that through this approach you can easily find these passages in whatever edition you have. Follow the leads. Read the surrounding context. Take the time and space to contemplate. And breathe.

In parts 2 and 3, as we begin to offer experiments and practices that you can use to explore mindfulness informally and formally, we change our language accordingly. We wish to offer you as much freedom in your experience as is possible in your encounter with written "instructions," and to help to keep your experience in the present moment. To that end, practice instructions are written in a style that may seem a little strange when you first encounter it. Much is drawn from the approaches used in "Mindfulness-Based Stress Reduction"* and the practice of "Sensory Awareness."† We use the present participle to suggest that what you're being prompted to do is happening both now and without a demand from us. (Bring*ing* your attention to the breath . . .) We have significantly reduced the use of personal pronouns such as *you* and *your,* to bring your focus to the experience of the moment rather than the "I" that is having the experience (. . . noticing sensations in the chest and abdomen . . .). Further, we offer wide-open questions that, we trust, will carry you more deeply into the practice rather than into analytical thought. (How is it for you right now?)

We hope that you will engage again and again with the practices in this book and that the language and substance will enrich, expand, and deepen your experience of new world mindfulness.

---

*Kabat-Zinn, J. "The Uses of Language and Images in Guiding Meditation Practices in MBSR." AudioRecording from 2nd Annual Conference sponsored by the Center for Mindfulness in Medicine, Health Care and Society at the University of Massachusetts Medical School. March 26, 2004.

†Selver, C., and C. V. W. Brooks. *Reclaiming Vitality and Presence: Sensory Awareness as a Practice for Life.* Berkeley: North Atlantic Books, 2007.

PART I
___

GETTING SITUATED
IN TIME AND SPACE

1

MINDFULNESS
IN EARLY AMERICA

Mindfulness is spectacularly unspectacular. It's a practice of showing up in the nitty-gritty of your life: feeling your body in this chair, your feet on this floor, as your breath moves your belly and sounds arrive at random from the next room. It's a practice of context, of being exactly where you are—the place where there's possibility, choice, and freedom—in the now.

There is also a larger context that may help in understanding just how nitty-gritty and *everyday* mindfulness practice really is: its history in the West. There is nothing new about meditative and contemplative practice, and nothing exclusively Asian, Buddhist, or otherwise exotic. Alan Watts, one of the most articulate and popular promoters of Asian spiritual traditions in America in the last great blossoming of meditative practice in the 1950s and '60s, was himself astonished at this:

> One of the most surprising things that has happened to me in my study of Eastern philosophy over the years, is to find that, as I thought I was studying something that, at first, seemed wholly foreign to the Western world, at the same time, I discovered all kinds of relatively new forms of thought and exploration of man's consciousness arising indigenously within the Western world, which in various ways paralleled the approaches of Eastern philosophy to the problems of human life.[1]

In a profound sense, mindfulness belongs to us. Looking out over the history of contemplative practice in America, you will see how homegrown insights and Asian traditions have steeped, and stewed, and blended together for many hundreds of years to yield a culture that offers us the concepts, language, and motivation to build our own unique ways of living in the now.

We might begin by reflecting on the unique experience of the silence and solitude of the early American wilderness, where walking was a necessity and a meditative practice. We might also look for antecedents in European history that influenced what arose in America.

It is possible to date a European intellectual connection to Asian spiritual thought and practice as early as the ancient Greek histories of Herodotus, Alexander the Great's Indian campaign in 327–325 BCE,[2] or the Italian poet Petrarch's description of Hindu ascetics in his *Life of Solitude,* written in 1345–47.[3] A more substantive beginning, however, would be 1784, which marks the founding by British scholars and magistrates of the Asiatic Society of Bengal, from which quickly flowed the first translations of Hindu scriptures directly from Sanskrit texts into English. Sir William Jones was the preeminent member of the group. His tireless work included translations of Kalidasa's *Sakuntala* (1789), Jayadeva's *Gitagovinda* (1792), and the influential *Institutes of Hindu Law* (1794). His early tutor in Sanskrit, Charles Wilkins, holds the distinction of making the first translation of the *Bhagavad Gita* (1785). In 1788, the group founded a journal, *Asiatik Researches,* which was widely circulated among the intelligentsia, including the second United States president (and first resident of the White House), John Adams, and the third president, Thomas Jefferson, who were enthusiastic readers and subscribers.[4] Thus, one can imagine sacred Asian texts gracing the White House library from its earliest beginnings. This flow of scholarly and objective information about Indian culture and religion began a profound shift in Europe and Early America's view of the East—"from the earlier presupposition of the East as barbarous and despotic, to a vision of an exotic and highly civilized world in its own right."[5]

The new language, ideas, images, and narratives embedded in such texts immediately touched something in poets, philosophers, and artists, particularly in England and Germany as the eighteenth century became the nineteenth. These became powerful influences on the development of American culture. In England, the Romantics embraced all things "Oriental" as a celebration of the irrational and exotic. Their use of the scriptures, stories, lyrics, and images becoming ever more available to them from Hinduism, Buddhism, Confucianism, and Islam was not discrete, but rather an amalgam. Their drive was not for a practical use of these new language elements to express insights that had been inexpressible; on the contrary, "their Orientalism was not serious [scholarship] but rather a matter of exotic settings for poems."[6] Herder, Goethe, and the Romantics who followed them in Germany found "Oriental" thought a refreshing alternative to the stifling rationality of their time. Yet, again, their usage of the new material available was not entirely pragmatic. The subsequent confounding of international relations in the nineteenth and twentieth centuries by "Orientalism" was an unforeseen serious geopolitical consequence.[7]

American Religious Tolerance: Big and Early

Right from the start, Americans were interested in Eastern religions. The great seventeenth-century puritan Cotton Mather was well-read for his time in the religions of Middle Asia—the Turkish Empire and greater India. Of course, his interest was focused on possibilities of missionary work. In contrast, at the end of the eighteenth century, one of the most inspiring figures in the nascent rapprochement with Eastern thought was Hannah Adams, a cousin of John Adams. She is credited as the first woman to make a living as a writer and as having written the first book on comparative religion in America, *A Dictionary of All Religions*, which was first published in 1784, was highly popular, and ran to several editions. The later editions contained material about Hinduism, Buddhism, Taoism, and Confucianism. A professing Christian, Adams nonetheless held herself to a principled approach in her presentations of other religions, emphasizing balance, fairness, and nonjudgment, and allowing the religions to speak for themselves. She exemplifies a spirit of openness and freedom that is one powerful current in Western culture today.[8]

The Romantics' philosophical and poetic insights could also have been expressed in the preexisting Western discourse of Christian mysticism, neo-Platonism, and Hermeticism and the charismatic movement. The use of Oriental religious discourse by a poet of spiritual power such as Novalis (Freidrich von Hardenberg) was able to suggest that the full range of both Eastern and Western varieties of religious and spiritual expression pointed to a transcendent reality, and that *all—in essence—* offered transcendental *truth*.[9] It is this last point that brings us back to early-nineteenth-century America, the Transcendentalists, and, at last, the pragmatic use of the Eastern discourses to better understand and express a personal tacit knowledge.

EMERSON, THOREAU, AND THE TRANSCENDENTALISTS

In writers such as Ralph Waldo Emerson and Henry David Thoreau, and the utopian vision of the Transcendentalist Brook Farm and other utopian communities, the influence of Eastern thought is evident.[10] Through the *Dial,* their journal, which did much to shape American transcendentalism, they brought out translations of Hindu, Buddhist, and Confucian texts, and of the Sufi poets, such as Hafiz, Rumi, and Saadi. In these "transcendentalations" a new, rich brew began to find ways to give voice to tacit experience.

Throughout this book, we will be relying on Emerson and Thoreau as natural contemplatives whose entwined literary and spiritual lives reflect experiences that demanded more pointed language than the West provided, for more explicit understanding and more elaborated communication. Their ways of articulating experience have been—and continue to be—influential in our Western, particularly American, culture. Emerson's early book,

Nature, written in 1836 *before* his deep engagement with Eastern thought, contains a description of such an experience in its first chapter:

> Crossing a bare common, in snow puddles, at twilight, under a clouded sky, without having in my thoughts any occurrence of special good fortune, I have enjoyed a perfect exhilaration. Almost I fear I think how glad I am. In the woods, too, a man casts off his years, as the snake his slough, and at what period so ever of life is always a child. In the woods, is perpetual youth. Within these plantations of God, a decorum and a sanctity reign, a perennial festival is dressed, and the guest sees not how he should tire of them in a thousand years. In the woods, we return to reason and faith. There I feel that nothing can befall me in life,—no disgrace, no calamity, (leaving me my eyes,) which nature cannot repair. Standing on the bare ground,—my head bathed by the blithe air, and uplifted into infinite space,—all mean egotism vanishes. I become a transparent eye-ball. I am nothing. I see all. The currents of the Universal Being circulate through me; I am part or particle of God.[11]

As Emerson began reading the available Oriental writings in earnest, a project that consumed him for the rest of his life, he began to distill and integrate the insights that supported his experience and vision on both a personal and a cultural scale. "For Emerson . . . the significance of Asian religions—of all human history—consists of assimilation into the present, into this individual here and now."[12] He was reading and feeling and thinking his way toward a universal, literally Unitarian religion.

It seems that Thoreau had a different project in mind, using the same materials. Where Emerson was grappling with universals and theory to make sense of the world, Thoreau was intent that particulars and practice would make sense of his own world—a perspective that is poignant today, as our culture once again integrates meditative practice through the engagement with mindfulness in health care and education. Although Thoreau only had translated texts to guide him, he did more than just *imagine* himself as an Eastern contemplative practitioner. He wrote to his friend, H. G. O. Blake, in 1849, "Rude and careless as I am, I would fain practice the yoga faithfully. . . . To some extent, and at rare intervals, even I am a yogin."[13] Thoreau offers descriptions of his experience, such as this from the "Sounds" chapter of *Walden:*

> I did not read books that first summer; I hoed beans. Nay, I often did better than this. There were times when I could not afford to sacrifice the bloom of the present moment to any work, whether of the head or hands. I love a broad margin to my life. Sometimes, in a summer morning, having taken my accustomed bath, I sat in my sunny doorway from sunrise till noon, rapt in a revery, amidst the pines and hickories and sumachs, in undisturbed solitude and still-ness, while the birds sang around or flitted noiseless through the house, until by the sun falling in at my west window, or the noise of some traveller's wagon on the distant highway, I was reminded of the lapse of time. I grew in those seasons like corn in the night, and they were for me far better than any work of my hands would have been. They were not time subtracted from my life, but so much over and above my usual allowance. I realized what the Orientals mean by contemplation and the forsaking of works.[14]

Like Emerson, Thoreau read the words of the Orientals back into his own experiences, to help express that which was inexpressible without them. A journal entry from 1851 states, "Like some other preachers—I have added my texts—(derived) from the Chinese and Hindoo scriptures—long after my discourse was written."[15] That original, inarticulate discourse of ecstasy in nature was capable of transformation with the insights he found in the translations of Jones and Wilkins. It was the here-and-now value of the new language, images, and stories that counted. An emphasis on the moment-to-moment particulars of nature and his own experience was the central concern of his later life. He became, in his own words (from his journal, February 22, no year given), a "self-appointed inspector of snow-storms and rain-storms," which is, perhaps, as cogent a description of a contemplative practitioner as any from the Eastern traditions.

AMERICA'S ENGAGEMENT WITH ASIA

While Indian and, particularly, Hindu thought have taken the prime place in the discussion so far, America's engagement with the East by the middle of the nineteenth century also included East Asian culture, with Chinese, Korean, and Japanese arts, literature, and religion—including the Buddhism of these areas—shaping the intellectual direction of an emerging American modernism.

For example, the work of Ernest Fenollosa, an American scholar of East Asian art and literature and a convert to Tendai Buddhism, brought this spirit into wider intellectual discourse.[16] Fenollosa represents a more specific, scholarly, but no less engaged use of the East by an American. A few lines from Fenollosa's poem, "East and West," his Phi Beta Kappa address at Harvard in 1892, reflect a growing need of Western thought for contemplative space. Addressing a Japanese mentor, Fenollosa says, "I've flown from my West / Like a desolate bird from a broken nest / To learn thy secret of joy and rest."[17]

At Fenollosa's death, his widow gave his unpublished studies of the Chinese written language and notebooks of translations from the classical Chinese poet Li Po to the American poet Ezra Pound, for whom a whole new world opened. Pound's Chinese translations drawn from Fenollosa's work radically transformed the art of the time. Indeed, Pound had, arguably, the most powerful influence of any single poet in shaping the poetry, not only of his modernist contemporaries, but also of the generation that would come to maturity in the middle of the twentieth century.

While Pound's use of Eastern influences was mainly stylistic, a very different sort of poet, Wallace Stevens, used his own encounter with the East—studying Buddhist texts and translating Chinese poetry with his friend, the scholar-poet Witter Bynner—to better understand and express his tacit experience.[18] Perhaps "The Snow Man," an early poem (written in 1908 and first published in 1921), suggests this.

> *One must have a smind of winter*
> *To regard the frost and the boughs*
> *Of the pine-trees crusted with snow;*

And have been cold a long time
To behold the junipers shagged with ice,
The spruces rough in the distant glitter

Of the January sun; and not to think
Of any misery in the sound of the wind,
In the sound of a few leaves,

Which is the sound of the land
Full of the same wind
That is blowing in the same bare place

For the listener, who listens in the snow,
And, nothing himself, beholds
Nothing that is not there and the nothing that is.[19]

Here is the description of an alternative, meditative stance, using an image from the poet's Connecticut landscape, and rhetoric from his East Asian studies, perhaps. Yet, it is possible that this is *also* an articulation of personal experience. Stevens did not study meditation formally, but, like Thoreau, he was a prodigious walker. In any season or weather, a perambulation of fifteen miles or so—in a business suit—was a common prelude to writing.[20] This is neatly captured in a few lines from "Notes for a Supreme Fiction." "Perhaps / The truth depends on a walk around a lake, / A composing as the body tires, a stop / To see hepatica, a stop to watch / A definition growing certain and / A wait within that certainty, a rest / In the swags of pine trees bordering the lake."[21]

A transparent eye-ball. An inspector of snowstorms. A mind of winter. These are powerful metaphors to describe experiences that became more clear and easier to describe as the authors deepened their acquaintances with the range of Eastern thought. For these individuals, there was a willingness to use whatever came to hand—from whatever culture or tradition suggested itself or was available—to understand what happens in the here and now. This stance reflects a perennial American pragmatism, which endures today in the ways that mindfulness is being taught in the mindfulness-based interventions: hatha yoga mixes with Buddhist meditation, while Sufi poetry and Native American stories illuminate teaching points, and the expressive language of the Christian and Jewish contemplative traditions hovers in the background.

This pragmatic approach is personified in William James, America's first psychologist and public philosopher, who makes a bridge from the Transcendentalists to modern thought. He was deeply influenced by Emerson, whom he knew from childhood—Henry James, Senior, his father, was a friend of Emerson. In fact, a precocious gift to the young William from his father was a complete edition of Emerson's works.[22]

William James's psychological explorations, in his seminal *Principles of Psychology,* led to his exploration of religious experience, for which he cast his net widely, in his *Varieties of Religious Experience.* He moved from psychology into philosophy, defining pragmatism, radical empiricism, and pluralism—resting everything on experience (in the moment!), and understanding that there is not a single *Truth,* or even particular *underlying* truths, but rather that there is simply *what works* in the particular situation. He understood and appreciated the resonances of his thought with Emerson's and with Buddhism, and his considerations of what he called "pure experience" sound much like Buddhist texts. Take in these lines from chapter 6 of *A Pluralistic Universe*:

> The essence of life is its continuously changing character; but our concepts are all discontinuous and fixed, and the only mode of making them coincide with life is by arbitrarily supposing positions of arrest therein. With such arrests our concepts may be made congruent. But these concepts are not parts of reality, not real positions taken by it, but suppositions rather, notes taken by ourselves, and you can no more dip up the substance of reality with them than you can dip up water with a net, however finely meshed.[23]

James's intuitive insights combined with his specific understandings and sympathies with Asian religions and particularly their ways of practice—of seeing the world in the flux of the moment—suggest him as a guide for us as we pursue everyday mindfulness. We will meet him again and again as this book unfolds.

Buddhism Comes to the Fore

Of the major traditions in the Oriental fusion, Buddhism appears to have been the least understood and the most scorned during the earlier part of the nineteenth century. Reasons include Christian defensiveness and hostile reporting from the mission field; a portrayal of Buddhist doctrines as atheistic, nihilistic, passive, and pessimistic; and even the contagious anti-Buddhist biases of the Hindu scholars who taught Sanskrit to the English translators of the Asiatic Society of Bengal.[24]

The "opening" of Japan to the United States in the 1850s, commencing with Commodore Perry's visit, and the subsequent travels, study, and writing of American artists, scholars, and sophisticates, including Ernest Fenollosa, Henry Adams (great-grandson of the aforementioned John Adams), John LaFarge, and Lafcadio Hearn (all had direct contact with Buddhism) did much to increase interest and sympathy for Buddhism. Then, the 1878 publication of *The Light of Asia,* Edwin Arnold's poetic retelling of the life of the Buddha, drawing parallels with the life of Jesus, turned interest into enthusiasm. The publication was, interestingly, facilitated by the Transcendentalist Bronson Alcott.[25] Sales estimates of between five hundred thousand and a million copies put it at a level of popularity matching, say, *Huckleberry Finn*[26] or the number-one bestseller of that time, *Ben Hur,* by retired Civil War general and adventurer Lew Wallace.

Buddhism became a new possibility for those at the bare edge of the culture who intuited the tidal shift of Christian believing that Matthew Arnold had poignantly articulated in "Dover Beach" in 1867.

> *The Sea of Faith*
> *Was once, too, at the full, and round earth's shore*
> *Lay like the folds of a bright girdle furled.*
> *But now I only hear*

Its melancholy, long, withdrawing roar,
Retreating, to the breath
Of the night-wind, down the vast edges drear
And naked shingles of the world.

For some, Buddhist belief became a formal identity. Madame Blavatsky and Henry Steele Olcott, founders of the Theosophical Society, were long engaged with Buddhism. In Ceylon in 1880, they made ritual vows in a Theravada temple to live by the five precepts and take refuge in the Buddha, the teachings, and the community. The most powerful events, however, were face-to-face encounters with Buddhist masters during the Parliament of World Religions in 1893, particularly the Theravadin Anagarika Dharmapala and the Rinzai Zen Master Soyen Shaku. Both of these teachers continued to raise interest in Buddhism through subsequent visits. In fact, Soyen Shaku bears significant responsibility for the popularization of Buddhism through the present day. The vision of Buddhism that he presented fit perfectly with the early modern scientific and moral outlooks. The themes he presented—"an embrace of science combined with the promise of something beyond it, and a universal reality in which different religions and individuals participate, but which Buddhism embodies most perfectly"—still resonate.[27] He also had a "second-generation" impact through the 1950s and '60s, as he encouraged his student and translator for the parliament visit, the articulate Zen scholar D. T. Suzuki, to maintain a dialogue with the West through visits and writing.[28]

A Prophecy about Buddhist Psychology

The Theravada Buddhist teacher Anagarika Dharmpala made an impression on Americans at the Parliament of World Religions in Chicago in 1893 and revisited the United States in the first years of the twentieth century. He came to Harvard and attended one of William James's scheduled lectures on psychology, which turned into something else entirely. James gave up his place for Dharmpala, saying something like, "You are better equipped to lecture on psychology than I." And after Dharmapala's talk James declared, "This is the psychology everybody will be studying twenty-five years from now."[29]

It is important to note that the character of Buddhist "believing" during this period was an engagement with philosophy and doctrine, a search for a replacement for the Judeo-Christian belief system that some felt was no longer sustaining. Consider that two other Buddhist bestsellers beside Arnold's *The Light of Asia* were Olcott's *Buddhist Catechism* and Paul Carus's *The Gospel of Buddha,* whose titles even reflect a Christian-style, belief-oriented approach to Buddhism. In the best Evangelical Protestant tradition comes the story of the first "Buddhist conversion" in America. In Chicago in 1893, Dharmapala was speaking on Buddhism and Theosophy to an overflow crowd in a large auditorium. At the end of the talk, Charles Strauss, a Swiss-American businessman of Jewish background, stood up from his seat in the audience and walked deliberately to the front. One can imagine the hush and expectancy. As planned in advance, he then—to use an Evangelical Protestant phrase—"accepted" Buddhism, repeating the refuge vows for all to hear.[30]

The connection of most of the two or three thousand Euro-American Buddhists and the tens of thousands of sympathizers at this time was, with a few exceptions, intellectual.[31] The popular appeal of Buddhism was as a form of *belief,* not as a form of spiritual *practice.* According to Tweed, the fascination with Buddhist believing reached a high-water mark around 1907 and declined precipitously thereafter.[32] A small nucleus of Euro-Americans interested in the academic or personal study of Buddhism maintained organizations and supported specialized publishing, but few Asian teachers stayed in the United States, and the impetus for growth was lost. Dharmapala, in 1921, wrote in a letter to an American supporter, "At one time there was some kind of activity in certain parts of the U.S. where some people took interest in Buddhism, but I see none of that now."[33] Charges by the status quo religious and cultural powers that Buddhism was passive and pessimistic—terrible sins in a culture fueling itself on activism, optimism, and progress—drowned dissenting Buddhist voices.

***

Three Buddhisms in America

It is important to note that the narrative that has shaped the discourse of mindfulness today sidelines the story of ethnic Asian Buddhism in America. Religion scholar Richard Hughes Seager describes three Buddhisms in America:

1. Old-line Asian-American Buddhism, with institutions dating back into the nineteenth century.
2. Euro-American or convert Buddhism, centered in the Westernized forms of Buddhism, often generically parsed as Zen, Tibetan, and Theravada (also known as Vipassana or Insight) Buddhism, which are centered on meditation practice; and Soka Gakkai International, an American branch of a Japanese group, which with a rich mix of Asian Americans, Euro-Americans, and substantial numbers of African Americans and Latino Americans is the most culturally diverse group, and is centered on chanting practice rather than meditation.
3. New immigrant or ethnic Buddhism, which is most easily parsed by country of origin.[34]

MEDITATION AND MASS CULTURE

In the aftermath of World War II, the applications of Eastern thought to Western experience developed a powerful momentum. The war had exposed Western soldiers, many drawn from professional life into active duty, to Asian cultures from India, Burma, and China. During the occupation of Japan, physicians, scientists, artists, and intellectuals held posts that exposed them to a culture that included the aesthetic, philosophical, and spiritual manifestations of Japanese Buddhism, particularly its Zen varieties. Some stayed to study, and East-West dialogues that had been suspended were resumed, such as those with D. T. Suzuki and Shinichi Hisamatsu.

Most important for the discourse of mind-body medicine and psychotherapy, American military psychiatrists were exposed to Japanese psychotherapy, particularly that developed by Shoma Morita, which is based on a paradox that had enormous repercussions in Western practice. Instead of attacking symptoms as in Western approaches, Morita asked his patients to allow themselves to turn toward their symptoms and fully experience them, to know them as they are.[35]

Morita therapy was of interest and intellectually available to those Westerners in Japan for two powerful reasons. First, it is a highly effective treatment for what Western practitioners would identify as anxiety-based disorders; reports of cured or improved rates greater than 90 percent are common.[36] Morita developed a diagnostic category of *shinkeishitsu* for the disorders he targeted, which he describes as anxiety disorders with hypochondriasis.[37] Second, Morita did not develop his work in cultural isolation. Working contemporaneously with Jean-Martin Charcot, James, Freud, and C. G. Jung, Morita read, referenced, and critiqued Western developments. He was particularly interested in the therapies that paralleled his own in certain ways, such as Freud's psychoanalysis, S. Weir Mitchell's nineteenth-century rest therapy (also known as the rest cure, "west cure," and nature cure), Otto Binswanger's life normalization therapy, and Paul DuBois's persuasion therapy.[38] Morita therapy integrated East and West—from an *Eastern* perspective.

While the entire regimen of Morita therapy, a four-stage, intensive, residential treatment, has rarely been used in the United States (although David Reynolds has adapted it and other Japanese therapies for the West), two of its basic insights had immediate and continuing effects.[39] The first is the paradox of turning toward rather than away from symptoms for relief. The second is the insistence on the nondual nature of the body and mind. Although the influence of Zen is easily seen in his therapy, Morita did not wish to promote a direct religious association, fearing that it might be seen as somehow less serious, exacting, and effective.[40] Paradoxically, perhaps the Zen connection actually drew the interest of the Westerners.

MEDITATIVE THOUGHT IN POST–WORLD WAR II AMERICA, FROM A TO ZEN

Zen had a double-barreled influence in America, particularly in the postwar "Zen boom" years of the 1950s and '60s, touching both the intellectual community and the popular culture. With the first barrel, it had significant impact on the serious discourse of scholars, professionals, artists, and Western religious thinkers. One person was so profoundly influential in conveying the spirit of Zen that he epitomizes this impact: D. T. Suzuki. As a young man, you'll remember, Suzuki had played a role in the Buddhist enthusiasm of the 1890s and 1900s, as translator for Soyen Shaku. Suzuki had then lived for a time in the United States, working with Paul Carus at Open Court, a publishing company specializing in Eastern thought, and had returned to Japan after a European tour, by 1909. In 1911 he married an American woman, in Japan. Many of his influential books in English were written in Japan. It was not until after World War II that Suzuki returned to the West, where he continued to write books of both scholarly and popular interest on Zen and Pure Land Buddhism, traveled and lectured extensively in the United States and Europe, maintained a voluminous correspondence, and affected an incredibly varied range of thinkers. Three short examples give a glimpse into the effects of Suzuki's Zen on intellectual discourse: Thomas Merton, John Cage, and Eric Fromm.

The Trappist monk Thomas Merton was greatly influenced by Suzuki's work, which he had first known in the 1930s before entering the monastery. An engagement with Eastern religious and aesthetic thought—particularly Zen, and particularly through Suzuki's work—shaped Merton's conception of and practice of contemplative prayer, which has had a powerful influence on Christian spiritual practice to the present day.[41] Merton began a correspondence with Suzuki in 1959, asking him to write a preface for a book of translations of the sayings of the Desert Fathers. Merton's superiors felt such collaboration in print was "inappropriate," yet in practice, they encouraged Merton to continue the dialogue with Suzuki, one telling him, "Do it but don't preach it."[42]

This stance represented a reversal of the earlier Buddhist fusion of *belief* without *practice*. The dialogue did indeed continue, each endeavoring to explore and understand Christianity and Zen from his own perspective. The relationship meant so much to Merton that, although his vocation had kept him cloistered in the Monastery of Gethsemane in Kentucky from 1941, he sought and gained permission from his abbot to meet Suzuki in New York City in 1964, Merton's first travel in twenty-three years.[43] Suzuki summed up the burden of their two long talks this way: "The most important thing is Love."[44]

The composer John Cage, who was deeply influenced by Hindu, Buddhist, and Taoist philosophy and practice, regularly attended Suzuki's lectures at Columbia University in the 1950s. His statement that in choosing to study with Suzuki he was choosing the elite ("I've always gone—insofar as I could—to the president of the company")[45] suggests the value of Suzuki's thought to him and to much of the avant garde. The Zen influence on Cage's work is captured in his conception of his musical compositions as "purposeless play" that is "not an attempt to bring order out of chaos, nor to suggest improvements in creation, but simply to wake up to the very life we are living, which is so excellent once one gets one's mind and desires out of the way and lets it act of its own accord."[46] Suzuki's expansive sense of play is reported by Cage in an anecdote: "An American lady said, 'How is it, Dr. Suzuki? We spend the evening asking you questions and nothing is decided.' Dr. Suzuki smiled and said, 'That's why I love philosophy: no one wins.'"[47]

The psychoanalyst Eric Fromm (the author of *Escape from Freedom*, about the social attraction of Fascism before and during World War II) was one of many in the psychoanalytic community of the time to be drawn by Zen and Suzuki's exposition of it. At a conference held in Mexico in 1957 titled "Zen Buddhism and Psychoanalysis," attended by about fifty psychoanalytically inclined psychiatrists and psychologists, Suzuki was a featured speaker and engaged in dialogue, particularly with Fromm and the religion scholar Richard DeMartino. A book of the lectures was published after the conference.[48] Fromm suggests that psychoanalysis and Zen both offer an answer to the suffering of contemporary people: "[T]he alienation from oneself, from one's fellow man, and from nature; the awareness that life runs out of one's hand like sand, and that one will die without having lived; that one lives in the midst of plenty and yet is joyless"[49] The answer, then, would not be a cure that removes symptoms, but rather *"the presence of well-being"*[50] (Fromm's italics). Fromm defines *well-being* as:

> to be fully born, to become what one potentially is; it means to have the full capacity for joy and for sadness or, to put it still differently, to awake from the half-slumber the average man lives in, and to be fully awake. If it is all that, it means also to be creative; that is, to react and respond to myself, to others, to everything that exists.[51]

For Fromm, the work was not just to bring the unconscious into consciousness, as Freud suggested, but rather to heal the rift between the two. What was most intriguing for Fromm in the possibilities Zen offered for such a project was *koan* practice—the use of paradoxical or nonrational questions, statements, and stories to back the student's ego-bound intellect against a wall, until the only way out is through. This process of amplifying the root contradiction of ego consciousness, leading to its overturning—*satori,* or enlightenment—was the subject of DeMartino's contribution to the conference and book. Fromm drew a parallel between this process and the work of the analyst, suggesting that the analyst should not so much interpret and explain, but rather should "take away one rationalization after another, one crutch after another, until the patient cannot escape any longer, and instead breaks through the fictions which fill his mind and experiences reality—that is, becomes conscious of something he was not conscious of before."[52]

Love, play, and well-being: it was not just Suzuki's erudition that attracted so many, it was his embodiment of what he taught. Alan Watts, the scholar-entertainer to whom we shall turn next, who got to know Suzuki at the Buddhist Lodge in London in the 1920s, described him as "about the most gentle and enlightened person I have ever known; for he combined the most complex learning with utter simplicity. He was versed in Japanese, English, Chinese, Sanskrit, Tibetan, French, Pali, and German, but while attending a meeting at the Buddhist Lodge he would play with a kitten, looking right into its Buddha nature."[53] Suzuki should have the last word on his way of being and what he wished to communicate to others.

> We cannot all be expected to be scientists, but we are so constituted by nature that we can all be artists—not, indeed, artists of special kinds, such as painters, sculptors, musicians, poets, etc., but artists of life. This profession, "artist of life" may sound new and quite odd, but in point of fact, we are all born artists of life and, not knowing it, most of us fail to be so and the result is that we make a mess of our lives, asking, "What is the meaning of life?" "Are we not facing blank nothingness?" "After living seventy-eight, or even ninety years, where do we go? Nobody knows," etc., etc. I am told that most modern men and women are neurotic on this account. *But the Zen-man can tell them that they have all forgotten that they are born artists, creative artists of life, and that as soon as they realize this fact and truth they will all be cured of neurosis or psychosis or whatever name they have for their troub*le (our italics).[54]

Certainly, such a vision of unfettered creativity and immediate relief from the pains of living would be resonant in postwar American culture.

It should be noted, however, that in the 1950s and '60s, despite his tremendous stature, Suzuki was criticized and continues to be. He is accused by the *academic* Buddhist community as a reductionist "popularizer" of Zen, and dismissed by the *practice* community as one who did not sit in meditation with enough discipline and regularity. On one hand, these may be valid charges, yet on the other, they may be significant reasons for Suzuki's influence. This was a time when Western intellectuals were in search of new rhetoric and new philosophy to help express and ground their shifting experiences and intuitions; for many, it was a time of wide-ranging dialogue, of exploring possibilities, of framing a debate, rather than a time of grounding, of digging in, of focusing on details.

Indeed, the charges might simply be moot, when Suzuki's enterprise is cast in the mode of his teacher, Soyen Shaku, or even the mode of Ralph Waldo Emerson, of attempting to universalize spiritual experience. In his dialogue with Christian mysticism, for example, Suzuki found it possible that "Christian experiences are not after all different from those of the Buddhist."[55]

2

MINDFULNESS
IN LATE AMERICA

Just as Suzuki epitomized the intellectual reach of the Zen boom, it may be possible to capture the more popular facets of the time and continue the story through the 1960s by focusing on a single character: the transplanted Englishman Alan Watts. Watts's eccentric career as a scholar-entertainer traveled a ragged arc from the 1930s to the early 1970s, along the way touching most of the important figures and movements in the meeting of Eastern and Western religious thought and practice. The arc described here is drawn with the help of his 1972 autobiography, *In My Own Way,* whose punning title suggests the paradox of sustaining a powerful public self-image in order to earn a living while discussing the dissolution of the ego, and Monica Furlong's 1986 feet-of-clay biography, whose original title, *Genuine Fake,* carries an ambiguous truth.

An intellectually precocious and sensitive religious seeker, Watts spent his early years at King's School, Canterbury, which is next to the ancient cathedral. There, the history-steeped atmosphere and rich liturgical expression cast a spell and created a love of ritual that never left him. In his adolescent years at the school, he developed an interest in Buddhism, which he was able to defend on a very high level in debates with faculty. He corresponded with Christmas Humphries, the great promoter of Buddhism and Theosophy and the founder of the Buddhist Lodge in London, who assumed the letters were from a faculty member. When they finally met,

Humphries became a mentor, providing guidance for reading and practice, and connecting Watts to other Asian scholars, including D. T. Suzuki. Watts passed up an Oxford University scholarship to, instead, study the Asian traditions that appealed to him. In 1935, Watts published his first book, *The Spirit of Zen,* a kind of guidebook to Suzuki's densely packed *Essays on Zen.* Watts's studies expanded; he came to read and write Chinese at a scholarly level, and he read deeply in Taoism, as well as in Vedanta, Christian mysticism, and C. G. Jung's psychology.

Through the Buddhist Lodge, he met Ruth Fuller Everett and her adolescent daughter Eleanor. Ruth had been a member of the ashram-cum-zoo, as Watts called it, of Pierre Bernard—known as Oom the Magnificent—who catered to the New York society ladies by teaching hatha yoga and tantrism. Through that association, she learned of Zen Buddhism, and, taking Eleanor as a traveling companion, set off for Japan. The two became the first Western women to sit in meditation in a Zen monastery. Years later, Ruth married a Zen teacher and eventually became a teacher herself. Watts and Eleanor courted, in a way, and attended meditation sessions together.

Watts's practice at the time was simply to be in the present moment, which he had learned from the independent spiritual teachers J. Krishnamurti (who called it "choiceless awareness") and G. I. Gurdjieff (who called it "constant self-remembering"). He was becoming frustrated with his inability to concentrate on the present and discussed this with Eleanor on their walk home from a session at the Buddhist Lodge. Eleanor said, "Why try to concentrate on it? What else is there to be aware of? Your memories are all in the present, just as much as the trees over there. Your thoughts about the future are also in the present, and anyhow I just love to think about the future. The present is just a constant flow, like the Tao, and there's simply no way of getting out of it."[1] That was *it.* He came to think of this as his true way of life and continued to practice in this way in various guises throughout his lifetime.

The couple married and moved to the United States, just ahead of World War II in Europe. At this point in his development, after all the resistance and protest, Watts felt drawn to try to fit himself into a vocation that made sense in the West. With his rich Anglican background, the logical choice was the priesthood of the Episcopal Church. Although he had no undergraduate degree, Watts proved the depth of his learning and entered Seabury-Western Seminary in Chicago for a two-year course of study. In his second year, his standing was so far advanced that he was excused from classes and undertook expansive theological reading in personal tutorials. His researches resulted in the book *Behold the Spirit,* which brought insights from the Eastern religions into profound dialogue with a Christianity he painted as in need of refreshment. Reviewers inside and outside the church greeted it warmly. Ordained, he was made chaplain of Northwestern University, where his feeling for ritual, his skills as a speaker, and his ability to throw a great party brought quick success. Yet tensions in his growing family and his own tendency for excess ended his career; the church in 1950 did not take extramarital affairs and divorce lightly.

Spontaneous Arising:
The Work and Practice of Sensory Awareness

In the opening years of the twentieth century, in Germany, a *Harmonische Gymnastik* teacher named Elsa Gindler was diagnosed with tuberculosis. She did not simply accept the dire prognosis given her, but rather chose to make a gentle study of her own breathing and the working of her organism. Her attitude was something like, "If this disease came by itself, it can go by itself."[2] As she simply gave her full attention to her own functioning—particularly her breathing—in each moment, she was able to find, and choose, what needed to be allowed in the body for fuller functioning. This was an indigenous form of consciousness exploration coming into the culture from an independent, highly original insight.

In a year of this quiet work, Gindler exchanged her diseased state for health, puzzling her physicians. She then began to teach—or to work with—others in this gentle, permissive way. There was no technique and, indeed, no goal for the participant but finding out "how it is" with each person in the moment. There was no real name for what she did. It was often simply referred to as "the work." Later, Gindler met the music educator Heinrich Jacoby, whose philosophy meshed with hers—he wished to carve over the door to his music school, "Here you should have fun making mistakes." The two together taught what is known in Europe as the Gindler-Jacoby work.

One Gindler student of the many who left Germany before World War II was Charlotte Selver, who began teaching the work in America. Through the 1940s and '50s she met and taught—and greatly influenced—such leading lights in the arrival of humanistic psychology as psychoanalyst Eric Fromm and Gestalt therapy founders Laura and Fritz Perls. In 1950, Fromm introduced her and the work—soon to be called Sensory Awareness—at the New School for Social Research in New York City. She was the only woman to present at Fromm's "Zen Buddhism and Psychoanalysis" conference in Mexico in 1957. And in 1963 she gave the first experiential workshop at the Esalen Institute in California.

The indigenous work was also being informed by and was informing the practice of Zen in America. Selver also met, taught, and astounded the leading lights in the nascent Zen boom, particularly Watts. Together, they presented many workshops, first in New York, later in California. Watts said of her, "She does what I only talk about." Her Zen students (who also taught her) included Paul Reps, Shunryu Suzuki Roshi, Richard Baker Roshi, and Zoketsu Norman Fischer.[3]

The influence of Sensory Awareness on the development of American spiritual practice is difficult to overestimate—a great many teachers and students have been touched. Sensory Awareness brings participants into their embodied experience with profound simplicity. In just turning the head or raising an arm with attention and without expectation, layers of conditioning may be recognized and allowed to subside. New clarity comes with exploring how posture, movement, and attitude affect the breath, how the body responds to gravity, and how energy and intention develop and manifest within.

With a new wife and no job, Watts's prospects were, indeed, uncertain as he began work on a new book, *The Wisdom of Insecurity* (1951). An influential friend, Joseph Campbell, the scholar of universal mythologies, managed to get Watts a grant from the Bollingen Foundation, funded by one of Jung's wealthy patients to support research on myth, psychology, and Oriental philosophy. The book, fueled perhaps by the indigence and indignities of his situation, brought Watts to the directness and clarity of expression that characterizes his work from here on. Here is a description of working with pain by trusting that the mind "has *give* and can *absorb* shocks like water or a cushion."[4]

> [H]ow does the mind absorb suffering? It discovers that resistance and escape—the "I" process—is a false move. The pain is inescapable, and resistance as a defense only makes it worse; the whole system is jarred by the shock. Seeing the impossibility of this course, it must act according to its nature—remain stable and absorb.
>
> . . . Seeing that there is no escape from the pain, the mind yields to it, absorbs it, and becomes conscious of just pain without any "I" feeling it or resisting it. It experiences pain in the same complete, unselfconscious way in which it experiences pleasure. Pain is the nature of this present moment, and I can only live in this moment. . . .
>
> This, however, is not an experiment to be held in reserve, as a trick, for moments of crisis. . . . This is not a psychological or spiritual discipline for self-improvement. It is simply being aware of this present experience, and realizing that you can neither define it nor divide yourself from it. There is no rule but "Look!"[5]

In no time, Watts landed on his feet. He was invited into a position at the founding of the American Academy of Asian Studies in San Francisco, a precursor of today's California Institute of Integral Studies. He also landed in creative ferment. Instead of the business people and government officials who were the anticipated students for learning Asian languages and culture, the academy drew artists, poets, and religious and philosophical thinkers who were open to the kind of exploration for which Watts and his faculty colleagues had prepared their whole lives. Students included the Beat poet Gary Snyder, with whom Watts struck up a deep friendship, Michael Murphy and Richard Price, who would found the Esalen Institute, and Locke McCorkle, who would become a force in Werner Erhard's est training. As Watts added administrative duties to his teaching, he brought in an amazing range of guest lecturers, including old friends such as D. T. Suzuki; his ex-mother-in-law Ruth Fuller Sasaki, who spoke on Zen koan practice; Pali scholar G. P. Malalasekera, Theravada Buddhist monks Pannananda and Dharmawara; and the Zen master Asahina Sogen. As the academy found its place in the community, local connections were made with Chinese and Japanese Buddhists. Through the academy, the Zen master Shunryu Suzuki came to understand the need for a Western Zen institution, later creating the San Francisco Zen Center. Watts himself spoke and gave workshops up and down the West Coast and began a relationship with the Berkeley radio station KPFA, the first community-funded station in the United States, broadcasting regularly, and appeared as well on the educational television station KQED. He was stirring what was fermenting, and that would soon distill itself as a kind of renaissance.

AND THE BEAT GOES ON

The core of the Beat writers coalesced for a moment in 1956 in San Francisco, and Jack Kerouac captured it in his novel *The Dharma Bums* (1958). Its central character is the poet and Zen student Japhy Ryder (Gary Snyder), whom the narrator, Ray Smith (Kerouac), idolizes for his "Zen lunatic" lifestyle, combining Zen discipline and aesthetics with freewheeling sensuality. One scene in the novel recounts the Six Gallery poetry reading, at which Snyder, Philip Whalen, Michael McClure, and Philip Lamantia read, and Allen Ginsberg's incantation of his poem "Howl" did, indeed, scream for a generation about the agonies of 1950s fear and conformity (and fear of conformity, and conformity as a form of dealing with fear). *The Dharma Bums,* coming fast on the heels of Kerouac's bestselling *On the Road* (published in 1957), drew a huge readership of the young and aspiring hip, who saw in Ryder/Snyder a new template for living, a chance to go beyond the confines of suburban expectations. This fueled the Zen boom from the popular culture side, prompting complaints from the Western Zen community of practitioners and academics about the authenticity of the Beat's Buddhism. Both the popular and elite outlooks drew a chastening commentary from Watts in his essay "Beat Zen, Square Zen, and Zen," as he showed that their differences arose from the same fundamental background and impulse:

> The Westerner who is attracted to Zen and who would understand it deeply must have one indispensable qualification: he must understand his own culture so thoroughly that he is no longer swayed by its premises unconsciously. He must really have come to terms with the Lord God Jehovah and with his Hebrew-Christian conscience so that he can take it or leave it without fear or rebellion. He must be free of the itch to justify himself. Lacking this, his Zen will be either "beat" or "square," either a revolt from the culture and social order or a new form of stuffiness and respectability. For Zen is above all the liberation of the mind from conventional thought, and this is something utterly different from rebellion against convention, on the one hand, or adapting to foreign conventions, on the other.[6]

Watts, already a friend and admirer of Snyder, whom he exempted from his criticisms due to Snyder's level of Zen scholarship and practice, soon came to count the rest of the Beats as friends and accepted many of them as "serious artists and disciplined yogis."[7] He had connections to many seemingly disparate worlds. There were old guard spiritual seekers, like expatriate friend Aldous Huxley (author of *Brave New World*); members of the highest circles of art, music, and literature; Asian meditation teachers from many different traditions and cultures; psychotherapists of every stripe; and the old guard bohemians, the Beats, and the students—all of whom, as the 1960s began, would come together to create a culture into which Watts was not fitted, but built.

In the revolutionary 1960s, a catalyst of the new culture was the beginning of experimentation with lysergic acid diethylamide (LSD) and other psychedelic drugs in the 1950s, and the publicity surrounding it. Huxley's descriptions of his experiences in *The Doors of Perception* (1954) were illuminating, but for Watts, it was about *embodiment*—that his once ascetic and severe "Manichean" friend had been transformed into a more sensuous and warm man made the promise real. Watts's own controlled experiments, in which he found his learning and understanding of the world's mystical traditions and meditative practices extremely helpful, resulted in powerful experiences, followed (inevitably) by enthusiastic essays and broadcasts, as well as by a book, *Joyous Cosmology: Adventures in the Chemistry of Consciousness* (1962). His position as a proponent of the drugs for experienced, disciplined explorers of consciousness helped fan interest—the more so when Watts coincidentally was given a two-year fellowship at Harvard just as Timothy Leary and Richard Alpert (later known as Ram Dass) were beginning their engagement with psychedelics there. The spread of psychedelics beyond the specialists added a key facet to what social critic Theodore Roszak, in 1969, dubbed the "counter culture." "It strikes me as obvious beyond dispute, that the interests of our college-age and adolescent young in the psychology of alienation, oriental mysticism, psychedelic drugs, and communitarian experiments comprise a cultural constellation that radically diverges from values and assumptions that have been in the mainstream of our society since at least the Scientific Revolution of the seventeenth century."[8]

Just as the 1950s Zen boom can be captured in the Fromm-Suzuki meeting in Mexico in 1957, the 1960s can, perhaps, be captured in a meeting (admittedly much larger), the "Human Be-In" in the Polo Field in Golden Gate Park, San Francisco, in 1967. A procession led by Snyder, Ginsberg, and Watts, among others, circumambulated the field as in a Hindu or Buddhist rite to open the day. Tens of thousands found their way there, dressed in colorful finery, raising banners, dropping acid, listening to the Grateful Dead, Jefferson Airplane, and Quicksilver Messenger Service, and digging the mix of the crowd; the inclusion of Leary and Alpert, political radical Jerry Rubin, Zen master Shunryu Suzuki, and activist/comedian Dick Gregory suggests the organizers' intention to unify "love and activism." The Be-In became a model for gatherings around the United States and the world. The color, light, and promise of the day were captured by Paul Kantner of Jefferson Airplane in "Won't You Try/Saturday Afternoon." The soaring harmonies and instrumental arrangement convey a fuller experience, but if you can't listen, try to visualize this stanza:

> *Saturday afternoon,*
> *Yellow clouds rising in the noon,*
> *acid, incense and balloons;*
> *Saturday afternoon,*
> *people dancing everywhere,*
> *Loudly shouting "I don't care!"*
> *It's a time for growing,*
> *and a time for knowing love.*[9]

And another shift had already begun. At the leading edge of cultural change, seekers had learned what was to be learned from psychedelic experience and were turning toward the practice of meditation. As Watts put it in his unique blend of the pontifical and the plain, "When one has received the message, one hangs up the phone."[10] Where an infrastructure for the teaching and practice of Zen Buddhism already existed, such as in San Francisco, seekers turned in that direction, following Watts and Snyder.

Another infrastructure had also been building, since 1959, using a mass marketing model to encompass much of the Western world: The Maharishi Mahesh Yogi's Transcendental Meditation (TM). This was an adaptation of Hindu mantra meditation for Western practitioners, in which the meditator brought the mind to a single pointed focus by repeating a word or phrase; in TM, the mantra was secret, potently exotic, and specially chosen for the meditator.[11] The Beatles, among many other celebrities, discovered (or were "recruited" into) TM in 1967, bringing it to prominence on the world stage. The connection seemed direct. Perhaps the psychedelic experience linked more directly to Hindu meditation than Zen, as well. Watts describes this from his own experience:

LSD had brought me into an undeniably mystical state of consciousness. But oddly, considering my absorption in Zen at the time, the flavor of these experiences was Hindu rather than Chinese. Somehow the atmosphere of Hindu mythology slid into them, suggesting at the same time that Hindu philosophy was a local form of a sort of undercover wisdom, inconceivably ancient, which everyone knows at the back of his mind but will not admit.[12]

The TM movement was able to aggressively take advantage of the publicity available to it. In 1965 there were 350 TM meditators in the United States, by 1968 there were 26,000, by 1972 there were 380,000, and by 1976 there were 826,000. (Later Deepak Chopra was able to vault onto the *New York Times* bestseller list with appropriated ancient ayurvedic wisdom by asking each of the TM meditators to buy ten copies of his first book.) The marketing strategy targeted specific populations, giving the practice and its benefits a spiritual spin, a political-change spin, or a pragmatic "self-help" spin depending on the target. The pragmatic approach, designed to reach the middle-class, middle-management heart of the market, was given impetus through scientific research into TM's physical and psychological outcomes, which subsequently captured the attention of the medical establishment.[13] The result was the development of and research on medicalized versions, such as the Relaxation Response at Harvard[14] and Clinical Standardized Meditation.[15] The factors at work here—translation into Western language and settings, popular recognition, adoption within scientific research in powerful institutions, and the use of sophisticated marketing and public relations techniques—represent a model for success in the building of new social movements.[16]

On both the substantive and popular levels, then, the market for Eastern and Eastern-inflected spiritual practices grew steadily. Looking from 1972 back to himself in 1960, Watts provides perspective on this growth:

In my work of interpreting Oriental ways to the West I was pressing a button in expectation of a buzz, but instead there was an explosion.

Others, of course, were pressing buttons on the same circuit, but I could not have believed—even in 1960—that [there would be] a national television program on yoga, that numerous colleges would be giving courses on meditation and Oriental philosophy for under-graduates, that this country would be supporting thriving Zen mon-asteries and Hindu *ashrams,* that the *I Ching* would be selling in hundreds of thousands, and that—wonder of wonders—sections of the Episcopal church would be consulting me about contemplative retreats and the use of mantras in liturgy.[17]

At the turn of the decade of the 1960s, through political dislocations, waves of immigration, and economic opportunism, new teachers from many of the Eastern traditions became available to offer instruction in the West. At the same time, Westerners of the post–World War II cohort who studied in the East, or with Eastern teachers in the West, began to find their own approaches and voices for teaching as well.

The 1970s were a time of institution building at an unprecedented scale, a time in which, for example, Buddhism in America took its essen-tial shape. Watts only flashed on this, only saw the promised land from afar. He died in 1973, at age fifty-eight, of a heart attack. His health had been in decline for some time, due to overwork and problems with alco-hol. And in that, his example was again prophetic, foreshadowing the rev-elations in the 1980s of many spiritual teachers' feet of clay.

3

AMERICA WENT
FAR TO FIND WHAT
IT LEFT AT HOME

The injunctions to relieve suffering and to live a more integrated, creative life by paying attention to what is arising in the present moment and turning toward discomfort—mindfulness and acceptance—are easily located within the three Abrahamic religions. The ones closest to home. But the encrustation of tradition and the carelessness of familiarity hide them quite well.

In Judaism, there is the marvelous text from Ecclesiastes (3:1–8), here in the King James Version, which may ring in your ears with the "To everything turn, turn, turn" motion of the chorus of the song by Pete Seeger.

> To every thing there is a season, and a time to every purpose under the heaven: a time to be born, and a time to die; a time to plant, and a time to pluck up that which is planted; a time to kill, and a time to heal; a time to break down, and a time to build up; a time to weep, and a time to laugh; a time to mourn, and a time to dance; a time to cast away stones, and a time to gather stones together; a time to embrace, and a time to refrain from embracing; a time to get, and a time to lose; a time to keep, and a time to cast away; a time to rend,

and a time to sew; a time to keep silence, and a time to speak; a time to love, and a time to hate; a time of war, and a time of peace.

There is also the tradition that everything should be blessed. Indeed, when one hears good news the blessing traditionally said is, "Blessed are you G-d, Sovereign of the Universe (who is) good and does good." On hearing bad news, such as the death of a friend or relative one says, "Blessed are you G-d, Sovereign of the Universe, true judge." Such blessings acknowledge G-d as the source of everything, good or bad.

In Christianity, the natural mode for many is to do for others, to focus outward. This "Letter to a Christian Lady" from C. G. Jung, which was made into a text for speaking by Jean Vanier, is a refreshing corrective:

> *I admire Christians,*
> *because when you see someone who is hungry or thirsty,*
> *You see Jesus.*
> *When you welcome a stranger, someone who is "strange,"*
> *you welcome Jesus.*
> *When you clothe someone who is naked, you clothe Jesus.*
> *What I do not understand, however,*
> *is that Christians never seem to recognize Jesus*
> *in their own poverty.*
> *You always want to do good to the poor outside you*
> *and at the same time you deny the poor person*
> *living inside you.*
> *Why can't you see Jesus in your own poverty,*
> *in your own hunger and thirst?*
> *In all that is "strange" inside you:*
> *in the violence and the anguish that are beyond your*
> *   control!*
> *You are called to welcome all this, not to deny its*
> *   existence,*
> *but to accept that it is there and to met Jesus there.*[1]

The Christian contemplative teacher Richard Rohr suggests that, for him, Jesus' refusal of the drugged wine as he hung on the cross is a model of the radical acceptance of what is happening in the moment.[2]

The Sufi poet Rumi makes the injunction for acceptance come alive in "The Guest House," a poem translated by Coleman Barks that has become a very common teaching:

> *This being human is a guest house.*
> *Every morning a new arrival.*
>
> *A joy, a depression, a meanness,*
> *some momentary awareness comes*
> *as an unexpected visitor.*
>
> *Welcome and entertain them all!*
> *Even if they are a crowd of sorrows,*
> *who violently sweep your house*
> *empty of its furniture,*
> *still, treat each guest honorably.*
> *He may be clearing you out*
> *for some new delight.*
>
> *The dark thought, the shame, the malice.*
> *meet them at the door laughing and invite them in.*
>
> *Be grateful for whatever comes.*
> *because each has been sent*
> *as a guide from beyond.*[3]

Buddhism in America began to grow and define itself as the '60s became the '70s—a time when a great variety of teaching and practice became available at the turn away from psychedelic culture to more disciplined and thoughtful practice began. There were a range of Eastern and Western teachers in Hindu, Buddhist, Sufi, and the independent and occult traditions. There were new takes on Western traditions such as the Jesus people or Jesus freak manifestation of Christianity or the resurgence of interest in the mysticism of Kabbalah in Judaism. Yet, in tracing the discourse of mindfulness, by far the most influential tradition was Buddhism. This turn-of-the-decade moment is a fruitful place to focus, as all of the elements at play today came into view.

This was a time of growth. For example, the San Francisco Zen Center, which had been started for Western students under the teaching of Shunryu Suzuki Roshi in 1961, expanded in 1967 to include a country retreat center at Tassajara Hot Springs, for which more than a thousand people had contributed money, By 1969, the center had moved to larger quarters in the city and had established a series of satellite locations. The Zen presence in the United States was the most well-established, while Tibetan and Theravada-derived teaching and practice infrastructures were in earlier developmental stages. It is these three generalized traditions that represent the shape that Buddhism in America has taken.

The task of characterizing and defining something that could be called American Buddhism is an enormous task, as it requires the parsing of, at minimum, two phenomena under that title. Charles S. Prebish suggests that two approximate divisions, Asian immigrant Buddhism and American convert Buddhism, can be informative. He notes, however, that there is considerable disagreement among researchers about how and if such distinctions can be made.[4] For our purposes it might reasonably be said that the former group is more interested in preserving religious and community traditions, while the latter is more interested in transforming religious traditions for an elite population.

American convert Buddhism is the preserve of an elite. This is indisputable and is an extremely important factor in the development of the popularity of mindfulness in medicine and mental health care. The group of Western practitioners is highly educated, economically advantaged, politically and socially liberal, and overwhelmingly of European descent. This was as true of the crowd at the Parliament of World Religions in 1893, as it was of the students and intellectuals who made the shift from psychedelic experience to meditative experience, and as it is now of the professionals exploring the roots of alternative medicine. Indeed, there is continuity, not just of types, but of persons.[5]

The signal characteristic of the American converts is a focus on meditation, almost to the exclusion of other forms of Buddhist practice and expression.[6] It is not surprising, then, that the expressions of world Buddhism they have "imported" for their use (as Nattier would characterize it)[7] are the meditation-rich Zen, Tibetan, and Theravada-derived traditions. A quick overview of the development and essential practice of each in the United States may be of value.

Zen was the first wave and the "boom" of Buddhism in America. In keeping with the elite nature of American interest, the highly aristocratic Rinzai sect, represented by Soyen Shaku and D. T. Suzuki, was influential until the 1960s. Rinzai emphasizes koan practice leading to satori or *kensho*—concentrating on a paradoxical question or story to heighten intensity and anxiety until a breakthrough occurs. This is central in the dialogues of D. T. Suzuki, Eric Fromm, and Richard DeMartino, for example.

In the '60s, however, the Soto Zen sect, which is far more popular in Japan, began to reach out of the Japanese-American communities to American converts. Two of the most important figures in this shift, and in the development of Buddhism in America, are from this community: Shunryu Suzuki and Taizan Maezumi. Maezumi Roshi founded the Zen Center of Los Angeles in 1967 to reach Western students. He was in the Harada-Yasutani lineage, which includes koan practice and significant intensity and push for enlightenment. Two Western teachers were also part of this lineage and began their teaching at this same period: Robert Aitken founded the Diamond Sangha in Hawaii in 1959, and Philip Kapleau founded the Rochester Zen Center in 1966. Suzuki Roshi, of the San Francisco Zen Center, was of a more traditional Soto lineage and presented an approach that must have clashed with what most of his students would have read or known about Zen. His focus was not on enlightenment, but on what he presented as the heart of the matter, just sitting. That is, "Our zazen is just to be ourselves. We should not expect anything—just be ourselves and continue this practice forever."[8] Zen in its original Chinese form, Chan, as well as Korean (Son) and Vietnamese (Thien) forms, arrived much later than Japanese Zen in the United States.

Yet, teachers such as the Korean Seung Sahn and the Vietnamese Thich Nhat Hahn have had significant influences on Buddhism in America—particularly the "genuine witness" of "engaged Buddhism" advocate Nhat Hahn, who was nominated for the Nobel Peace Prize by Martin Luther King for his peace work during the Vietnam War.

The foundational teachers mentioned here have authorized others to carry on their lineages of teaching. These teachers have often gone on to found their own centers. Some have hewn closely to their teachers' approaches, while others have continued to make adaptations to bring Zen to more Americans. To suggest the flavor of this process, in the Maezumi line, John Daido Loori founded Zen Mountain Monastery in Mt. Tremper, New York, keeping more toward traditional monastic training, yet creating a highly advanced computer-based communications and marketing infrastructure. Bernard Glassman Roshi, Maezumi's heir, has extended not simply Zen training, but also a deeply felt social engagement, from highly successful initiatives to bring education and employment opportunities to the homeless in Yonkers to the founding of the Zen Peacemaker Order.[9] In Kapleau's line, Toni Packer, who had been his successor in Rochester, became disillusioned by the traditional hierarchy and protocols and left that all behind to form an independent center with a Zen spirit all but devoid of the tradition—including that of lineage.[10]

If it were possible to characterize "typical" Zen practice, one might see most of the following protocols for meeting teachers and entering and leaving meditation halls, including bowing; chanting, often in the original Asian language; ceremonial marking of changes in status, anniversaries of events, and the like; and a meditative engagement with manual work around the center.[11] Central to Zen is the sitting practice, *zazen,* in which the adherence to correct physical posture is considered extremely important. Initial instruction may be to count one's breaths—say, to ten—and when the attention has wandered, to just notice that this has happened and begin the count again. When the capacity for concentration has grown, one may begin *shikantaza,* "just sitting" with full awareness, without directing the mind.[12] Retreats, or *sesshins,* are intensely focused on sitting meditation, with short periods of walking meditation in between; retreats are rarely longer than seven days.

Tibetan teachers began to leave Tibet in response to the Chinese repression in the 1950s that killed or drove more than a third of the population into exile. Buddhism's central role in the culture made teachers and monastics a major target. While a few scholars had come to the United States in the '50s—notably Geshe Wangal, the first teacher of the American Buddhist scholar Robert Thurman—it was not until 1969 that Tibetan teachers reached out seriously to American students. Tarthang Tulku established the Tibetan Nyingma Meditation Center in Berkeley. The basic approach was very traditional, with students asked to undertake hundreds of thousands of prostrations, vows, and visualizations before meditation instruction is given. He also created the Human Development Training Program to teach Buddhist psychology and meditation techniques to a professional health care and mental health care audience, as well as the Nyingma Institute to support Buddhist education and study. In 1971, Kalu Rinpoche, who had been asked by the Dalai Lama to teach in North America, came first to Vancouver to start a center, and later created a center in Woodstock, New York.[13]

Chögyam Trungpa, who had escaped from Tibet to India in 1959, came to the West to study at Oxford University; during the years he spent in the United Kingdom, he moved away from the traditional monastic teaching role and eventually gave up his vows. In 1970, as a lay teacher, he came to the United States, where he had an instant effect. He had arrived after the "boom," after the Beats, but "Beat Zen" described him better than any other current phrase. Allen Ginsberg became a student, and many of the original beat contingent taught at the Naropa Institute (now Naropa University) in Boulder, Colorado, which Trungpa founded. The appeal to the counterculture was swift and far reaching. In a very short time, he created a thoroughgoing infrastructure, including a network of practice centers (now worldwide), and developed a "secular path" called Shambhala Training to make the benefits of meditation practice and Buddhist psychological insights more available. Trungpa's approach to teaching was not the traditional one, but an amalgam that included much that he had learned from his Oxford education in comparative religion as well as his wide-ranging exposure to Western psychology. He not only powerfully shaped Tibetan Buddhism in the West, he offered spiritual perceptions that had a much wider reach—particularly the idea of "spiritual materialism," which he defined in this way: "The problem is that ego can convert anything to its own use, even spirituality. Ego is constantly attempting to acquire and apply the teachings of spirituality for its own benefit."[14]

Tibetan Buddhist practice in America is richly varied; characterizing it in a paragraph is a hopeless challenge. It is the most exotic and sensual of the three traditions under consideration. The iconography and rituals are complex; the teachers are often Tibetan, rather than Westerners, as is common in the other traditions. There is considerable emphasis on textual study. The relationship of student to teachers is hierarchical and devotional. Many of the difficult issues of "belief" that are subdued in the other traditions are right at the surface in Tibetan doctrine and practice—karma, rebirth, realms of supernatural beings. And the practices themselves are guarded, only revealed by initiation, face-to-face with an authorized teacher. Vajrayana or Tantric practice, roughly conceived, includes visualization by the meditator of himself or herself as a particular enlightened being. Less traditional teachers work differently; Trungpa began his students with sitting meditation much like that of his friend Shunryu Suzuki. The *dzogchen* teachers have an approach that seems easily accessible to Western students, a formless meditation akin to shikantaza in Zen. Within the tradition, this is considered a high teaching, available only after years of preparation. In the West, however, it is offered differently. Lama Surya Das, a Westerner, explains, "One surprise is that people are a lot more prepared than one thinks. Westerners are sophisticated psychologically, but illiterate nomads (as in Tibet) are not."[15] Retreats in the Tibetan tradition may be adapted for Americans as day-long, or weeks-long, or more traditional lengths such as three months or three years.

Vipassana meditation is the latest tradition to flower in North America. It is drawn from Theravada Buddhist practice, the tradition most directly connected to the historical Buddha, and perhaps the most conservative. Theravada was an early and profound influence on the development of Buddhism in the United Kingdom and Europe, dating back to the nineteenth century, through colonial connections. In the United States, the connection came much later, in the Buddhist Vihara Society of Washington, D.C., founded in 1966, with teachers Dickwela Piyananda and Henepola Gunaratana, and also as young Americans in the Peace Corps or traveling in southern Asia in the 1960s came into contact with Theravada teachers, such as Mahasi Sayadaw, S. N. Goenka, and U Ba Khin. The influential Vipassana, or Insight, movement in the United States can be said to have begun when two of those young Americans, Joseph Goldstein and Jack Kornfield, came together to teach Vipassana at Chögyam Trungpa's request at Naropa Institute in 1974. Their connection, which also included Goldstein's friend Sharon Salzberg, another of the travelers to become a teacher, deepened. In 1975, under their leadership, the Insight Meditation Society was founded, in rural Barre, Massachusetts. It grew quickly into a major retreat center as the Insight approach found broad appeal. In 1984, Kornfield left the society for California to found Spirit Rock Meditation Center, which quickly became a second wing in American Vipassana practice.[16]

The Insight movement is the most egalitarian and least historically conditioned of the three traditions under consideration. Ritual, ceremony, and hierarchy are deemphasized, and meditation is of central importance. In contrast to Zen orderliness and Tibetan richness, there is ordinariness and a very American democratic, individualistic atmosphere. Students and teachers alike wear casual clothes and are known by first names. Teachers are less authority figures than "spiritual friends," and language is more psychological than specifically Buddhist. Vipassana is highly psychologized; in fact, many, if not a majority, of Vipassana teachers in the Insight movement are trained psychotherapists.

Meditation practice commonly includes two forms, concentration on the breath and open awareness (insight) of whatever is arising in the moment. Practices for cultivating loving kindness, as well as compassion, sympathetic joy, and equanimity, are also a part of training. Retreats are commonly ten days in length, with long days of intense practice in silence.

A typical schedule would find retreatants rising at five in the morning and moving through periods of sitting and walking (walking periods are as long as sitting periods, in contrast to the short breaks in Zen), with breaks for meals, until ten in the evening.[17]

Perhaps most important for the discourse is not the differences in these three traditions, but rather the essential similarities. Stephen Batchelor neatly summarizes:

> The distinctive goal of any Buddhist contemplative tradition is a state in which inner calm (*samatha*) is *unified* with insight (*vipassana*). Over the centuries, each tradition has developed its own methods for actualizing this state. And it is in these methods that the traditions differ, *not* in their end objective of unified calm and insight.[18]

If the 1960s and '70s were the period of foundation and growth, the 1980s and '90s could be seen as the painful passage to maturity. In the many Buddhist centers around the United States, large but intimate communities had grown up, often with charismatic leaders. In most instances, the sharp discipline of Asian monastic practice, with celibacy and renunciation at its core, had been replaced by a more casual, worldly, "extended family" types of community. As Suzuki Roshi told the San Francisco Zen Center, "You are not monks, and you are not lay people."[19] In his book *Shoes outside the Door*, Michael Downing construed this as a warning. There was no map as communities sought ways forward. Perhaps the scandals around sexuality, alcohol, finances, and power that began to plague these institutions could not have been avoided and were necessary in catalyzing change. By 1988, Kornfield could write, "Already upheavals over teacher behavior and abuse have occurred at dozens (if not the majority) of the major Buddhist and Hindu centers in America."[20] None of the three traditions was spared. A précis of a scandal from each will help illustrate the commonality of the problems and the importance of their aftermaths and resolutions.

At the San Francisco Zen Center, Suzuki Roshi appointed Richard Baker his successor, not just as abbot, but as principal authority over the entire enterprise, which included associated meditation centers and successful businesses such as Tassajara Bakery and Greens Restaurant. Following Suzuki's death in 1971, Baker held a tight rein over the institution, with little input from board members or other authorized teachers. In 1983, the board called a meeting, and the outcome was Baker taking a leave of absence. This was precipitated by an incident in which it became obvious that Baker, married himself, was having a sexual relationship with a married female student—indeed, the wife of a friend and benefactor. This was not an unprecedented situation; Baker had a considerable history of infidelities with students. There was more: in a community where the residents willingly worked long hours for low wages, Baker spent more than $200,000 in a year, drove a BMW, and had his personal spaces impeccably furnished with antiques and artwork. Further, Baker had surrounded himself with an inner circle of "courtiers" and failed to treat other senior members who had been ordained by Suzuki Roshi as valued peers. The most painful thing for the community was Baker's reaction: he did not comprehend that he had done anything wrong. More than ten years after "the apocalypse," as it came to be known, he stated, "It is as hard to say what I have learned as it is to say what happened."[21]

In Chögyam Trungpa Rinpoche's organization, excess was framed as *"crazy wisdom"* and accepted by many; in fact, failure to accept it was framed as failure to understand the teaching. Trungpa's sexual liaisons with female students, his destructive meddling in students' lives and relationships, his drunkenness, and his aggressive, even violent outbursts were well known. He was both open and unapologetic about his behavior.[22] Trungpa chose a Westerner, Osel Tendzin, as his heir. When Trungpa died in 1987, Tendzin became what amounted to supreme ruler of the enterprise, holding untouchable spiritual and executive power. In 1988, it was revealed to members that Tendzin was HIV positive, and that although he was aware of his condition, he had continued to have unprotected sex with male and female members. Not only had Tendzin known of his condition, but board members had known as well and kept silent.[23] Tendzin, at the urging of a senior Tibetan teacher, went into retreat, and died soon after.

At the end of an Insight Meditation Society retreat taught by an Asian Theravada teacher, Anagarika Munindra, a woman came forward to say that she had had sex with the teacher during the retreat. The woman had been psychologically troubled, and this had traumatized her further. The society's guiding teachers were divided as to how to handle the situation—how much to reveal publicly and how to deal with Munindra, who had returned to India. Kornfield pushed for complete disclosure and an immediate confronting of Munindra. As he put it, "If parts of one's life are quite unexamined—which was true for all of us—and something like this comes up about a revered teacher, it throws everything you've been doing for years into doubt. It's threatening to the whole scene."[24] Eventually, Kornfield was sent by the board to India to speak directly with Munindra, who agreed to apologize to the community.

In the aftermath and resolution of all of these incidents, American Buddhism lost its idealized self-image and came to the maturity it carries now. In this process common themes and practices arose. Leadership power moved away from the charismatic models, and was rationalized and distributed more widely, with checks and balances, and boards accountable for oversight. Ethics were addressed formally with statements and policies. The model of teacher-student interaction was scrutinized, and methods for diluting intensity were developed and instituted, as possible. Of course, this remains the most difficult of all relationships to manage, as meditation training carries the teacher-student dyad into areas of intimacy and power differential analogous to those in psychotherapy.

A universalizing and secularizing discourse draws together four themes. The first theme is the need for an expanded vocabulary of words, images, and ideas with which to express tacit experience. As more experience comes into shared language—verbal or nonverbal—the possibilities for teaching expand. The second theme is the drive for universalizing the experiences and the language surrounding them. This may emerge as explicitly spiritual language, as with Emerson or D. T. Suzuki, or in more secular language, as in the mindfulness-based interventions. The third theme, which is more specific, is the discovery/rediscovery of the principle of turning *toward* suffering and taking on the attitude of acceptance. This is a universal insight that is both spiritual and psychological in nature and may be talked about in either form. Thus, as the verbal (and nonverbal) discourse of mindfulness continues to expand, universalize, and secularize, the potential communicative resources for teaching expand as well. But this is only possible if the fourth theme is considered: the fact that this discourse is predominantly a product of an elite social group with significant socioeconomic advantages and a level of education that is "right off the charts."[25] As professionals and members of an elite, we teach from our own experience and give voice to it in language that may reflect our elite position. Therefore, we must continually be sensitive to, and learn from, the language of our clients, patients, and students.

One window into the possibilities of expanding discourse is suggested in the work of the postmodern theologian Don Cupitt, who undertook an exercise in "ordinary language" theology. He collected and analyzed more than 150 idiomatic expressions in English that use the term *life*. His hypothesis was that these idioms have arisen as the overall population's reaction to the shifts in religion or spirituality from the midnineteenth century onward—the era of the development of the East-West discourse under consideration. He suggests that for a great many people, *life* has become the privileged religious object. Consider, for example, the switch since the mid-twentieth century from funerals oriented toward the deceased's place in the hereafter to a "celebration of the life of" the deceased. It might be said of the deceased that "she loved life." Phrases like "the sanctity of life," "the value of life," and "the quality of life" have become current since the 1950s; in fact, in health care, there are scales to measure quality of life. And then there is the imperative phrase "get a life!" which became so popular in the 1990s: what are its implications as a spiritual phrase?

The usual rhetoric about spirituality and religion in contemporary Western culture is that it has been *secularized*. Cupitt suggests just the reverse, that ordinary life has been *sacralized*. We can trace the roots of this shift back again to the mid-nineteenth century, when Thoreau recorded this new attitude in *Walden,* as he went to the woods to "live deliberately," as he puts it. Says Cupitt:

It is clear straightaway that Thoreau is not going to live in the wilderness for any of the Old World's traditional reasons. He's not going into the desert like Elijah or Muhammad to listen out for the voice of God; he's not going like Jesus or Anthony to be tempted of the devil; and he's not going, like Wittgenstein or Kerouac, in order to seek relief for his own troubled psychology. He's going to try to find out for himself what it is to be a human being with a life to live.[26]

This attitude is of considerable importance. For example, a poem such as Mary Oliver's "The Summer Day," with the last lines, "Tell me, what is it you plan to do / With your one wild and precious life?" when dropped into the silence of a class creates a sacred space and a sacred pause for reflection. It is secular liturgy.

Another window into the further possibilities is suggested by the sociologist of religion Robert Wuthnow. In *After Heaven: Spirituality in America since the 1950s,* he maps out three approaches to spirituality that may suggest language, images, metaphors, and assumptions that will promote the connection of contemporary Americans to alternative practices.[27] The approaches he names follow the arc of the narrative of this chapter: the traditional *spirituality of dwelling,* the contemporary *spirituality of seeking,* and the emerging *spirituality of practice.*

Dwelling spirituality dominates in settled times in history, when it is possible to create stable institutions and communities, when sacred spaces for worship can be *inhabited.* The metaphor of this spirituality is a *place.* In the narrative we've been following, the hundred years from the mid-nineteenth to the mid-twentieth century were dwelling times. In America, the overwhelming majority of the population identified with Jewish or Christian tradition. Towns were small, church buildings and synagogues were central, often a " common" occupied the center of town, and one—and one's entire family—simply *belonged.* Lives were spent from infancy to funeral within a community, a place. The few people at the end of the nineteenth century who saw and felt the withdrawal of the tide of the sea of faith—the first Buddhists—were anomalous harbingers.

Seeking spirituality dominates in unsettled times, when meaning must be negotiated and all that is on offer may be explored. Wuthnow notes that a major shift was beginning in the America of the 1950s, as the culture became more fluid, complex, and threatening to individual identities. The opening to new possibilities from the East and from the culture of recovery and self-help brought new products and perspectives into the spiritual marketplace. The seeking of the 1960s and 1970s was pervasive, and continues today, as the market becomes more fragmented and the culture more unstable. *The metaphor for seeking spirituality is a journey.*

Practice spirituality is the new bright edge in the culture. In a profound way, it integrates both dwelling and seeking. It requires setting aside a sacred space/time for the practice, yet that space/time is potentially fluid. Further, practice spirituality begins to reconcile or mediate the split between dwelling and seeking. Practice encourages both discipline and wide-ranging exploration, and can be undertaken within the shelter of an organization and community or pursued independently. There is not a metaphor for practice, but rather an impulse and attitude to "live deliberately," as Thoreau and Cupitt suggest.

It is here, now, in this emerging moment, with a democratic and ethical view of spiritual teacher-student relations, a secular spirituality of life, and a drive for the paradoxical fluidity and stability of spiritual practice that alternative medical interventions are growing and evolving. With one hundred and fifty years of evolving discourse behind and within alternative thought and practice, we may finally be ready to enter into practice on our own terms.

4

ARE YOU WAITING
FOR AN INVITATION?

Today's calls, promises, and invitations for you to take up meditation practice may seem to be coming faster and from more different quarters than ever before. The calls in the popular media tell you how stressed-out you are (as if you didn't know) and how you need to "slow down" and find time to "care for yourself." We have been subtly influenced by a couple of centuries of engagement with Asian meditative and contemplative tradition. Now, those calls are coming through more clearly than ever. And people are responding.

The response is perhaps more dramatic now because of two tightly linked phenomena. First, meditative and contemplative practices, such as hatha yoga and mindfulness meditation, have been successfully *secularized.* In this latest cultural-spiritual environment, Don Cupitt suggests that "your life" is the "privileged religious object," and Robert Wuthnow indicates that practice is now more an expectation than an option. Thus, there's less drive to take on new beliefs or a new identity than there is to find a way to make sense of your everyday experience and improve your physical and psychological well-being. You no longer have to seek out an exotic teacher, visit rooms filled with strange smells and paraphernalia, or change your clothes or your name. That is, you can try something new the way Thoreau advises in the "Economy" chapter of *Walden:* "I say, beware of all enterprises that require new clothes, and not rather a new wearer of clothes. If there is not a new man, how can the new clothes be made to fit? If you have any enterprise before you, try it in your old clothes."[1] (paragraph 36)

You can easily find a yoga or meditation class at your local hospital or other medical center, or the adult education program at a high school or college near you. Your employer may even sponsor classes in such practices to help reduce employee stress and increase productivity. A therapist or counselor or even a business coach could teach you to meditate in individual sessions. If you're in school, you may find that mindfulness courses are part of the curriculum; it's a trend—from K through 12 to law school and medical school, from public schools to the Ivy League.[2]

The second phenomenon is a major driver, supporter, and product of this secularization: the scientific evidence of the effectiveness of meditative interventions in medicine and mental health care that has been amassed since 1980 and the particularly great volume of evidence—continually expanding—gathered in the twenty-first century. Figure 4.1 shows the steep "hockey-stick" curve of growth in interest in mindfulness in psychological intervention, while figure 4.2 suggests the acceleration of applications in health care.

Another way of assessing the transformative power of the information that scientists are generating is to monitor government funding of health

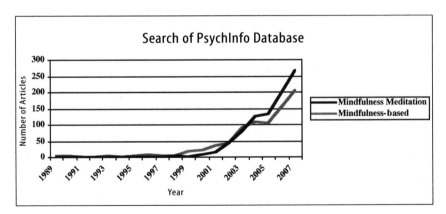

Figure 4.1. The growing use of mindfulness for mental health care applications. The number of articles reporting on and interpreting research studies about the use of mindfulness for treating psychological disorders absolutely took flight following the startling success of Mindfulness-Based Cognitive Therapy for Depression: A New Approach to Preventing Relapse, written by Segal, Williams, and Teasdale, and published in 2002.

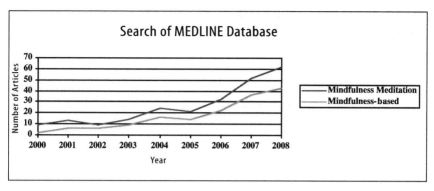

Figure 4.2. The growing use of mindfulness for medical applications. The incline of these lines demonstrates that specific mindfulness-based interventions and other clinical applications of mindfulness meditation have made their way into the mainstream in medicine.

care research up to now. Little money is spent by governments on speculative ideas; they want to fund things that they already think *work*. As study after study has suggested the effectiveness of mindfulness, the United States government, through the National Institutes of Health, has increased its willingness to invest in "randomized clinical trial" studies of mindfulness, a format for research that is considered the most objective possible, the gold standard that is used to measure the safety and effectiveness of new pharmaceuticals. At the turn of the latest century, the National Institutes of Health were funding just three studies involving mindfulness; by 2008, they were funding forty-four, both in medical and mental health care applications.[3] A selected recent list of conditions being investigated in clinical trials will give you an idea of where there is both interest and great potential for effectiveness: asthma, bone marrow transplant, breast cancer, chronic pain, chronic obstructive pulmonary disease, fibromyalgia, HIV, hot flashes, hypertension, immune response to human papilloma virus, irritable bowel syndrome, lupus, myocardial ischemia, obesity, prostate cancer, rheumatoid arthritis, solid organ transplant, type 2 diabetes, and other medical conditions, as well as psychiatric disorders, including anxiety disorders, delusional disorder, depression, drug abuse and dependence, eating disorders, personality disorders, post-traumatic stress disorder (PTSD), schizophrenia, suicidality, and more. It is fortunate for the future of mindfulness that these studies are being conducted, because in the future it is very unlikely that government funding for anything—including medical research—can possibly continue at the present levels.

The evidence for the effectiveness of mindfulness truly is exciting reading—and it's not often you can say that about statistical outcomes and medical imaging. But before we turn to look at a couple of watershed studies, we need to get a sense of how this scientific undertaking got started and how it began growing in its characteristic ways and directions.

Some Things Never Change . . .

The calls today for folks to reduce their stress and increase their wellness echo throughout history. In the nineteenth century, William James, the founder of American psychology, was one of many voices. He called particularly loudly and articulately in his lecture "The Gospel of Relaxation," reprinted in his bestselling book (which made his fortune) *Talks to Teachers on Psychology and to Students on Some of Life's Ideals*. He speaks of the American way of carrying ourselves as "bottled lightning," bringing to our attention the amplified level of bodily tension that people walk around with, he suggests, because it's a social expectation, even a social habit. He even notes its sham medical name, *Americanitis*. Maybe you can relate: do you feel like you're "on" continually, like you must always be ready to perform? Do you feel as if you never have enough time to do what needs to be done?

Here's what James has to say about this habit that we still seem to share after more than a century.

> The general over-contraction may be small when measured in foot-pounds, but its importance is immense on account of its *effects on the over-contracted person's spiritual life*. . . . [James's italics] For by the sensations that so incessantly pour in from the over-tense excited body the over-tense and excited habit of mind is kept up; and the sultry, threatening, exhausting, thunderous inner atmosphere never quite clears away. If you never wholly give yourself up to the chair you sit in, but always keep your leg- and body-muscles

half contracted for a rise; if you breathe eighteen or nineteen instead of sixteen times a minute, and never quite breathe out at that,—what mental mood *can* you be in but one of inner panting and expectancy, and how can the future and its worries possibly forsake your mind? On the other hand, how can they gain admission to your mind if your brow be unruffled, your respiration calm and complete, and your muscles all relaxed?[4]

Of course, we can look further back over more centuries—millennia, in fact—to the ancient medical traditions West and East, Hippocrates and the Yellow Emperor, say, whose efforts were often channeled to just these points: how to make the most energy free and available for healing. So, nothing new here. We're still human. We're still easily overwhelmed by the demands of our lives. And we're still looking for help.

THE START OF A PHASE

The growth of mindfulness that we've been describing has a distinct beginning—a personality, a place, and a program that stirred up our East-West cultural soup once again. Jon Kabat-Zinn, a scientist and meditator working at the University of Massachusetts Medical Center, noticed that there were patients who seemed to be falling through the cracks in the medical system. Many of them had chronic issues that they were told they would have to "live with" by their physicians. But the question that went unanswered was, "*How do I live with this?*" Kabat-Zinn's answer was the patient education program that he developed in 1979. In a stroke of marketing genius, he named it Mindfulness-Based Stress Reduction (MBSR), tying it to a phenomenon we all know and share—stress. There is no stigma to suffering from stress, since we all do it, making it easy and appealing for recruiting participants.

MBSR uses mindfulness practices to help participants "turn towards" their symptoms (stress)—towards their actual experience in the moment—and paradoxically to find relief from suffering. Together, the content of the curriculum, the range of meditative practices, the we're-all-in-this-together attitude of the group, and the non-judgmental stance of the teacher may result in profound shifts in the physical and psychological well-being of participants. Kabat-Zinn, as a scientist educated at Massachusetts Institute of Technology, made sure the shifts were not only profound, but also *measured* to provide *quantitative* evidence of MBSR's effectiveness.

Early studies showed that participants in MBSR improved significantly in their ability to live with chronic pain conditions[5] and reduced the severity and frequency of anxiety and panic attacks.[6] What's more, participants maintained their gains and continued to connect to mindfulness practice in their lives three and four years, respectively, after completing the MBSR course.[7] These kinds of dramatically positive outcomes drew attention to the MBSR program, both in medical and mental health care circles.

In 1990, Kabat-Zinn published *Full-Catastrophe Living: Using the Wisdom of Your Body and Mind to Face Stress, Pain, and Illness,* a book-length treatment of MBSR, offering a class-by-class description of the curriculum and appealing anecdotes from actual encounters in the classroom. Not much later, in 1993, MBSR got a huge boost when Bill Moyers featured Kabat-Zinn and the MBSR program on the *Healing and the Mind* public television series. Interest by medical and mental health care professionals and by the public grew dramatically thereafter. Five years after the Moyers series, more than 240 hospitals and clinics in the United States, and many in other countries, were offering MBSR programs.[8] Ten years after the series, meditation and mindfulness had climbed to new heights in cultural recognition (even acceptance), with cover features appearing in both *Time* and *Newsweek.*[9] It's no wonder that Kabat-Zinn is credited with bringing the term *mindfulness* into current use.[10]

As a result of the cultural wave, and far from being "banned in Boston," participants flocked to the MBSR courses at the University of Massachusetts and other locations around the country and the world. More important for the growth of mindfulness, professionals also arrived in droves to learn more about MBSR, and, possibly, eventually, to teach the course themselves in their own locations to their own populations of participants. At last count, more than nine thousand professionals have received some level of training in teaching MBSR through the Center for Mindfulness at the

University of Massachusetts, and training for professionals is now offered by other entities in the United States and internationally.

What Happens in MBSR Classes?

The MBSR program is a group-based, educational, and experiential course. Participants attend a two-and-one-half-hour session once a week for eight weeks, and a full-day (seven-hour) class between the sixth and seventh sessions. Class time, apart from a very few didactic presentations by the teacher on mindfulness, stress physiology, and interpersonal communication, is divided between formal meditation practice, small- and large-group dialogue, and inquiry with individual participants about their present-moment experiences.

Four formal mindfulness practices are taught:

1. **Body scan:** a lying-down practice in which you move your attention progressively through your body, dwelling with sensations as they arise and subside.

2. **Sitting meditation:** in which, when it's first introduced, you're asked to concentrate attention on the sensations of the breath entering and leaving your body, and when your practice is more established, you expand your focus of attention to include other domains of experience—body sensations, sounds, thoughts, emotions/ moods—until you're allowing "choiceless awareness" of whatever is arising in the moment.

3. **Hatha yoga:** based on simple, nonstrenuous stretches, which give you a structure for attending to your body in motion.

4. **Walking meditation:** a formal practice in which you attend to the sensations of movement while walking slowly without a destination, which can be brought easily into daily life for just a moment, from desk to water cooler, or for longer periods, helping to bridge formal and informal practice.

In addition, the curriculum offers an introduction to eating meditation in class one, a practice of compassion for self and others during the full-day session, and imaginative practices of a mountain and a lake meditation to help point out ways of relating to experience in meditation and in daily life. However, these practices are not encouraged as formal daily home practice during the eight weeks.

Class discussions, which comprise much of the class time, focus on group members' experiences in the formal meditation practices and their applications of mindfulness in daily life. Home practice is an integral part of MBSR. Participants are asked to commit to formal practice, supported by audio recordings that guide the meditations, once a day, six days a week.

The Mindfulness-Based Interventions Keep Expanding

As professionals encountered MBSR, they began to consider how they might offer the benefits of mindfulness to the populations for which they care. By starting with the basic curriculum for learning mindfulness practice that MBSR captured so well, medical and mental health practitioners were able to craft new "versions" of MBSR to target particular cohorts of people. And, of course, the new versions also were subjected to research, helping to further build up the evidence base.

One such adaptation is Mindfulness-Based Cognitive Therapy (MBCT) for prevention of relapse in major depression.[11] The developers were mental health clinicians and researchers who had come to appreciate MBSR's effectiveness and could see that there were parallels and openings for incorporation of cognitive therapy content into the curriculum as well. Once they learned the lesson that it was absolutely necessary for the teachers to have in-depth experience of mindfulness practice themselves, their work was quite successful, with MBCT participants showing a dramatically smaller rate of relapse compared to usual treatment.

The success of MBCT and its embrace by academic and clinical psychologists and other psychotherapists naturally (following the MBSR pattern) led to elaboration of MBCT-based curricula for a quickly growing list of populations and disorders. Targets include children, the elderly, stroke survivors, and people with bipolar affective disorder, conversion disorder, eating disorders, generalized anxiety disorder, suicidal behavior, and co-occurring addictive and mood disorders. MBCT, then, like MBSR, acts as a basic structure for expanding the use and visibility of mindfulness—particularly in clinical settings.

The Ongoing Elaboration of
the Mindfulness-Based Interventions

With MBSR and MBCT offering inspiration and training for medical and mental health professionals, variations to reach specific, different populations continue to be developed and researched. Here's a list that's guaranteed to be outdated:

Mindfulness-Based Stress Reduction (MBSR)[12]

Mindfulness-Based Cognitive Therapy (MBCT)[13]

Mindfulness-Based Relapse Prevention (MBRP)[14]

Mindfulness-Based Eating Awareness Training (MB-EAT)[15]

Mindfulness-Based Art Therapy (MBAT)[16]

Mindfulness-Based Relationship Enhancement (MBRE)[17]

Mindfulness-Based Childbirth and Parenting (MBCP)[18]

Mindfulness-Based You Name It (MB-ETC) (Our little joke!)

Roughly contemporary to Kabat-Zinn's development of MBSR, two other interventions were independently developed for mental health care applications: Dialectical Behavior Therapy (DBT) and Acceptance and Commitment Therapy (ACT; pronounced as the word *act,* rather than as an acronym). These two interventions also are deeply connected to mindfulness as it is defined within the Buddhist traditions, but neither one teaches formal meditation as a main practice. Rather, DBT and ACT help their participants understand and use the insights of mindfulness through very short, concrete demonstrations, stories, and metaphors. In essence, they make mindfulness accessible and possible for populations that might not find formal meditation attractive.

Dialectical Behavior Therapy

Psychologist Marsha Linehan developed DBT originally to treat chronically suicidal patients who have the symptoms of borderline personality disorder.[19] It synthesizes strategies for change from the cognitive-behavioral therapy tradition and strategies for acceptance from Eastern and Western contemplative traditions. It is a yearlong, multimodal program that incorporates weekly individual therapy and group-based skills training sessions, plus individual skills coaching by telephone when needed. The key is mindfulness: "It is both the practice of the therapist and the core skill taught to clients."[20]

The client population has difficulties complying with extended formal mindfulness practices, so mindfulness in DBT is instead taught as an interlocking set of skills through structured exercises. The first and perhaps most important of the skills is *wise mind,* which is the result of integrating two more commonly accessed states of mind, *emotion mind* and *reasonable mind.* In emotion mind, the client feels controlled by emotional reactivity, while in reasonable mind, the client can apply logic and critical thinking. Wise mind arises, then, when clients know what they feel and can think clearly about it—a capacity that DBT trusts is inherent in everyone.

The evidence base for DBT's efficacy as a discrete intervention is very strong, and, of course, it shares the evidence of the efficacy of mindfulness. DBT was one of the first manualized treatments to place mindfulness at its core. Linehan's imaginative and effective translation of formal meditation practices into easily taught skills significantly broadens the applicability of mindfulness to challenging populations.

Acceptance and Commitment Therapy

ACT, developed originally as a general approach to individual therapy that allows for brief, targeted interventions for specific issues, arises directly from within the cognitive-behavioral therapy tradition. In fact, its developer, the psychologist Steven Hayes, refers to its position as a "third wave" in cognitive-behavioral therapy.[21] ACT proposes that people suffer from psychological disorders because they become psychologically rigid. They can't think their way out of the language of their problem. The logic of a statement such as, "I can't change careers because I need to keep paying the mortgage," creates a vicious circle that never results in action. As well, people avoid the inner and outer events that cause them distress, and they often do so in harmful ways. For example, one may drink alcohol to excess to suppress painful memories, or isolate oneself to avoid social anxiety.

ACT's goal, then, is to create psychological flexibility—the capacity to turn toward and accept what each situation or moment brings and, when possible, to choose to change in the direction of one's closely held values. The core processes of the ACT model of therapy can be evenly divided between the processes for mindfulness and acceptance and the processes for commitment and behavioral change.

ACT does not include explicit meditation practices. However, it has extracted principles from meditative experience, and presents them as experiential exercises, metaphors, paradoxes, and stories. In fact, teachers within the other mindfulness-based interventions intuitively recreate or approximate many of these in their own work. So, there is a kindred sense of ACT as a mindfulness-based intervention. ACT's growing evidence base and its continually widening range of applications, including group approaches, also contribute to the overall interest in and expansion of mindfulness-based interventions.

Plus, History Is Still with Us

The use of meditation in earlier forms of psychotherapy, as we described in earlier chapters, could easily be redefined as mindfulness to fit the current context. In fact, as the media talk of meditation and mindfulness heated up in the 1990s, Mark Epstein's *Thoughts without a Thinker* was published in 1995 with the imprimatur of a foreword by the Dalai Lama, bringing a higher cultural profile to the idea that analytic psychotherapy and meditation practice are complementary, that each can provide tools and insights to make the other more fruitful.

In addition, mindfulness is historically ingrained in a panoply of other approaches to therapy, particularly those that were born or came of age in the earlier surge of interest in meditative practices in the 1950s and '60s. The privileging of present-moment experience and embodied knowing in today's mindfulness-based approaches resonates with the practice traditions of existential, Gestalt, transpersonal, humanistic, and systemic therapies, as well as the expressive and body-based therapies. All of these approaches stand to benefit from the multifaceted ways in which empirical evidence for the efficacy of mindfulness is accumulating, as well.

Quantifying the Benefits of the Mindfulness-Based Interventions

By the early 2000s, enough rigorously scientific studies had been done to allow scientists to analyze the data and begin to see what the trends in outcomes looked like. This type of research, called *meta-analysis,* was undertaken just as the interest in mindfulness started to surge—and contributed to it. Analysis of the studies that were most highly controlled showed good "effect sizes" for both mental health and physical health variables. The conclusions drawn from meta-analysis, in science-speak, are actually quite strong: "Thus far, the literature seems to clearly slant toward support for basic hypotheses concerning the effects of mindfulness on mental and physical well-being."[22] The table below shows the variables and effect sizes measured in one of the meta-analyses.

Variables	N	Mean Effect Size*
Mental health variables		
Pre-post	18	0.50
Between groups	10	0.54
Physical health variables		
Pre-post	9	0.42
Between groups	5	0.53

*At post-treatment
N = number of studies included in the meta-analysis
Between Groups (controlled studies) includes both wait-list controls (WLC) and active controls (AC).
No difference in mean effect size noted between WLC and AC.
Source: Paul Grossman et. al., 2004.

This meta-analysis by Paul Grossman and colleagues from 2004 helped to solidify the positive trend—and excitement—building in the mindfulness-based interventions. The study looked at all the most scientifically strict research that had been done. Its results revealed effect sizes that supported the idea that patients in the studies were receiving substantial benefit from participation. Effect size is a way of comparing the outcomes for treatment and control groups by considering the size of the difference between the groups, rather than the more common route of statistical significance of the outcomes.

WHAT THE EXCITEMENT IS ALL ABOUT

With just a couple of studies, you'll be able to see how this latest phase of attention to meditation is capturing the attention of both the helping professions and the popular media. The two studies we'll review here are based on work with MBSR.

The first is a rigorous scientific study that has several different points of appeal. Its subjects are not people with medical or psychological diagnoses, rather they're just employees—with work and home stress like all those who work for someone else—recruited from a corporation. Further, the study looks at three different variables that, again, concern all of us: the level of stress we're walking around with *every day,* the closer or further we are from being happy, and the potential impact of mindfulness on our health.

The researchers used questionnaires to track any changes in "trait anxiety," which we'd call stress. Then they used recordings of brain activation to track changes in "positive affect," which we'd dub happiness. What they looked for in the brain was more activation in the left anterior regions of the prefrontal cortex—left front—which has been shown to reflect a more positive "set point" for emotional response. They measured this immediately after the eight-week MBSR course and again four weeks later. Further, they expected that the immune systems of the more mindful subjects would respond more strongly to a challenge. They investigated this by giving subjects an influenza vaccination at the end of the eight weeks, and then measuring the level of antibodies generated in response at about a month and two months after the course.

Compared with the control group (who actually got to take the course later), the subjects who had been trained in mindfulness through MBSR showed significantly less trait anxiety at the end of the course and four weeks later, and also showed a significant change in their happiness set point at the two post-course measurement times. Their response to the flu vaccine was also much greater.

The study tells a very appealing story that you can reduce your stress and become happier and healthier through mindfulness.

The second study (or rather, pair of related studies) is exciting for the way it reports its findings. Certainly, there have been many studies of MBSR outcomes that show that participants feel less stressed at the end of the eight-week course, and there are many reports of an improved capacity to regulate emotions and to think more clearly and critically. However, what we find here is the association of those findings with measurable changes in the structure of the brain.

In a paper published in 2010, Hölzel and colleagues reported on images of the brains of a group of twenty-six "healthy but stressed" subjects made via magnetic resonance imaging (MRI) before and after an MBSR course.[24] The subjects reported through questionnaires that they felt less stress, and the pictures of the subjects' brains showed that there was, indeed, less gray matter (functioning brain cells) in the right amygdala (the part of the brain that is most responsible for perceiving threats and reacting to them). In 2011, the same group published another paper reporting on magnetic resonance images from sixteen healthy participants in an MBSR course.[25] This time, they saw changes in the amount of gray matter in brain regions involved in learning and memory, in regulating emotion, in relating to the self, and in taking "perspective" on experiences.

We didn't even know it was possible to change the structure of the brain until very recently. Modern medicine and science had labored under the assumption that we are born with all the brain cells we would have for life and that, other than loss, there was no possibility of change. As we've come to understand neuroscience much better—the

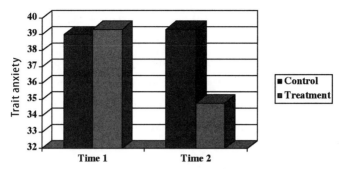

4.3a. *Reduction in mean trait anxiety. The y-axis shows the measure of trait anxiety from the Speilberger State-Trait Anxiety Inventory; increasing numbers equate to increasing anxiety. Time 1 is prior to intervention. Time 2 is immediately after the eight-week intervention.*

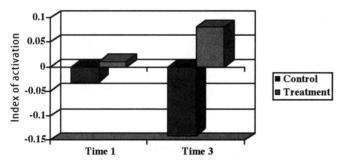

4.3b. *Means of asymmetric brain activation. Measure is a standard index of asymmetric activation—the higher the number, the greater the left-sided brain activation. Time 1 is prior to intervention. Time 3 is four months after end of eight-week intervention.*

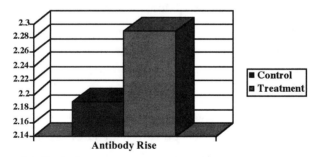

4.3c. *Means of antibody rise*

Figure 4.3. The results of a study by Davidson, Kabat-Zinn, and colleagues show that healthy subjects who completed an eight-week MBSR course reported that they were less nervous and worried day-to-day (4.3a).[23] The electrical activity in their brain showed that they had shifted their "emotional set point" more toward the positive (4.3b). And their immune systems responded more strongly to threat of infection than those of the control subjects (4.3c).

U.S. government actually named the 1990s the "decade of the brain" to encourage research—the principle of neuroplasticity (brain change) has become a focus of expanded understanding of what happens in healthy (and unhealthy) brains. This new way of measuring and talking about "real" change in our thinking and acting can perhaps help motivate us to take up mindfulness practice—and to keep at it!

IT'S TIME TO TAKE SOME PERSPECTIVE

The language of neuroscience is just one of many that we've been speaking in this chapter. We've also been using the languages of Western medicine and mental health care. All of these ways of talking about mindfulness can seem exciting, interesting, and even inspiring. Yet there is an increasing possibility that in the current cultural conversation we may be losing some valuable perspectives that are not easy to express in these languages.

In the neuroscience discussion, which includes all the beautiful color images of brains that the media love and that we find so fascinating, we may become so caught up in the new, ever-improving ability to track activity in different parts of the brain that we close down our focus on experience. What we can now see happening in the brain has *always* happened; it's just a new *description,* not a new *event.* More important, to keep our perspective, we must remember that it is just one event among an uncountable cascade of events that are just as real and important. Mindfulness practice is not just about what happens in our heads; rather, it involves body, mind, and world in infinite interconnections.

As we listen to the language of medicine and mental health care, it is easy to hear a litany of deficits, diagnoses, and disorders. Mindfulness becomes a prescription, a way to fix what is broken in you. As each new mindfulness-based intervention is rolled out, we may lose a little more perspective, a little more sense of the whole. Emerson well knew how easily this happened. In his lecture, "The Transcendentalist," he notes, "Each 'Cause' as it is called . . . becomes speedily a little shop, where the article, let it have been at first never so subtle and ethereal, is now made up into portable and convenient cakes, and retailed in small quantities to suit purchasers."[26] The professional and scientific mindfulness community is aware of this potential for loss and reduction, and individuals have been raising concerns *inside* the community. Nevertheless, with each new study or intervention, the message that goes *outside,* into the popular media and culture, is, "Look what else mindfulness can *fix.*" Mindfulness practice is not on offer here *to fix you*; you're not broken, just human. A better verb, perhaps, is *to explore.* Mindfulness practice is your ongoing opportunity to explore your experience of the moment. Not to learn "who you are," but to understand "how it is." When you know how it is, you're free, because you have a choice. You can be with how it is, or you can work to change it.

The language of professional expertise is the one speaking down to you. Because the current mindfulness-based cultural conversation was started and is maintained by a highly educated cohort of physicians, psychotherapists, academics, and other professionals, it may seem like they have the answers. After all, they have the statistics, the costly technologies, and the color pictures of things inside us that we've never seen before. Yet, that expertise is a phantom phenomenon. The practice of mindfulness is humbling—particularly for those who think they know something. Among professionals who practice and are trained in teaching mindfulness, each one would tell you that the only useful answers are *yours.*

"Right Off the Charts"

In his sociological study of American Buddhists (converts, not ethnic Buddhists), James Coleman gives us a demographic snapshot that explains how mindfulness has taken its academic and professional turn. Published in 2001, just as mindfulness began to assume a high profile in medicine and mental health care, Coleman's work shows just who is involved: more than 80 percent of American Buddhists in his survey were college graduates, over 90 percent had attended some college, and more than 50 percent held graduate degrees. As he puts it, the educational level of these folks was "right off the charts." Further, when it comes to occupation, the number of psychotherapists is second only to the number of college professors.[27]

NOW IT'S TIME FOR THE INVITATION

Although the authors are *professional experts,* we have been humbled by mindfulness practice and by watching with astonishment as clients and patients connect to what is whole and healing within their own experience and are transformed. The approach of this book, then, is a humble one. It's simply to support your mindfulness practice. There are no prescriptions. There's no pretence of expertise. There's just information that we hope will be useful, and encouragement to find out what works for you.

Certainly, we'll provide instructions for the formal mindfulness practices used in the mindfulness-based interventions. You may find that setting aside a time each day for formal practice has great appeal for you and that you want to learn more and build the formal practice into your life. That would be wonderful. Contrariwise, you may find that formal practice is not calling out to you so strongly, that you may sometimes fit it in, but that you can't build it in to your life. That's actually wonderful too.

This is a book to help you make your everyday mindfulness practice truly *every day*—as ordinary as the everyday miracles of waking up, drinking coffee, washing the dishes, or slouching on the couch. It's what you bring to any experience (or don't bring!) that makes it mindfulness practice. We're asking you to take up the invitation that all the historical figures and commentators we've considered, and all the practicing professionals as well, hold out to you: to *turn toward your life with curiosity and kindness.*

Having and/or Being

In his essay on Plato, Emerson describes it in metaphorical, yet practical, terms: "The experience of poetic creativity is not found in staying home, nor yet in travelling, but in transitions from one to the other, which must therefore be adroitly managed to present as much transitional surface as possible."

In the mindfulness-based interventions, formal home practice is considered an integral part of the course. Participants in many programs are encouraged to practice for forty-five minutes a day, six days a week. But what you ask for and what you get can be quite different. The average practice session rarely approaches the requested time, ranging from about sixteen to twenty minutes per day for sitting meditation and yoga, to thirty-one to thirty-five minutes per day for the body scan practice, versus the requested forty-five.[28] Programs that ask for less time in practice, ranging from fifteen to thirty-five minutes, actually show the same levels of relief as the programs that ask for forty-five minutes.[29]

There is no consensus in the research on the relationship between home practice duration or frequency and participant outcomes. Some have found no relationship,[30] while others have found specific correlations.[31]

Whether or not researchers find consensus on this question matters little to us. In a sense, they are asking their question in the wrong dimension. Clock-time and calendar-time only map out the horizontal dimension of *having;* they tell us nothing about the vertical dimension of *being.*[32] So, in science, you can reduce *having* a mindfulness practice to how many days, months, and years you've practiced; how often each week or day you practice; and for how many minutes you practice. But, you can't reduce a moment of *being* mindful. Clock-time only measures minutes, not moments. It may be that moments of mindfulness are what catalyze the changes researchers measure. When we punctuate our anxious, horizontal, *having* of a life with a vertical moment of being alive, possibilities abound.

PART 2

NAVIGATING
YOUR BUSY LIFE

5

YOU'RE NEVER LOST IN THE PRESENT MOMENT

Once you're determined to enter more deeply into your life and to reap the benefits of such a move, there is only one place to start, and only one time to begin. You start in your awareness. And you begin now.

Emerson, in an address titled "The Method of Nature," offers imagery that may help you to find and define the full scope and size of awareness. He suggests that you could envision experiencing your world as a rushing stream, even as a waterfall with such volume and power that its surface of cascading drops and sheets and rivulets appears smooth. Encountering this cataract without some preparation and understanding may be overwhelming, notes Emerson. "If anything could stand still, it would be crushed and dissipated by the torrent it resisted, and if it were a mind, would be crazed; as insane persons are those who hold fast to one thought and do not flow with the course of nature."[1]

Yet being overwhelmed is just one possibility in encountering the flow of experience within awareness, and Emerson immediately offers a counter-description. He calls it the "dance of the hours" and describes it as graceful, complete, and balanced in beauty. "Like an odor of incense, like a strain of music, like a sleep, it is inexact and boundless. It will not be dissected, or unravelled, or shown. . . . Known it will not be, but gladly be loved and enjoyed."[2]

In entering the vast wildness *and* stillness of awareness, then, the recommended disposition seems clear: a way of being that promises not only survival, but also joy. In this way we could notice our resistance and work with it to better "flow with the course of nature." As well, it would be a way of openness and respect for experience as it is—a way of love. Such a way is only possible, only workable, in the present moment.

We can bridge (over the rushing stream) from Emerson to Thoreau at this point. The present moment was Thoreau's great theme in his *Walden* experiment. He defines it as the line of meeting of two great eternities, the past and the future. In full transcendentalist rhetoric in the "Where I Lived, and What I Lived For" chapter, he states that "God himself culminates in the present moment."[3] In contemporary parlance, we could say that the present moment is the only time in which our life happens and in which we can share it with others. This line of meeting is easy enough to find. The challenge is finding a way to stay there.

Mindfulness practice is the attempt to "toe that line,"[4] as Thoreau put it in Walden's "Economy" chapter. Whether hoeing beans, walking the woods, reading, writing, or just sitting in the cabin's doorway throughout the morning, he kept his toes as close as he could to that moving target—providing a continual opportunity to flow with and stay open to his unfolding experience of life. We can do the same. The activities may be transposed or translated from the nineteenth to the twenty-first century, yet tending spreadsheets, walking the supermarket, cruising the Internet, cooking a meal, or sitting in traffic are just as worthy of attention and care. *No action or experience was outside Thoreau's practice, and nothing need be outside ours.*

This is a wonderful undertaking, to choose to pay attention to your ongoing experience as it rushes, falls, and dances from moment to moment. This book, from this moment on, is designed to support and guide you through the exploring, experimenting, and building of a mindfulness practice that fits your life and personality. Of course, it's also meant as a resource you may return to, again and again, to renew, adjust, and transform your practice as life flows on.

What will be helpful right at the start is to have a working (and workable) definition of mindfulness—just a little history and theory to keep your exploration grounded. Because the Buddhist description of mindfulness is relatively more clear and accessible than in other spiritual traditions, it makes sense to offer a basic set of Buddhist terms and definitions pertaining to mindfulness. And because so much of the contemporary medical, psychological, and scientific research on mindfulness is making its way into popular culture, it seems right to provide an overview of how mindfulness is defined for research and clinical applications—in secular language.

Further, because you've seen how big and wild awareness can be, we'll be presenting some tools to help you navigate it. We'll start with an overlay of three dimensions—sensation, thought, and emotion—that does not divide awareness, yet allows you to speak and reflect about your experience more easily. To help characterize these dimensions memorably, we'll enlist some of the historical figures who have eased mindfulness into our culture. Then, we'll introduce two useful instruments that we'll discuss in detail over the five following chapters: a compass and a chart. Finally, we'll describe an ancient classification scheme that can help you find ways to build mindfulness into your life, regardless of the position or posture in which you find yourself at any moment—the four meditation postures of reclining, sitting, standing, and walking.

DEFINING MINDFULNESS
IN THE BUDDHIST TRADITION

The life of the Buddha is an ancient story, enchanting in its mythic and psychic resonances, and alive in its historical reality. A prince, Siddhartha Gautama, is raised in royal retreat from the pains of the world. His father ensures that he sees only beauty and cannot witness suffering or death. Yet the prince intuits that there is more to the life of the world than satisfaction and sensual pleasure.

At last, approaching the age of thirty, he comes face-to-face with reality in the three forms of an old person, a diseased person, and a corpse. He understands that he too must come to this. Then he sees a religious ascetic, and his path opens up for him. On a day of joy, at the birth of his son, he leaves the palace to follow the ascetic disciplines in hope of transcendence.

He spends the next six years wandering. He studies every doctrine and system of thought with the wisest of teachers. He practices dramatic austerities that leave his body emaciated and broken. But he comes at last no nearer to the truth of life that he was seeking. It's up to him, alone.

He cleans himself up, eats a little, and sits down under a fig tree to work it out for himself. He does: he wakes up; the light goes on. And then he faces a challenge. How can he explain this to others? In fact, he thinks he may not bother—they'll never understand. After fifty days of sifting through what he realized, he decides that teaching is worth the risk. He begins by finding his most recent ascetic companions and bringing his experience into language for them. He speaks of the "middle path" that led to his awakening, running between his former ways of royal indulgence and extreme renunciation. He speaks of what he awoke to as four noble (or ennobling) truths.

The Four Ennobling Truths

After more than 2,500 years, it is challenging to hear the Buddha's struggle to bring his experience into words in a way that is meaningful. His first pronouncements have become tenets of belief for a billion followers today—across the many different flavors of Buddhism found worldwide. They are hallowed by time—or sometimes, hollowed out by it. A dip into history, into Dwight Goddard's *A Buddhist Bible,* first published in 1932, translates and formulates these truths this way: (1) the Noble Truth of Suffering, (2) the Noble Truth of the Origin of Suffering, (3) the Noble Truth of the Extinction of Suffering, and (4) the Noble Truth of the Path that Leads to the Extinction of Suffering.[5]

Stephen Batchelor helps resuscitate these tenets by making them the answers to a different question: not What do you believe? but What did you do, and how did you do it? as the Buddha's first audience might have asked. Framed in this way, the Buddha's first teaching is revealed as essentially relational and experiential. It is possible to imagine him actually saying, "Don't take my word for it; check it out for yourself!" Therefore,

Batchelor prefers the term *ennobling truths.*[6] The invitation is for engagement. By testing the Buddha's process, one can realize the outcome oneself and be awakened, raised up, edified, *ennobled.*

These four truths provide a flowchart for a process of investigation. The steps are interdependent.[7] The first two truths state the problem, so you could see them as a *diagnosis.* The second two truths are the resolution of the problem, so you can consider them a treatment or *prescription.* Here's the process: first, by fully understanding suffering that stems from the mind, you notice that it comes from craving. Second, this understanding suggests a "letting go" of craving. Third, when you let go, the result is a (usually very, very small) relief of suffering, that is, liberation. Fourth, this relief leads you, naturally, to want to continue to cultivate the path to liberation (see figure 5.1). That path, of course, is the Buddha's middle way, an eightfold group of moral and practical disciplines—right view, right resolve, right speech, right conduct, right livelihood, right effort, right mindfulness, and right concentration. And those last two take us right back to our practice—the development of mindfulness and concentration.

The Three Marks of Existence

Buddhism's view of the world of our experience calls out three characteristics that apply to *everything.* These "marks" are hard for many of us to see because we'd rather do just about anything than look for them. Yet, if we could bring ourselves to "turn toward" our experience and face it squarely, this is what we might report. (More likely we'd report in English, rather than in Pali, yet it may be useful to see the original terms.)

1. *Anicca* (**impermanence**): That is, *everything changes; nothing is always* there for you. You may find this true for the things you want to hold onto as well as the things that you want to wish away.
2. *Dukkha* (**unsatisfactoriness**): That is, your relationship with anything—even the most beautiful object or most exquisite experience—is ultimately unsatisfying.
3. *Anatta* (**nonself**): That is, things are not what you think. There's nothing essential or enduring that makes a chair, a chair, or even

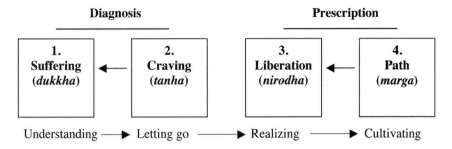

Figure 5.1. *The Four Ennobling Truths as a Process. The arrows point to relationships of cause and effect. Look at the top layer of arrows, which point from right to left. You can see that craving causes suffering, and that the path leads to liberation. Now look at the bottom layer of arrows, pointing left to right. Now you can see that understanding suffering leads to letting go of craving, which leads to realizing relief of suffering, or liberation, which in turn leads to cultivating the path. This model is not linear. It doesn't map out stages of progress. Instead, it creates a loop of integrated practice—the impulse to cultivate the path carries you right back to a deepening understanding of suffering.*[8]

that makes you, you. There's nothing essential you can put your finger on; there's just the way it is right now.

The Four Foundations of Mindfulness

The Pali term *sati* is most often translated now as "mindfulness." In the eightfold path, it is referred to as *samma-sati,* "right mindfulness." It is the instrument, so to speak, for the process of investigation suggested in the four ennobling truths. We are encouraged to cultivate mindfulness formally in the practice of meditation and informally at all times. It helps us to understand suffering, let go of craving, and experience liberation.

A word study helps to define it. *Sati* originally denoted "remembering"— not so much *recalling* the past, but *remembering* where we are and what we're doing *right now.* So it carries connotations of a kind of attention that led Buddhist scholars toward terms such as *self-possession* or *mind development.*[9]

As an overview of the attitude and practice of mindfulness, this description of "bare attention," a term used by Nyanaponika Thera, is technical and concise:

Bare Attention is the clear and single-minded awareness of what actually happens *to* us and *in* us, at the successive moments of perception. . . . Attention or mindfulness is kept to a bare registering of the facts observed, without reacting to them by deed, speech or by mental comment which may be one of self-reference (like, dislike, etc), judgement or reflection.[10]

Then the tradition goes on to prescribe what to pay attention to and how, elaborating four foundations of mindfulness.

1. **Mindfulness of body** typically begins with bare attention to the sensations of the breath, bringing the body and mind together and calming them. Then, other body sensations may be observed in all the potential postures and movements of formal practice and daily living.

2. **Mindfulness of feelings** brings bare attention to the feeling-tone of the experience of each moment. Feelings are identified as pleasant, unpleasant, or neutral and are simply observed as they arise, stay, and pass away.

3. **Mindfulness of mind** directs bare attention to the quality of the activity of the mind, registering awareness of states or dispositions, such as distraction and concentration, or one of the three roots of suffering—desire, hatred, or delusion. And these can be observed in their arising, presence, and passing away.

4. **Mindfulness of mind-objects** points bare attention toward what the mind encounters within and without. Someone once said that some religions have God, but Buddhism has lists. The fourth foundation is defined by lists, as the traditional instructions are to observe the arising and passing of the five hindrances (sense-desire, anger, sloth and torpor, agitation and worry, and doubt), the five aggregates (material form, feeling, perception, mental formations, and consciousness), the six sense factors (listed as subjective/objective: eye/form, ear/sound, nose/smell, tongue/taste, body/touch, and mind/concepts), the seven factors of enlighten-

ment (mindfulness, investigation of reality, energy, enthusiasm, tranquillity, concentration, and equanimity), and, coming around again at last, the four ennobling truths.

DEFINING MINDFULNESS
IN CONTEMPORARY PRACTICE

In the current scientific literature about mindfulness, the most commonly quoted definitions of mindfulness come, not surprisingly, from Jon Kabat-Zinn, developer of Mindfulness-Based Stress Reduction:

- "Paying attention in a particular way: on purpose, in the present moment, and non-judgmentally."[11]
- "Mindfulness meditation is a consciousness discipline revolving around a particular way of paying attention in one's life. It can be most simply described as the intentional cultivation of nonjudgmental moment-to-moment awareness."[12]

The three key elements of these definitions—intentionality, present-centeredness, and absence of judgment—align quite closely with the description of "bare attention" you just read in the Buddhist section. They are repeated and reinforced in the ongoing scientific research–oriented discussions of mindfulness, and they continue to shape the thinking, practice, and experience of the ever-changing and ever-expanding secular mindfulness community in medical centers, schools, and other venues around the world.

One deliberately science-oriented model uses the above-quoted Kabat-Zinn texts as a touchstone.[13] This model, shown graphically in figure 5.2, posits three axioms, or principles: intention, attention, and attitude. These principles are not a sequence and are not related by cause and effect, but rather are in play simultaneously in mindfulness practice. Each one captures a part of direct experience.

Intention is not simply using the will to direct attention; it also includes the motivation for initiating and continuing mindfulness

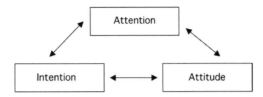

Figure 5.2. Three Axioms of Mindfulness. The three axioms of intention, attention, and attitude are not sequential, but rather are engaged simultaneously in the process of mindfulness.

practice. Such motivation is unique for each person, and over time may shift. It may begin as a need to reduce stress or deal with specific suffering, which we might call a need for self-regulation. As practice develops, the motivation may shift to focus on learning more about one's habits, reactions, and ways of encountering experience, which we might call self-exploration. Further along still, the motivation may be to free oneself from the habits and reactions that impose limits, which we might call self-liberation.

The axiom of attention refers to the capacities necessary to attend to your present-moment experience—sustained focus and flexibility of focus. Both can be cultivated through formal meditation practices. The usual sequence first emphasizes the capacity to focus, and then later opens to increase flexibility.

The axiom of attitude makes it clear that nonjudgment in secular mindfulness is not an affect-free "bare awareness," but rather an accepting, open, and kind curiosity toward one's own experience.

Attitude: The Translations of Nonjudgment

The term *nonjudgment* can sound cool and calculating, yet it is an incredibly important axiom of mindfulness as taught in the secular interventions today. It sounds passive, but it's actually active, so it has a slippery meaning that you need to grab and translate for yourself. The word and meaning you choose (and use) will shape your practice. Such words and meanings have the power to bring you closer to your own experience or, to put it another way, to expand your awareness beyond your ingrained limits.

Perhaps a translation of *nonjudgment* into "kindness" works for you, bringing a warmth and gentleness to formal and informal practice.

Or maybe the figures of *lover* and the *beloved* would add richness to the way you attend to your world. The lover wishes to know *everything* about the beloved. That openness, that willingness to be "moved" and "touched" by the presence of the beloved can help you in turning toward any experience and in sustaining your practice over time.

It may be that a different emotional tone resonates better with you. So *nonjudgment* may mean "friendliness" or "friendship" for you—making friends with how it is with you in each moment. A metaphorical (or real) smile and extended hand in greeting to whoever (or whatever) is here is a transformative disposition for formal and informal practice.

What will your translation be? Is there a word, an image, or even a person who embodies nonjudgment that you can summon when you notice that judgment has once more come to visit your experience?

In the descriptions of outcomes of mindfulness practice, a major emphasis is placed on a particular shift in the practitioner's relationship to self and experience—the awareness of an observing consciousness that is both *a part of* and *apart from* the ongoing experience.

In many scientific accounts of meditation and mindfulness, this shift has been identified as a central mechanism. Early studies in meditators identified mechanisms such as: (1) *de-automatization* of "the psychological structures that organize, limit, select and interpret perceptual stimuli";[14] (2) increased *field independence,* as evidenced by the ability to discern the hidden shapes in embedded figures tests;[15] and (3) *dehabituation* to stimuli, which Zen masters described as "constant refreshing of perception of the moment."[16] Later attempts at definition include the concept of the *observing self,*[17] and terms such as *deautomization,* in which habitual modes of perception are suspended, and *decentering,* in which a capacity to view experience from "outside" is cultivated.[18]

Kabat-Zinn uses the phrase "orthogonal rotation in consciousness," in which conventional and new dimensions coexist, and "everything old looks different because it is now being seen in a new light—an awareness that is no longer confined by the conventional dimensionality and mindset."[19] Shapiro and colleagues propose a meta-mechanism of *reperceiving* that does not create distance and disconnection from one's experience, but rather enables one to look, feel, and know more deeply.[20]

The Self in "Song of Myself"

Walt Whitman describes a mindful mode of experiencing early in his long poem "Song of Myself." In part 4, he describes the daily demands and muddle of life in work, love, family, society, and even memory and fantasy, and notes:

> Apart from the pulling and hauling stands what I am,
> Stands amused, complacent, compassionating, idle, unitary,
> Looks down, is erect, or bends an arm on an impalpable certain rest,
> Looking with side-curved head curious what will come next,
> Both in and out of the game and watching and wondering at it.

Whitman's extraordinary creative force both arises from and reflects his innate capacity for encountering his life mindfully—for being both in and out of the game. As we read his work, we feel his presence, his ongoing knowledge of how it is with him in the moment.

It is interesting that Whitman came *later* to his encounter with Eastern thought and practices. As Thoreau related to a friend, on a day when Whitman presented Thoreau with a copy of the second edition of *Leaves of Grass,* Thoreau asked if Whitman had read the "Orientals." Whitman replied, "No, tell me about them." Yet, Whitman reports that it was Emerson's work, more than any other influence, that shaped him in his beginnings as a poet—the self that wrote "Song of Myself." So, it may well have been there was a direct transmission of American mindfulness from Emerson to Whitman, or Whitman may have been an independent eruption.

As we consider this mechanism, it becomes clear that, whichever fancy term we might use, it is wonderfully practical. It's practical in just the way that the Buddha suggests and to which traditions around the world attest—it helps relieve our suffering. As humans who don't particularly like to feel hurt, we nevertheless assume the default position of "I am having this pain or this uncomfortable thought." And the "I" that is speaking is *identified* with the pain or thought. This is extremely limiting, and the well-worn ways of experiencing life that support "I *am* my pain" help to maintain the limits. And we judge the thoughts and events identified with this "I." We bring prediction, memory, and desire into the mix: this cold, hard hospital chair, this dim, unnatural lighting, this dull ache, these recurring thoughts of death, this pulse of fear—this is my world. My *little* world. There is a sense of constriction, almost a claustrophobic quality to the experience, as graphically suggested in figure 5.3.

Yet, with an "orthogonal rotation" or through "reperceiving," it becomes possible for an expansive "I" to see the constricted "I" that is suffering and to know that "I" *am not* this pain, this uncomfortable thought, or this frightening emotion. The event becomes observable. The larger "I" is a step away from the little one, suggesting an expanded space in which events can be reflected upon. What's more, if this second "I" can see the first "I," the way is opened for a third "I" to see the second seeing the first—and on back and back, like the ever-receding images created when two mirrors face each other. These observing "I's," then, are neither solid nor central. Nor are they

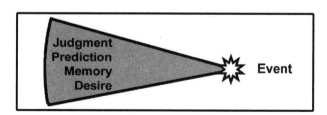

Figure 5.3. Experience before the Shift to Mindfulness. The little "I" observing an event, say a thought or a pain, identifies directly with it: "This is my pain." Judgment based on prediction, memory, and desire intensifies identification, and, in the case of pain, constricts in suffering, as the narrowness of the band suggests. Pleasant and neutral events also have this structure, yet the felt quality of the "pinch" is often less evident—at least for a time.

separate. Each is simply a temporary, albeit useful, platform for observation within a unity of awareness. After this shift of mindfulness, the constricted "I" is part of a much larger context and has room for expansion, as suggested in figure 5.4.

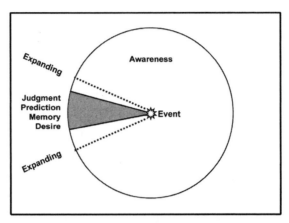

Figure 5.4. Experience after the Shift to Mindfulness. Another "I" observing the little one creates a larger context for the event and the little "I." It is a context in which awareness expands around the little "I," allowing exploration and offering space in which constriction can find relief. And, of course, that larger "I" can be seen by one in a still larger context—and on and on. (Note that the graphic convention of the circle makes a boundary where none is implied; awareness is boundless.)

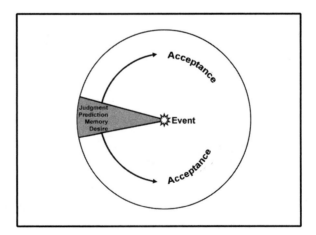

Figure 5.5. As Awareness Expands, Acceptance Becomes More Possible. The constriction of the little "I," defined by the limiting factors of judgment, prediction, memory, and desire, can be swept open through mindfulness practice. As the constriction opens into a larger and larger space of awareness, acceptance moves from possibility to actuality.

There is a space that opens as we explore, as we cultivate a capacity for observing. As we continue to work with it, the space can continue to open—to a vastness that we could call acceptance of how things are in the moment. So, in exploring our awareness with mindfulness, we are changing our relationship with our experience. You can see this happening in figures 5.5 and 5.6, which complete the sequence with the prior two figures.

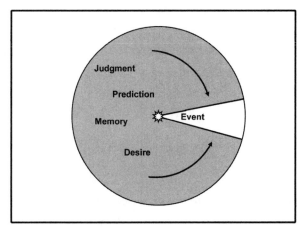

Figure 5.6. Expanding Awareness Allows Greater Ease. With the sweeping open of constriction, the space of awareness becomes a wide meadow in which the wild horse of the event—thought, sensation, and emotion—is free to run. In that boundless space, its energy, grace, and beauty become clear. Or, to use our other metaphor, when the limiting factors are dissolved as a handful of salt in a reservoir, they lose their bitterness.

Two traditional metaphors make this change of relationship clear in ways that appeal to the senses. In the first metaphor, you can see an event in awareness (particularly an unpleasant one) as a powerful animal, say a horse, restrained within a small enclosure. From up close to the fence, the bucking, rearing, and galloping are threatening— uncontrollable. Yet if you move the fences back farther and farther until the horse is in a large meadow, you gain a sense of calm—even of control. In fact, you may appreciate the grace and beauty of the horse's once-threatening actions and energy. In the second metaphor, the event in awareness is a handful of salt. If you add it to a glass of water, the taste is overwhelming. But if you throw it into a reservoir, it's undetectable. In fact, it's nothing but a tiny serving of a natural nutrient.

A TRANSPARENT
OVERLAY FOR THE AWARENESS

In practicing mindfulness formally or informally, you're bringing attention to awareness. This distinction between awareness and attention is very useful in understanding the practice. Awareness is the flow of "data" from the senses (including the conceptualizing mind—the sense that "makes sense" of experience). It is continuous and expansive—sight, sound, smell, taste, touch, naming, planning, emoting. As Emerson described, any given instant of this flow could be overwhelming. You can't take it all in, so choice is necessary. You might choose, for example, to feel the soles of your feet on the floor in this moment, leaving aside many other possibilities in current awareness. That's a clear description of an act of attention.

Mindfulness practice hews to Emerson's dictum that awareness "will not be dissected, or unraveled," yet will be "gladly loved and enjoyed." During practice, analysis is not encouraged, and judgment is swapped as much as possible for friendliness. In reflecting on experience, however, it may be helpful to invite more structured thought. What's more, if we have the opportunity to converse with others about our experience, it will be immensely valuable to have a shared grid—a set of coordinates we can use to point toward the source and course of whatever we notice.

Several senior teachers at the Center for Mindfulness at the University of Massachusetts Medical School have shared such a scheme, which they call the "triangle of awareness." The three dimensions they list—body sensation, thought, and emotion—are clear and simple. Even better, as you analyze and push the limits of any one dimension further and further, it reveals itself as overlapping and inextricably linked to the other two. So, any effort at dissection or unraveling ultimately results in an affirmation of the unity of awareness.

We will give each of the dimensions a more memorable description and a human face as we recall them through the rest of this book. We can link each of these dimensions to a historical personality involved in the introduction and diffusion of the meditative view into our popular culture and imagination. Furthermore, as we look more closely at each of these personalities, we'll come to see that, again, there is an ultimate unity—within each and among the three.

Body Sensation

Henry David Thoreau's practice, whether we consider him as writer, naturalist, or spiritual practitioner, was *walking*. For him, to walk was to enter his life, which was continuous with the life of the natural world. He was fed daily by what he experienced with his senses on his walks; the journal, poems, essays, and books all arose in walking. For sad proof, as his final illness overtook him and he could no longer take his daily walks, he ended his journal—there was nothing more to record or say.

In the essay "Walking," he makes a statement you might take to heart (and even learn by heart) for understanding the importance of the dimension of body sensation in mindfulness practice.

> In my afternoon walk I would fain forget all my morning occupations and my obligations to society. But it sometimes happens that I cannot easily shake off the village. The thought of some work will run in my head and I am not where my body is—I am out of my senses. In my walks I would fain return to my senses.[21]

Does this sound like a familiar dilemma? How often are you somewhere else, out of your senses? Yet, when you can catch up with your body—bring yourself back to what you see and touch and hear—you are suddenly, and by definition, present and mindful. The action of turning your attention to the dimension of sensation can turn your world around.

Thought

Ralph Waldo Emerson spent much more time attending to his *thoughts* than to the number of species of wildflowers in Concord's meadows or to the thickness of the ice on Walden Pond (although he was interested in those, too). From his observations he drew a powerful theme—*transition*. In the essay "Circles," he notes that everything is in motion, in nature and the mind. "[E]very moment is new; the past is always swallowed and forgotten; the coming only is sacred. Nothing is secure but life, transition, the energizing spirit."[22] He notices that when the mind settles on an idea or concept, it is immediately limited and must be unsettled for growing and flowing to continue. He says it this way (it may be a motto you'd like to consider): "I unsettle all things. I simply experiment, an endless seeker, with no past at my back."[23]

Transition is not merely a description, but as with walking for Thoreau, it is a crucial practice. You might think of the dimension of thought, as you attend to it, as a "transitional surface" on which, when judgment is abandoned, the strange may seem familiar and the familiar, strange.

Emotion

William James had little patience for the laboratory experiments favored by much of the psychology community in his day. Yet, he was, it would seem, infinitely patient in watching his own responsiveness to experience. His theory of *emotion* (The James-Lange theory, discussed in detail in chapter 9) makes the ultimate unity of awareness clear. He suggests that emotions are, first, body sensations. Here's the famous description: when we see a bear moving toward us in the woods, we have a physical reaction that includes running, breathing fast, increasing heartbeat, and maybe sweating or shaking. It is only after we've launched ourselves that we come to recognize the emotion of fear.

James invites his readers to observe what is happening with them. He did it himself, so subtly, so well, that all his descriptions are easily recognizable. So, with James, you can tune in to this dimension of emotion by noticing what is happening in your awareness.

LOOKING AT NAVIGATIONAL INSTRUMENTS AND FINDING A WAY TO GO ON

Perhaps it is becoming more obvious that the body is central to mindfulness practice. Even if we try to divide up awareness into three different dimensions, bodily experience asserts its unity again. Sensations (which we call feelings) and emotions (which we also call feelings) wrap right around thoughts (which may be about our feelings and may cause other feelings) and present us with a crushing or beautiful experience from moment to moment.

Finding your way about in such vast and shifting terrain is certainly a challenge. So, we've devised an *aid to navigation* that can help keep you oriented to the here and now (see figure 5.7). It is simple enough: a compass with cardinal directions based on *gravity* and *breath.* You know *up* and *down* through your relationship to the pull toward the center of the earth that you fight against or give in to; those two directions are trustworthy constants in your life. Gravity helps you to feel yourself in space, through what is called *proprioception.* It helps define the space you inhabit in the present moment. Most important, it will hold you, even comfort you, and asks nothing in return. You know *in* and *out* when you tune in to the breath using your sense of *interoception,* which is feeling from inside. More, the breath marks time for you. It has the capacity to bring you into the "eternal now," and can mark the passing of time as well. It is ever changing, yet always there—an inconstant constant.

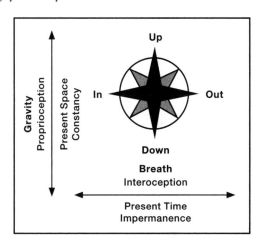

Figure 5.7. A Compass for Navigating Direct Experience. This simple instrument can be combined with the triangle of awareness to locate and approach your direct experience. You can use gravity to center your body in space, to come to a disposition of stillness and constancy. And you can use the breath to center the body in time, in the rush of the present moment. Then knowing your location at these coordinates, you have the physical and psychological freedom to look closely at the flow of sensations, thoughts, and emotions arising now.

Later, we will also introduce another aid to navigation through awareness: *disposition.* As you enter each present moment of your life, you may notice that yes, you do want to be there, or no, you don't. That yes or no may be revealed first in body sensation, thought, or emotion. (You may ultimately find it reflected in all three!) You can use your noticing of your disposition as a map, a reference to help you move closer or farther from your experience. When you know where you're located in the moment, you can determine which way you want to turn.

The final chapters are meant to help you fashion a daily (hourly, moment-to-moment) practice of mindfulness that fits the demands of your life. We'll help you apply the navigational tools to your life—which you experience in your body—as it unfolds when you are sitting, or standing, or walking, or lying down. In all these traditional meditation postures, you can enter into life in the present moment for as long or as little as you wish, to learn just how it is with you and choose how to work with it. We'll give you detailed instructions for formal practices, and hints for exploring, experimenting, and making practices of your own. Our ultimate goal is for you to be completely free when you choose to "toe the line."

As the next chapters unfold, we'll be offering thick descriptions of gravity and breathing. We'll provide facts and concepts from history, science, and spiritual practice, trusting that greater knowledge will improve your orientation. Just as Thoreau was both poet and naturalist—his journal entries lurching from invocations of the old gods to exhaustive catalogs and minute descriptions of wildflowers and trees—we will explore and explain both extremes of experience: the practice of love and enjoyment and the analysis of fact. In mindfulness, nothing is discounted, everything belongs. And to give Thoreau the last word, in "The Natural History of Massachusetts," he observes, "Let us not underrate the value of a fact; it will one day flower in a truth."[24]

6

GRAVITY

North and South on Your Compass

In 1845, Edgar Allan Poe published *The Purloined Letter,* bringing into detective fiction a marvelous device that continues to generate satisfying tales—the object hidden in plain sight. In the story, a government minister has concealed a blackmail-worthy letter somewhere in his room. The police use every method at hand to find it—disassembling every piece of furniture, paging carefully through every book, taking a microscope to every inch of the house—and ultimately coming up empty and perplexed. C. Auguste Dupin, Poe's amateur detective, with the sensibilities of both poet and mathematician, finds the letter where no one has thought to look—on the letter rack in the minister's office, hidden in plain sight. As Dupin describes the process that brought him to the discovery, he offers the narrator several analogies. This one seems helpful for our explorations. Dupin asks,

"[H]ave you ever noticed which of the street signs, over the shop doors, are the most attractive of attention?"

"I have never given the matter a thought," I said.

"There is a game of puzzles," he resumed, "which is played upon a map. One party playing requires another to find a given word—the name of town, river, state, or empire—any word, in short, upon the motley and perplexed surface of the chart. A novice in the game generally seeks to embarrass his opponents by giving them the most minutely lettered names; but the adept selects such words as stretch, in large characters, from one end of the chart to the other. These, like the overlargely lettered signs and placards on the street, escape observation by dint of being excessively obvious. . . . But this is a point, it appears, somewhat above or beneath the understanding of the Prefect [of police]. He never once thought it probable, or possible, that the Minister had deposited the letter immediately beneath the nose of the whole world by way of best preventing any portion of that world from perceiving it.

And so it is with us and gravity. The pull of the earth on our bodies is precisely under our noses. It's written in the largest possible letters over the door of our experience. It's the name of the empire that spans the edges of the map on our table. This paradox of ubiquity and invisibility makes gravity a wonder-full object of meditation and contemplation. Gravity is constant—suggesting either security or captivity, and even prompting spiritual or religious reflection. It is also defining—giving us a nearly unfailing navigational sense of up and down, a ground on which to meet each other, and a wealth of metaphors that undergird human culture and communication. And it is revealing—bringing our very aliveness into awareness, with a potential focus on the smallest and the largest of body movements and processes.

As we investigate these wonders, it may be helpful to integrate within ourselves the two sensibilities that make Dupin so insightful, those of the mathematician and the poet. As you read, see if it is possible for you to analyze and interrogate the facts and concepts presented in this chapter as you simultaneously intuit and sense your way through the experiments you'll be asked to undertake. You may come to a deeper understanding of how gravity can shape your mindfulness practice moment by moment and for your life long.

Friendly Physics

As mindfulness practitioners, we, like Poe's detective, Dupin, balance the sensibilities of poet and mathematician. So, dipping into the discipline of physics at least as far as classical mechanics can be useful in expanding our ability to put our embodied experience into language. Here's a quick overview of essential terms and concepts, as a way of opening the field of inquiry and clearing up misconceptions for working with gravity in our own quiet, personal way.

Getting the terms straight at the outset, we're concerned with gravity, not with gravitation. The term *gravitation* usually refers to the force by which all matter attracts other matter. It's not a force that would figure in our practice: human bodies have nowhere near enough mass to attract each other or a chair or a book at any discernable level. You need mass like a planet to get any action. The term *gravity,* then, refers to the force our planet exerts, drawing us and all loose change toward the center of the earth. We're continually falling, accelerating at approximately 9.81 m/sec^2. The shorthand for this familiar feeling is 1g, one gravity. The force itself is felt at a great distance; it's holding the moon in orbit. So, the experience often spoken of in manned space flight as zero gravity or micro-gravity, 0g or µg, is not escape from the pull of Earth, but rather a condition in which the effects of gravity are not in evidence because the bodies are in free fall. An orbiting vessel or object could be described as continually falling over the curve of the earth. The embodied experience of a person in such a situation is most clearly described as *weightlessness.*

On Earth, we feel our own body's apparent weight through a reaction force: the surface beneath you exerts a counterforce to your acceleration toward the center of the earth. Without this counterforce, you'd be in free fall and experiencing weightlessness. The ground, the floor, the chair in which you're sitting are keeping you from continuing your fall. They are also allowing you to feel your body's weight—that's the sensation of compression of your bottom on the seat and your feet on the floor. You can tune in to it right now, if you'll take a moment to come to quiet.

CONSTANT WONDERS

In our mindless moments, we may wander through our world less like Poe's Dupin and more like the prefect of police, with an understanding of the world that is "somewhat above or beneath" what is already in our awareness. Our body's encounter with gravity is seamless, providing no clues, no tell-tale signs. The pull we sense toward the center of the earth doesn't blink or fade as we go from bed to breakfast to work to play and back to bed again. Even as we float in our dreams, the bed, the ground, holds the full weight of our bodies.

So, unless we enter a space program, we have little chance of experiencing our bodies as weightless. And even if we do undertake such an adventure, the joys of its novelty are likely to be tempered by the woes of space motion sickness in the short term and a host of physiological atrophies and ailments in the long term, from cardiovascular deconditioning and anemia to muscle loss and bone deterioration.[1] Humans need and miss our sense of connection with gravity—think separation anxiety, or withdrawal, or homesickness.

Our bodies are not suddenly *subjected* to gravity, as if our birth is an arrival on Earth from some weightless realm. Rather, gravity is knit in our very flesh, bones, and consciousness. Studies suggest that gravity is essential for embryo development: sea urchins, fish, salamanders, frogs, and mice (and, logically, humans, too) have all had a hard time developing as living beings without good old 1g.[2] On Earth, beginning in embryo, our developing sensors and central nervous system actually learn to tell gravity's constant acceleration from other movements. This discrimination allows us to learn how gravity affects our interaction with the environment very quickly. At just seven months of age, a baby can correctly anticipate the acceleration of an object rolling on an incline. Our knowledge of gravity, as we've seen, is hidden, tacit. The know-how has been built in. Just lifting and lowering an arm involves a tremendous number of calculations of the interplay of muscular forces with the effect of gravity in the ever-changing flow of the movement. And we deal with the most amazing complexity in a tacit way. For example, in preparing to catch a ball, our body-mind simultaneously processes not just the ball's velocity, mass, inertia, and angle, but gravity's influence on the ball *and* on our body's changing location and limb movements as well.[3] So, gravity is knit into the fabric of our embodied knowing, our experience, our existence, our being, our life. It is present whenever we are, wherever we are, and whichever way we turn.

When we deign to notice gravity, we wake up to something that is already there. We experience how it is possible to be completely oblivious to something that pervades our entire life, and how the shift into awareness of it brings clarity that rings out and continuously expands in our experience, like the sound from a bell or the ripples from a pebble splashing into a pond. As your mindfulness practice has no doubt disclosed, and will continue to show, this kind of waking up to the obvious is not once and done. Not with gravity. Neither with other forms of experience—for example, with the fear or anger or sadness or tenderness or joy that may saturate and control your experience in a moment or over a prolonged period of time. Whenever you mindfully notice your relationship to gravity—again—and bring it into awareness, you come to know just a little more about waking up to what is present. In that same way, you can mindfully notice a constant in your life, such as fear or tenderness, and simply hold it in awareness rather than identify with it, thereby sharpening your ability to "dry out" from the saturation of your experience.

A Theistic Exploration

We could consider gravity as prevenient in our sensing of the body in movement and stillness. That's from the Latin, meaning "coming before," and suggesting, to the theistically minded, the grace of God that anticipates our desire for the holy. Here is an analogy crying out for expansion and exploration. The sacred texts of Judaism and Christianity offer rich ground for such a practice. If you're so disposed, perhaps you can hold this book in your hands—knowing that with your grip you have arrested the book's inexorable descent toward the center of the earth—and reflectively engage with these lines from Psalm 139. Let the following questions, and your own, shape this experiment: How does your experience of gravity in this moment inform your reading? What words or images touch you? Where do you slow and stop? Is there a verse with new power for you? What will you carry away into your daily life?

O LORD, you have searched me and known me.

You know when I sit down and when I rise up; you discern my thoughts from far away.

You search out my path and my lying down, and are acquainte with all my ways.

Even before a word is on my tongue, O LORD, you know it completely.

You hem me in, behind and before, and lay your hand upon me.

Such knowledge is too wonderful for me; it is so high that I cannot attain it.

Where can I go from your spirit? Or where can I flee from your presence?

If I ascend to heaven, you are there; if I make my bed in Sheol, you are there.

If I take the wings of the morning and settle at the farthest limits of the sea,

even there your hand shall lead me, and your right hand shall hold me fast.

If I say, "Surely the darkness shall cover me, and the light around me become night,"

even the darkness is not dark to you; the night is as bright as the day, for darkness is as light to you.

For it was you who formed my inward parts; you knit me together in my mother's womb.

I praise you, for I am fearfully and wonderfully made. Wonderful are your works; that I know very well.

A Nontheistic Exploration

Playing with prefixes, gravity is undoubtedly *con*venient for exploring our world. Again, that's from the Latin, meaning "coming with" or "together," and suggesting, to the nontheistically minded, the insight of *dependent co-arising* to which the Buddha awakened and from which the resonances and radiations of the concept of *interdependence* have entered the West's consciousness and conscience. Here again is gravity as an analogy of how all is laced together. If you're inclined to, perhaps letting this book come to rest on your lap or table and sensing how the body, the trunk, the head, each limb—in fact, each cell—responds and reacts to the pull toward the center of the earth. Noting how all that's within your own experiential horizon responds and all within the expanding horizons of those around you responds as well. Letting the following image, which is central to Chinese Hua-yen Buddhism[4] and which has captured the intellects and imaginations of contemporary ecologists, systems thinkers, and environmental advocates, shape your "reflections." How do your body sensations of gravity affect your reading? What is stirred up in you? Does this practice prompt an action? What will you take from this into your daily life?

> Far away in the heavenly abode of the great god Indra, there is a wonderful net which has been hung by some cunning artificer in such a manner that it stretches out indefinitely in all directions. In accordance with the extravagant tastes of deities, the artificer has hung a . . . glittering jewel at the net's every node, and since the net itself is infinite in dimension, the jewels are infinite in number. There hang the jewels, glittering like stars of the first magnitude, a wonderful sight to behold. If we now arbitrarily select one of these jewels for inspection and look closely at it, we will discover that in its polished surface there are reflected all the other jewels in the net, infinite in number. Not only that, but each of the jewels reflected in this one jewel is also reflecting all the other jewels, so that there is an infinite reflecting process occurring.[5]

DEFINING WONDERS

On a foggy night in a deep forest, you've been blindfolded, spun around, and abandoned. Take a moment. Imagine it. How lost are you?

Certainly, you are *disoriented:* to take the word apart, *dis-* (deprive of) *orient* (east); you simply can't find the east. There is no sun or moon, no star to guide you. Yet even in the fog, in the dark, in the dense vegetation, you can locate yourself in two directions: you know *up*, and you know *down*. Whatever the conditions are, wherever in this world you find yourself, you can ground yourself, and thereby find the way to center. That's a clear indication of how precious gravity is, both as a catalyst for and an object of our mindfulness practice.

Gravity helps define so much of our experience: contact, balance, stillness, motion, touch, presence, even safety arise from our ongoing encounter with it. In the desolation of that forest experience, gravity first offers you a choice. You can follow the famously futile rule, "When in trouble, when in doubt, run in circles, scream and shout." Or you can feel in to what gravity has to offer, starting with the contact of the soles of your feet with the ground. Let's take this moment, right now, and experiment with the latter.

Placing both feet on the floor, whether you are sitting, standing, or lying down. Allowing the body to come to rest. Then allowing your breath to flow naturally. Allowing yourself to feel the emotions of the moment, being aware of whatever thoughts and body sensations are arising, without restricting or attempting to change them. Simply observing.

Then moving your attention to the soles of your feet. Feeling your heels on the floor or inside your shoes; feeling the curves of the arches, the balls of the feet, and the toes—perhaps moving the toes to help distinguish one from another. Feeling the sides and tops of the feet, perhaps the pressure of the socks or shoes holding them. Then sensing the entire body resting with gravity at this moment.

After two or three minutes of this practice, begin expanding your attention again to notice the quality of emotions, thoughts, and body sensations. This is a practice that doesn't end, so simply continue reading, mindfully.[6]

What do you notice right now? Take a look at the list of what gravity helps define. Do contact, balance, stillness, motion, touch, presence, or safety enter into your experience? Does it make sense that this practice can be a way of orienting yourself when you feel "dis-oriented"?

It is telling that the experiment we just did comes out of clinical work by psychologists trying to help manage anger and other strong emotions—there are dense forests in our emotional lives as well. The good news is that what gravity defines for us can be used for our own comfort. As we sense our bodies in contact with the ground and held by gravity—held in balance, held in stillness, held in the present moment—we may find a sense of security or even safety. So, we don't actually *get grounded* or *ground ourselves;* rather, we "re-cognize," understand anew, that gravity and the ground are constantly there for us.

Knowing up and down, we may find the courage and patience to work with ourselves, others, and our environment to *settle* a situation (impossible without gravity!) and to find a way *forward* (although up and down come first!).

What Do I Do When I'm Lost in the Forest?

A poem by David Wagoner, "Lost," is a version of a teaching story from the Native Americans of the Pacific Northwest, where to venture off the path in the old growth forests could be a disorienting, even life-threatening, experience. Think of these lines as instructions for the lost moments in your life.

> *Stand still. The trees ahead and bushes beside you*
> *Are not lost. Wherever you are is called Here . . .*

It is the same in an open field, a big city street, a mall parking lot, or even in your own home. You are one place, only. And there's only one thing to do, as Wagoner says. You must listen as the forest (or flowers, or black top, or furniture) speaks, saying:

> *I have made this place around you.*
> *If you leave it, you may come back again, saying Here.*
> *No two trees are the same to Raven.*

No two branches are the same to Wren.
If what a tree or a bush does is lost on you,
You are surely lost. Stand still. The forest knows
Where you are. You must let it find you.[7]

Gravity defines our uprightness, which in turn gives us the comfort of knowing where we stand. We sense front and back and right and left, as well as up and down. Our world is articulated by our embodied experience, both in space and time.

The unassailable facts of our physiology, especially the placement of our sense organs and the orientation of our limbs and joints, open for us a distant forward horizon, which is visual, which is light, which is a future that retreats forever as we move toward it. We are built both physiologically and psychologically for leaning into the future. We could say that one reason we have trouble staying in the present is because our eyes by nature seek the future. That may be why closing the eyes is often helpful in our practice of dropping into now. The up direction, too, is bright, expansive, and future-oriented. You can experience this expansiveness directly in this moment, if you'd like: Come into quiet awareness of your entire body; if you're reading while lying down, it might help to come to sitting or standing so the vertical is very evident for you. Now notice how it feels at the top of your head. This is where your body ends its upward thrust. Does it feel like a stopping point? What is this sensation of up? Now, raise one hand and gently place the palm on the top of your head, defining your upward physical limit. Do you sense the body differently now? Do you sense the body's up and down dimension now squeezed between the soles of your feet (or your seat) and the palm of your hand? Take your hand away. How does experience change?

Balance! Balance!

Anthropologist Kathryn Geurts, in her book *Culture and the Senses*, questions our underexamined idea that because sensation and perception are basic to the human body-mind complex, they are relatively unaffected by culture.[8] We might assume that others in the world frame their experience through the conventional five senses as well, so that our worlds map together. She shows, compellingly, that this is not so, and balance plays a big part.

Guerts reports on the Anlo-Ewe–speaking people of southwestern Ghana, whose sensory mode of encountering the world is suggested by their general term *seselelame,* which refers to acts of feeling in and through the body that are both sensory and cognitive. Balance has a dominant place in their sensorium. This is a people who walk with cargo balanced on their heads—the children walk to school balancing their desks. From the earliest days of a child's life, he or she is encouraged to "balance, balance!" The capacity to stand upright and balance is, for the Anlo-Ewe, an essential part of the definition of a human being. To never learn to walk upright is to be considered as an animal. And, in fact, they believe that loss of hearing is the worst that can befall someone, as it would include a disruption of the sense of balance.

The directions back and down, when you consider the design and disposition of the body, are dark, compacted, and reflective of the past. There is vulnerability in the back direction; our visual ability there is peripheral at best, however fluidly we can turn our necks. Other senses, particularly hearing and touch, are required to reconnoiter the space in back. In the dimension of time, as we walk into the future we leave the past behind, or trample it underfoot. The discipline of history reads its narratives toward the present, as if walking through time with eyes fixed ahead. We recount our personal narratives—to others and to ourselves—in the same toward-the-present mode. Even looking backward, we're tacitly oriented forward.

How do you experience the space behind you? Right now, while you're still reading, you can simply pause to try a moment's exploration. Come up to standing and look directly forward in the way you're facing. Notice how it is to see what's before you, seeing in full depth and width, out to the extreme periphery. Then, with your eyes still open, notice how it is for you to concentrate on the unseeable area directly behind you. What is there for you? What senses are active? Now close your eyes. Sense into the space in front of you first. What is that experience like? Then sense the space behind you. If you're in a familiar place, perhaps you know and can imagine what's back there in some detail. Is this different from your first encounter with the back? What senses are most at work (or play) for you now?

When front and back are defined, then left and right are defined as well. There is the same kind of unbalance, the same opposing feelings in these directions. For many, the right side is dominant, so its space is wide and bright and full of promise. The left side is narrow and shadowed and lacking control. Perhaps you can continue the exploration with eyes closed. What happens as you try to experience the full 360 degrees around you? Is there anywhere the space feels expansive? Anywhere it feels constricted?

Our bodies are the centers and measures of our worlds. Gravity defines up and down, acting as the stake driven in the ground that makes surveying possible, or as the compass needle that lets us navigate our lives. When we tune in to the pull of the earth, we know where we stand, and we can help others get where they want to go.

Living (in) Metaphors

As you're aware by now, there is a close tie between our simplest embodied experiences, such as our relationship to gravity and the ground, and ways of speaking that are "resonant," are "moving," and that "make sense." The inextricability, the interdependence, of body, mind, and environment is clearly on display in the primary metaphors that come from up and down, front and back, left and right. The work of George Lakoff and Mark Johnson has helped to shift the ways we think of metaphor from a specialized literary concern to a central feature in our understanding of the embodied mind—a shift of concern from artists to everybody.[9] The ideas and research in metaphor and neuroscience over the past three decades have led to a theory that primary metaphors are not just verbal constructions.

Rather, they are "neural maps," physical links from our sensory-motor experience to the brain's motor cortex and to other parts of the brain as well. These maps don't simply *represent how* we think, they *are a way* in which we think. Language comes later. Lakoff and Johnson state it powerfully:

> You don't have a choice as to whether to think metaphorically. Because metaphorical maps are part of our brains, we think and speak metaphorically whether we want to or not. Since the mechanism of metaphor is largely unconscious, we will think and speak metaphorically whether we know it or not. Further, since our brains are embodied, our metaphors will reflect our commonplace experiences in the world. Inevitably, many primary metaphors are universal because everybody has basically the same kind of bodies and brains and lives in basically the same kinds of environments, so far as the features relevant to metaphor are concerned.[10]

We encounter these metaphorical meanings with a virtual immediacy. Bidden or not, they are *already there* in our moment-to-moment awareness. It's valuable, then, to acknowledge and work with them consciously—question them, interrogate them—in our mindfulness practice. It's even more valuable to recognize that they are not in opposition, that one is not more or less to be courted or investigated than another. Rather, it is possible to notice what is dominant *at the moment* in experience and to know that the others are not merely implied, but present as well.

Here are a few primary metaphors that occur across a variety of cultures, reflecting the human experience of gravity and the ground:

Ground/grounded

- Foundation
- Home
- Security/safety
- Balance/calm

Up/rising

- More/greater quantity
- Importance
- In control
- Morality
- Superior status (Note that it's almost impossible to write this list without being tautological, as *superior* suggests the Latin for "up/higher.")
- Energized
- "Positive" emotional states (e.g., happy)
- Transcendent
- Sacred
- Salvation

Down/declining

- Less/smaller quantity
- Unimportant
- Out of control
- Immorality
- Inferior status
- Exhausted
- "Negative" emotional states (e.g., sad)
- Mundane
- Profane
- Damnation[11]

REVEALING WONDERS

As we become aware of the intimate relationship of our body-mind to gravity, what may be revealed to us, if we use Dupin's mode of investigation, is our own liveliness. Gravity draws down, and the body's living processes offer up. In commonsense and everyday language, we understand this as an opposition, a conflict, a battle for supremacy (for "above-ness"). A baby sits up by herself, or comes up to standing, and we celebrate the victory. We rise to our full height to stride out into the world, carrying an attitude of individual power and accomplishment. We arrive at our bedside at the end of a tiring day, and we capitulate, surrender ourselves to gravity and oblivion. We even conceive of the sun as rising and sinking, although we "know" better.

This sense of opposition is, as always with commonsense formulations, worth questioning through critical thinking and contemplation of direct experience. We've seen how gravity makes our body processes possible, how it's intertwined with our life functions so inextricably that living a weightless life causes debilitating deteriorations. Gravity is truly as supportive as it is oppositional or aggressive. Right now, if you come to quiet and then come to standing from wherever and however you are disposed with this book, perhaps you can notice that your engagement with gravity is not constant warfare. We exert our liveliness, and we arrive at standing. We can move again and find a way of sitting that is a comfort for a while. Indeed, we are always traveling toward truce. Or more than truce, toward balance, which is an embrace we recognize. In each of our movements, we return like a prodigal child to be met and held in a moment of rejoicing in which every cell of the body feels at home.

When walking, standing, sitting, or reclining, we are continually seeking and finding the truth of truce, the fluid embrace of balance. Sometimes for just milliseconds. Sometimes for long moments of relaxation or intensity. Balance is quotidian, as in standing at the kitchen sink snapping beans. And it is profoundly moving, as in a ballerina *en pointe* or your baby's first steps. Balance is as near and dear to us as vision or hearing or the others on our "official" list of five senses. We are as discomfited without it as without sight or hearing. It can be valuable to our mindfulness practice to investigate balance in Dupin's two modes—the analytic and the poetic—to understand through scientific insight, and to integrate those insights through direct experience. So, let's put balance in context, look at the physiology and neurology, and then put everything together in some informal practices that you can bring into your workday—at the kitchen sink or behind your desk.

Gindler on Gravity

Gravity can maintain or restore our liveliness when we court it, accept it, and give ourselves to it in a mindful way. The following little vignettes, which appear in "*Gymnastik* for Busy People," the only written work of Elsa Gindler published in her lifetime, make a big impact. She expresses not only how far away from our own bodies' liveliness we may find ourselves as "busy people," but also how close we are to an incredible source of refreshment.

> We read that the Arabs have a capacity through which, after trekking through the desert, they can lie motionless on the sand for ten minutes, and in this ten minutes to regenerate themselves so that they are then able to continue walking for hours longer. This is an example of relaxation. We hear that top businessmen often remain utterly motionless for a moment while directing all their senses inward. Then, suddenly, they seem to awaken and make decisions that are uniquely right. It is clear that in this moment of being with themselves relaxation has taken place. This is the kind of relaxation we are seeking. It can be most readily reached through the experience of gravity.[12]

Balance has been a purloined sense for those of us in the tradition of Euro-American science and thought. Our common understanding of sensation and perception is built on the five senses that school children learn by rote—sight, hearing, touch, taste, and smell. Four of the five are focused in the head; it's no wonder we spend so much time there and so little in our bodies. Even at more sophisticated levels of teaching and learning, the five senses undergird our classifications. A quick review of progressive editions of a couple of standard psychology textbooks, both titled *Sensation and Perception,* reveals that more than half the total number of chapters focus on vision, with hearing weighted next highest, and touch, taste, and smell rating far less real estate.[13] What is truly telling, and what is good news from the perspective of our mindfulness of body practice, is that in the very latest edition of each book, at last, chapters are allotted to our "sense" of orientation in space—including gravity sensing and balance.

As with other features of daily life too obvious to be noticed, balance mostly comes to consciousness through aberration or absence. Medical disorders, motion sickness, and other specific issues surrounding weightlessness in space are most responsible for the serious investigation of balance. For example, the Vestibular Disorders Association is engaged in a drive for recognition of balance as the "sixth sense." They note that almost eight million Americans report chronic problems with balance, that such disorders increase in prevalence with age, and they further highlight the costs, in both dollars and suffering, of the disorders and the harm associated with falls.[14] In weightless environments, our capacity to accurately know the body's orientation is challenged by the absence of the sense of gravity's pull. This is the dominant issue for space neuroscientists,[15] and focused research has helped to increase understanding of the ways in which the body senses gravity. What is most interesting for us, as mindfulness practitioners, is that more and more of the body is being found to be involved in noticing and knowing up and down. So, our own research can come not from aberration and absence but from awe, gratitude, and celebration of this embodied knowing.

How do we know? The current concept of the sense of balance is based on the "equilibrial triad," comprising the vestibular system, the visual system, and the somatosensory system. Let's get an analytic overview of each one, before we investigate how they come together in preconscious and conscious ways.

The vestibular system, which is part of the inner ear and is located in the skull's *vestibules,* or entryways, is made up of two sac-like structures, the utricle and saccule, and three semicircular canals (see figure 6.1 on page 104). The utricle and saccule deliver information about linear acceleration (like flooring it in your car, starting up in a fast elevator, or tilting your head down or up) and the relationship to gravity. Inside these sacs is a gelatinous mass suspending the *otoliths,* literally, "ear stones"—actually tiny grains of calcium carbonate. As the head moves, the otoliths shift

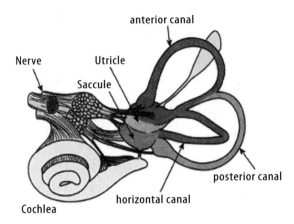

Figure 6.1. The vestibular system;
image by Thomas Haslwanter, Sensesweb

and bend the hair-like receptor cells lining the sacs, which report movement and alignment with gravity to the central nervous system. The three semicircular canals provide information about angular acceleration of the head. They are oriented to the *x, y,* and *z* axes—roll, pitch, and yaw—that is, angling forward and backward *(x)*, from side to side *(y)*, and turning around *(z)* the center of gravity. When the head moves on these planes, the inertial movement of the fluid in the canals excites hair-like receptor cells, which send information to the central nervous system about the speed, direction, and distance of the head's motion.

Upright from the Beginning of Time

The ability to sense gravity has been essential for life for the past four hundred million years or so. The most ancient single-cell organisms we've found are equipped with organelles called *statoliths*. These calcium carbonate particles suspended in the cytoplasm are acted on by gravity, and their movement provides a cue to the organism for the most beneficial orientation. Even some fungi and most plants have analogous equipment, *amyloplasts*, to find the way to down.

The visual system is integral to our sense of balance. The eyes provide cues for alignment up and down. We stand up by orienting the body perpendicular to the horizon, and may use the natural or the built environment as references. We assume that a tree or the corner of a building is vertical. When the visual cues are misleading in some way, we may follow them and be misled or may rely on the other gravity-sensing inputs (see the "Whose Clues?" box). The tilted room in a fun house confuses us because the angles of doors, windows, and walls are all in parallel but out of plumb. Right now, you can see just how important visual cues are to you, by standing up with your feet very close together. As you look out at the world, how well are you balanced? What happens when you close your eyes? Do you feel yourself come to greater stability when you open them and get visual cues again?

Whose Clues?

Different people rely more or less on the external cues from the visual system to find the subjective vertical. The concept was first described in the 1940s by Herman Witkin and Solomon Asch, who used physical tests such as the Rod and Frame Test to understand the importance of visual cues. In the test, the subject is seated in a tilting chair or tilting room in darkness, so there are no visual cues of vertical or horizontal. A tilting square frame is shown to the subject, and he or she is asked to adjust a rod in the frame to the vertical position. Such tests have revealed that some people rely on visual cues to perceive the vertical and place the rod in respect to those cues *only*, while others rely more on their direct sensations of gravity and place the rod *counter* to any misleading visual cues. Those who favor visual cues are classified as *field dependent*, and those who favor internal cues are classified as *field independent*. As the concept was elaborated, these preferences came to be seen as two poles of a continuum of cognitive style and personality. At the risk of oversimplification, field-dependent people have less capacity to focus, rely more on external cues, and are more easily persuaded by others, while field-independent people are capable of highly focused attention, rely more on internal cues, and are less easily swayed.[16]

There's a rather powerful suggestion that the practice of meditation may increase field independence: the vast majority of such studies reported in a bibliography of research from 1931 to 2002 on the effects of meditation have shown an increase in field independence for meditators.[17]

The somatosensory system comprises sensory receptors throughout the entire body that provide the capacity for such forms of sensing as *proprioception* and *kinesthesia* (knowledge of the body's position in space and of its movement, respectively), the whole category of *touch* (knowledge of contact, temperature, and pain), and *interoception* (knowledge of sensation inside the body). It is because all of these different functions or knowings are associated with a single area of the brain, the somatosensory cortex, that they can be grouped in this way.

Proprioception and kinesthesia rely on a number of specialized receptors, including neuromuscular spindles in the muscle fibers, which signal length and velocity of the stretch of the muscle, golgi tendon organs, which provide information on muscle tension, and joint receptors, which (along with touch sensations) signal the angles of joints. Knowledge of gravity and the vertical axis when standing can be related to, for example, the sensations of the joint angle and muscle activity in the ankles, feet, and lower legs.

The sense of touch, particularly the receptors that respond to "mechanical" contact such as pressure, vibration, and movement, contributes to our capacity to sense up and down. The mechano-receptors allow us to experience the effect of gravity on our body and on an object that we hold or that rests on us, like hefting a ball or feeling the weight of a leg when our legs are crossed. Except in freefall or weightlessness, there is pressure somewhere on the body, cueing us to our orientation to gravity. Such cues are powerful, particularly in ambiguous situations:

in experiments by Lackner and colleagues,[18] blindfolded subjects who were being turned at a steady rate on a "rotisserie" type of device were made to feel as if they were rising to a standing position when pressure was applied to the soles of their feet, and they could be made to feel as if they were sitting when pressure was applied to their buttocks.

Interoceptive information from the viscera may be more of a contributor to our sense of the vertical than has been thought. That is, there is increasing experimental evidence that our innards give us an "inner sense" of gravity.[19] Three candidates for these "gravi-ceptors" include the kidneys, which may act like statoliths suspended in us, the blood in the large vessels, which is distributed in part through gravity, and receptors associated with the hollow organs in the abdomen, since a full stomach appears to aid in accurately sensing the vertical.

Gravity Keeps Us in Touch with the Provinces

Our sense of the position of our arms and legs can signal the direction of gravity, and likewise, gravity can reveal the position of our arms and legs. In weightlessness and in the dark, astronauts have difficulty knowing where their limbs are. An Apollo astronaut describes the initial experience of drifting off to sleep in weightlessness this way: "I suddenly realized that I had lost track of . . . my arms and legs. For all my mind could tell, my limbs were not there. However, with a conscious command for an arm or leg to move, it instantly reappeared—only to disappear again when I relaxed."[20] Gravity keeps us in touch; even when we are still, we don't disappear. There's security and comfort, without effort.

So, we've identified many of the facts and facets of our sense of gravity and the vertical, as the mathematician sensibility of Dupin might suggest would be helpful. Yet this analytical approach is precisely counter to our own embodied way of knowing, which is an integrative approach, reflective of the poet—Dupin's other sensibility. As we walk through our world, our central nervous system is constantly responding to perceptions of gravity and the vertical and making automatic adjustments in the body as an ongoing dynamic response to keep us in balance. These adjustments are not processed consciously up in the brain, but rather automatically, low down in the brainstem. (Note the metaphor: high is heady and complex; low is bodily and simple). Messages from all of the gravi-ception systems must be integrated in these dynamic responses. These can be as simple as adjusting blood pressure depending on how gravity distributes the blood in the body, so that, if everything is working, you can move from lying down to standing up without passing out (orthostatic regulation). They can also be as complex as the total-body adjustments made in microseconds to keep you in balance as you run up a rock-strewn path in the mountains, where the vestibular, visual, and somatosensory inputs are flowing fast.

Let's take one of the truly purloined responses to experiment with and appreciate. It's visual, but we don't usually see it: the vestibular-ocular reflex is what makes it possible for you to read this book on the train or while the dog is settling down on the couch with you. It adjusts the eyeballs in their sockets as the head moves, to keep the image of the words steady on the retina. Here's the experiment: as you continue to read, move your head side to side, up and down, and any combination that appeals. Slower or faster. You're still reading; all that sensory input is processed automatically. Now, hold your head steady and move the book up, down, and around . . . Here's your place. You lost it, because you had less input to help you make the required compensation.

That little experiment is just one more way in which our relationship to gravity and balance reveals our essential liveliness. It's evident throughout the body. There is a distinctive tonicity—a readiness for response, movement, dance, flight—in many of our muscles that is the product of our constant conversation with the pull of the planet. As we investigate gravity, we investigate our living—and perhaps even our knowledge of the how and why of our living. This suggests why many of our clients and students name "paying attention to gravity" as a practice that can shift them from experiences of anguish, anger, or anxiety to a moment-by-moment sense of "this is my place in the world, and I can deal with what's happening," as one client put it. Two cases stand out in their surface disparities and essential similarity. Consider these two men: one in his twenties, one in his seventies; one who works with his hands, one engaged in intellectual effort; both struggling to control outbursts of anger that were destroying important relationships; both capable of road rage on their long daily commutes. As they began to practice with gravity, they brought it into their cars. They reported that feeling their feet on the floor and their hands on the wheel gave them a chance to check in, to feel themselves held by gravity in the seat. The rising anger often subsided. And the training of the long drive helped them to bring the practice into their workplaces and their homes.

A Toggle Switch
for Liveliness

Our otolith organs are responsible, in a way, for the muscle tone of our neck, back, arms, legs, and more. This *tonic labyrinthine reflex* is easily seen in babies. When a child is held horizontally, with the head up so that the otolith organs respond to gravity as if vertical, the reflex creates a muscle tone that allows the child to extend the arm, leg, and trunk muscles. When the head is pushed face downward, the child's muscles lose tone, and the body settles toward a fetal position. Without the stimulus of gravity on the otolith organs, a weightless astronaut assumes much the same posture. Gravity not only reveals, but also creates, our liveliness.

Casual Contact:
Meeting Gravity at Work and at Home

It's up to you to decide when and where to try these practices. Some have been designed through my own practice (Don), which centers on hobbies at home of walking, cooking, and outdoor work, and on a mostly seated work life, which consists of listening and talking, reading and writing. You'll know which fit your situations. Try them out and adjust them to explore more and more deeply your relationship to the vertical, the embrace of balance, and the constancy of gravity.

Hands and feet: I worked my way through college as a laborer on road crews. A full day of moving gravel or hot blacktop with a wide, flat shovel would put me to bed early. So I was fascinated by the year-round workers, whose pace and movements were slower and more measured than mine, and who by day's end had not only accomplished more, but were also ready to wash up and hit the bar that night.

If you work standing up, do it with gravity. That is, check in with the way your legs and feet are supporting you. How much energy do you need to expend to stay upright? Can you feel into the muscle tone required in feet, ankles, knees, and hips, to find a softness that lets gravity work for you—holding you up? Then tune in to the work with your hands. How much are you *opposing* gravity? How much can gravity *contribute* to the work? If you're, say, chopping vegetables, how does the knife fall? Washing dishes, how do you lift, lower, hold, scrub, rinse? How do you use the weight of the arms? What adjustments can you make for more ease—maybe even more power or efficiency? Most important, how is it to find that you are working *with* gravity? Is it grave? Or joyful? What's there for you?

Note, visceral work: Another time, explore the work above while sensing into the truncal gravi-ceptors. Is the body sensing the vertical to work with it and from it? Is there a gut feeling that goes with working this way?

Listening, to your legs: When you're sitting and in a conversation, how do your legs respond to gravity, and to the tenor of the conversation? Notice when the feet are bearing the weight of the legs. What is the conversation like then? Notice when you're holding the legs up, perhaps on toe points, perhaps even with the hands. What's it like for you then? What happens to the conversation if you deliberately shift to feeling both feet on the floor and letting the weight settle on them?

Note: What happens if, in the conversation above, you talk about your experience of feeling the relationship of your legs to gravity? If your conversation partner makes this exploration, too?

7

THE BREATH I

East and West, Inside and Outside

For the New Year, 1868, Ralph Waldo Emerson's gift to his daughter Edith and son-in-law William Forbes was an Aeolian harp. The aging philosopher-poet was sharing an instrument that had brought him much pleasure—spiritual insight and inspiration—through the years, both as sound and symbol. Named for Aeolus, the Greek "keeper of the winds," this type of instrument was first built by the seventeenth-century Jesuit scientist Athanasius Kircher. His was a long, narrow pine box with fifteen gut strings, set in the window of his museum in Rome, giving a sighing, singing, harmonious voice to the breeze. Aeolian harps came into popularity, though, at the middle of the eighteenth century in England, when Scottish violinist, composer, and entrepreneur James Oswald refined designs and produced Aeolian harps for home use, providing an effortless and convenient concert played by force of nature. As the harps made their way across Europe, they became both the background music to and a dominant symbol for the unfolding of the Romantic era. Coleridge and Wordsworth, Goethe and Schiller—all created powerful works with the Aeolian harp as a symbol of the poet's mind, and all helped to shape Emerson's thought profoundly. Emerson, as part of the gift to his daughter, wrote the poem "The Maiden Speech of the Aeolian Harp," in which the harp describes its own mission and intentions:

Soft and softlier hold me, friends!
Thanks if your genial care
Unbind and give me to the air.
Keep your lips or finger-tips
For flute or spinet's dancing chips;
I await a tenderer touch,
I ask more or not so much:
Give me to the atmosphere,—
Where is the wind, my brother,—where?
Lift the sash, lay me within,
Lend me your ears, and I begin.
For gentle harp to gentle hearts
The secret of the world imparts;
And not to-day and not to-morrow
Can drain its wealth of hope and sorrow;
But day by day, to loving ear
Unlocks new sense and loftier cheer.
I've come to live with you, sweet friends,
This home my minstrel-journeyings ends.
Many and subtle are my lays,
The latest better than the first,
For I can mend the happiest days
And charm the anguish of the worst.

As spiritual heirs of Emerson, we each have been gifted for new years, and for every new moment, not with a harp, but with the trembling resonance of our respiratory organs. The breath is an exquisitely sensitive instrument set within the window of our awareness. It has not simply come to live with us; it is our home, our life. As we bring our attention to it—lend it our ears, so to speak—it can impart the promised secrets, and mend and charm our days.

The breath is a rich and worthy focus for mindfulness practice, offering layer after layer of information, from direct sensory data, on to subtle emotional cues, and finally to elemental paradoxes that invite lifelong reflection. We can use these paradoxes as an organizing scheme for exploring this constant physiological process and our inconstant relationship with it. An abundance of these paradoxes can be nested within just three distinct pairs of opposites that point to basic characteristics of the breath. From each pair, an array of further pairs then cascades out, expanding our inquiries. First, the pair *outbreath* and *inbreath* yields outside/inside, wind/breath, and present moment/passing time, among its many possibilities. Second, the breath's position as the only physiological process that is both *intentional* (voluntary) and *automatic* (involuntary) yields such pairs as universal/unique, willful/willing, and continuity/disruption. Third, the link to emotion suggests the pair *revealing* and *regulating,* which yields heart/head, threat/safety, and chaos/creativity. The more we learn about and experience each of these core and cascading pairs, the easier it becomes to hold both sides, to resolve or dissolve the seeming paradox. Let's pick up again the metaphor of the Aeolian harp and begin exploring.

INSIDE/OUTSIDE

Emerson's own Aeolian harp was made of polished mahogany, an aesthetically designed and refined instrument for bringing the wind's voice inside, to be savored in the study or drawing room. Thoreau had a harp, too. His, however, was built to fit the wilder, outside strains of his life and thought. It affords us a clearly American version of the metaphor, as it compounds the romantic and the scientific, the spiritual and the commercial, and the natural and the built environments. Thoreau's Aeolian harp was new and monumental: the telegraph wire being strung in the late summer of 1851 through the Concord, Massachusetts, landscape, on poles along the railroad connecting Boston and Burlington, Vermont.

In the early summer, even before the wire was strung, a harp was playing in Thoreau's journal as rumor and metaphor. On June 21, he noted, "There is always a kind of fine Aeolian harp music to be heard in the air. . . . To ears that are expanded what a harp this world is!" By September 3, it was no longer abstract: "As I went under the new telegraph-wire, I heard it vibrating like a harp high overhead. It was the sound of a far-off glorious life, a supernal life, which came down to us and vibrated the lattice work of this life of ours."[1] Thoreau's expanded ears kept finding more volume and more subtlety in the reality of this metaphor as he walked with it and through it. The railroad had been built just a few years before, and a "deep cut" had been made through a hill near Walden pond, exposing the local geology and the natural processes of erosion in an edge-on view that grew in meaning over years for Thoreau. In fact, much of the "Spring" chapter of *Walden* is a minutely observed contemplation on the designs made by the freezing and thawing of the sand and clay of the bank, in which Thoreau's poetic mind shifts from the image of a leaf to an anatomical *lobe,* "a word especially applicable to the liver and lungs," as he points out. He feels as if he is standing "in the laboratory of the Artist who made the world and me." On that September 12, the place was flooded with the sound of the harp to become a site of spiritual and sensual insight. "As I was entering the Deep Cut, the wind, which was conveying a message to me from heaven, dropped it on the wire of the telegraph which it vibrated as it passed. I instantly sat down on a stone at the foot of the telegraph pole, and attended to the communication."[2]

The vastness and physicality of the telegraph harp shook him simultaneously at the cellular and cosmic levels, working into his being just the way the sound invaded the wooden poles. In the Deep Cut on a windy September 22, he reports, "I put my ear to one of the posts, and it seemed to me as if every pore of the wood was filled with music, labored with the strain—as if every fibre was affected and being seasoned or timed, rearranged according to a new and more harmonious law. . . . The resounding wood! How much the ancients would have made of it! To have a harp on so great a scale, girdling the very earth, and played on by the winds of every latitude and longitude, and that harp were, as it were, the manifest blessing of heaven on a work of man's! Shall we not add a tenth Muse to the immortal Nine?"[3] From wood fiber to the globe, from his ear to the gods, Thoreau's experiential metaphor encompassed inside and outside, breath and wind, self and world—cascading paradox pairs—in ways that stayed with him for the rest of his life (another decade), as the evidence of his last months suggests.

Dying of what would become known as tuberculosis (see the "A Plague in Both Your Houses" box on page 117), breathless and fevered, he could no longer leave the house. His lifelong inspiration, the natural world, was literally and figuratively unavailable to him. Without his outdoor walks and encounters, new writing seemed impossible. As his body shut down, he closed the journal that was his life's work, and allotted his remaining days to revising and proofing earlier work for publication. The final entry in his journal, November 3, 1861, finds him once again scrutinizing railroad geology, contemplating the wind and its effects, and generating meaning for himself and us. "After a violent easterly storm in the night, which clears up at noon, I notice that the surface of the railroad causeway, composed of gravel, is singularly marked . . . so that I can tell within a small fraction of a degree from what quarter the rain came. . . . Behind each little pebble, as a protecting boulder, an eighth to a tenth of an inch in diameter, extends northwest a ridge of sand in inch or more, which it has protected from being washed away." Then this short paragraph haunts the closing: "All this is perfectly distinct to an observant eye, and yet could easily pass unnoticed by most. Thus each wind is self-registering."[4] As with the wind, so with the man.

In his last days (Thoreau died May 6, 1862), he dreamed of wind in the Deep Cut—transformed. His friend and walking companion William Ellery Channing records, "Words could no longer express these inexplicable conditions of his existence, this sickness which reminded him of nothing that went before: such as that dream he had of being a railroad cut, where they were digging through and laying down the rail—the place being in his lungs."[5]

The conflation of wind and breath, landscape and lungs in Thoreau's walking and writing and dreaming points to ancient ways of perceiving and speaking about these essential forces—ways understood and intuited by those, like Jefferson and Adams, Emerson and Thoreau, who knew the classical literature of both the West and the East.

A Plague in Both Your Houses

Consumption, or phthisis (Greek for "wasting"), which we know as tuberculosis, might be thought of as the Romantic disease. Many of the European influences on the American Romantic movement and the Transcendentalists, such as Rousseau, Goethe, and Schiller, had respiratory consumption. Among English Romantics, poets Keats and Shelley were consumptive, and Byron, famously, wished he was— "Because the ladies would all say, 'Look at that poor Byron, how interesting he looks in dying!'" The bright, feverish eyes, the pale skin, and the rumor that creative genius attended the sufferer (a symptom known as *spes phthisica*) made consumption a social (and literary) asset rather than a social stigma in their time. In addition to these historical figures, consumption provided for the Romantic sufferings of many fictional characters in literature and opera of the nineteenth century. Reality and literature came together in the case of Edgar Allan Poe's mother and wife, who both suffered and died young from tuberculosis, providing inspiration for much of Poe's most moving poetry.

The disease was present in America even in the Colonial era (George Washington's brother Lawrence died of it). In fact, there is archaeological evidence in New England, uncovered by coauthor Marc Micozzi and others, that tuberculosis was massively introduced to Native American populations by the European settlers in the seventeenth century. Not until the opening of the nineteenth century did consumption reach the rampant state that earned it the epithet "white plague," as it doubly decimated families of every rank. It caused 20 percent of American deaths from 1800 to 1870. It was often seen as a familial disease. For example, Emerson's father and two of his adult brothers died of consumption; Ralph Waldo and his brother William were infected as well but recovered from its most perilous symptoms to live into old age. Emerson's first wife, Ellen Tucker, also from a consumptive family, was suffering when they married, and died less than two years after the wedding.

Thoreau's family was as heavily touched; his grandfather, father, brother, and older sister, as well as Henry himself, were infected or died of consumption. In Concord and throughout the land, the breath—its quality, quantity, continuation, and cessation—was on everyone's mind.

Both genius and sentiment were activated in America. Emerson's world was shaped by consumption and loss, and his work, which shaped America, was, as he would say, his compensation. Ellen Tucker Emerson found moments of freedom in her love of her young husband and in a *spes phthisica* outpouring of poetry that we might see as sentimental, but that was certainly compensatory. Poetry and song, so dependent on the breath as measure, became for many a form of therapy of the body and mind, though often shrouded in the conventions of the "graveyard school" of versification. As a famous case in point, the poetry of the Davidson sisters, Margaret and Lucretia, from Plattsburg, New York, received accolades from the likes of Poe and Washington Irving. Lucretia's method of composition speaks to the breath of those times. "Lucretia wrote in a dark room—to the music of an Aeolian harp in the window—strange and wild poems about the Near East."[6]

The pursuit of the cure and elimination of this disease yields some further resonant ideas. Before the identification of the tubercle bacillus in 1882, the causes of consumption were unknown and unproven. Treatments varied wildly, from bed rest in a dark room to the fresh air and "jolting" of carriage and horseback riding prescribed for Ellen Tucker Emerson. In keeping with ancient ideas of wind and weather, travel—to warmer and colder climes—was a great part of treatment regimens. Entire families removed to another state or country for the health of one or some members. In America, the South and West passed through vogues; the young Emerson in 1826 tried South Carolina and Florida to "escape the northeast winds," while the dying Thoreau in 1862 went to Minnesota, then much touted for its "dry air."

Treatment before the 1943 advent of antibiotics generated, among other approaches, the nature cure, the worldwide establishment of sanitariums, and close observation and experimentation with breathing. Of interest to us is the debate about whether patients should sit up or lie flat in bed for ease of breathing and optimum benefit of the fresh air they traveled to find. Gravity and the breath come together here. Consumption begins in the upper part of the lungs, and, as physicians found, the lying flat position allowed gravity to bring the greatest volume of air to the upper areas, allowed it to settle there, and also allowed maximum blood flow to that area. There's practice here: when you're next lying flat, how do you experience the fullness of the breath? The weight of the air?

WIND/BREATH

Once upon a time, people were embedded in a specific place, where they were vulnerable to the climate from season to season and to the weather from moment to moment. From which quarter the wind would blow next was a fundamental concern, a question of life or death.

This constant uncertainty of the all-important yields of crops, herds, game, fish, and distant trade—and of the safety of farmers, husbandmen, hunters, fishermen, ships, and caravans—is self-evident, even to those of us who live in climate-controlled glass houses. A vagrant winter storm tramples the new spring growth in the fields, setting back and endangering the harvest. An early snow traps sheep and shepherd still in the high mountain pasture. After hours of artful stalking, the hunter finds himself suddenly now *up*wind of the deer—who bound off with tail flags flying.

It is easy to understand how the wind, an invisible force revealed only through its effects, accumulated its metaphorical associations with the veering turns of change. In the tenth chapter of the *Odyssey,* for example, Homer tells how Aeolus gives Odysseus a mixed bag of winds for his journey home so he will always have a favorable breeze. And Homer only gets more adventures to recount because, when Odysseus is sleeping, his men open the bag hoping to find riches inside, and instead let all the winds out as a tangled gale that hurls the ship ever farther from home. The "winds of fortune" feel nothing like a metaphor to those clinging soaked and freezing to the pitching ship through the night and scanning uncomprehendingly the calm horizon at sunrise. When you're out in it, the wind is starkly real, and fortune and health come together where the wind meets the body.

Whole peoples were seen to be shaped by the wind prevailing in their lands. In the ancient Greek outlook, according to the Hippocratic treatise *Airs, Waters, and Places,* peoples influenced by the north wind are sturdy and lean, with fierce characters, while peoples living under more easterly and southerly winds have better temperaments and more intelligence.[7] Following the wind far around the globe, in ancient China, the term for the ways of being or customs of a people was *fengsu,* which contains the word for wind, *feng.* The great history, the *Hanshu,* spells it out: "[S]ome peoples are more rigid, others more flexible, some are relaxed, others tense, and their voices differ in pitch. All these qualities depend on the windy breath (*fengqi*) of the region."[8]

Ancient views also considered the wind's effects on the well-being of the individual. Wind, disease, and health are inextricably linked in medical and sacred texts. The direction and qualities of the wind are endowed with power and influence over illnesses. In the treatise *The Sacred Disease* (i.e., epilepsy), Hippocrates notes that changes of the wind are apt to bring on seizures, most likely "when the south wind blows, then the north wind, and then the others." The treatise contrasts the south and north winds, which are seen as "most opposite, not only in direction, but in power." The south wind is moist, thick, and warm. It is so influential that it dulls the light of sun, moon, and stars. In the body, it "moistens the brain and enlarges the veins."[9] The north wind is considered cooler and drier. It acts to condense and clarify, so that the sun and celestial bodies shine clear and bright, and the brain and body respond to it by concentrating and clearing out unhealthy moisture. The linking of wind and disease runs through many Hippocratic treatises—including *On Breaths, On Humors,* and the *Epidemics*—pointing out the wind's role in a catalog of illnesses. *Epidemics I,* for example, describes the wind and weather patterns from which arise a list of conditions, including miscarriages, dysentery, headaches, and "gangrene of the brain." Even in colonial America, when deaths were recorded by physicians, the weather conditions at the time of death were often recorded in more detail than were the medical findings.

In ancient India, the *rishis* (seers) to whom the Vedas were revealed watched the winds with infinite patience and in painstaking detail. In their regions, not merely health but life itself depended (and still depends) on the rain the monsoon winds bring to ensure a harvest. Awaiting the shift from dry westerlies to rain-bearing easterlies was an anxious time. The tensions of delay inspired rituals to petition the gods of wind and rain, as well as the development of highly refined systems of weather forecasting.[10] The rishis also knew wind as a purifier, diffusing contamination and promoting health. In the Vedic Hymns, the wind (called Vayu or Vata) is petitioned for health and longevity:

> *May Vata waft medicine, healthful, delightful to our heart;*
> *may he prolong our lives!*
> *Thou, O Vata, art our father, and our brother, and our friend;*
> *do thou grant us to live!*
> *O Vata, from that treasure of the immortal which is placed in*
> *thy house yonder, give us to live!*[11]

The ancient Chinese medical doctors suspected the wind as a cause of nearly all illnesses. The influence of *feng* (wind) brings on common issues such as dizziness, headaches, cramps, and vomiting. One who is *shangfeng* (wounded by wind) runs a fever. One who is *zhongfeng* (struck by wind) faints away. Again, the direction and quality of winds are instilled with power. For society, *fengzhan,* wind divination, predicted the quality of the harvest, the possibility of floods, the potential for epidemics, and war or peace, by the direction of the wind.[12]

Making the Ancient Present, Finding the Past Now

We're not presenting these ancient perspectives on wind and breath for historical interest only. Please don't think of them as just background or introduction. They're meant to carry you into the present moment, into your bodily experience. They're meant to prompt and support your informal and formal practice of mindfulness.

Our contemporary perspectives, understandings, and expectations may be dramatically different from those of the ancients we're describing here. We have, of course, created very different ways of being from the ways of those who came before us. Our culture in twenty-first-century America grants little importance to the everyday wind, and even to the every-moment breath. We cannot recapture the embodied meanings with which the ancients lived. The precise experiences that their words and images captured for them are lost to us; we cannot step entirely outside our cultural conditioning to make them live again. We can, however, step further into our bodies to search where they searched—our common physiology—and perhaps find something of what they found. We can use the language they've left behind to help us experience new possibilities as we come into the present moment with concentration and curiosity.

Are you more apt to notice the metaphor of "winds of change" in your life than the actuality of the breeze against your face? For many of us, that's how it is; we're not ancients, we're moderns. We open our doors and notice storm or sunshine, and don't necessarily connect to the direction of the wind. Here's a chance to come to mindfulness: step outside and notice the motion of the air. Turn toward it and feel it on your face. What are you facing in your yard or neighborhood? Maybe you know that you're looking south, or maybe you can just pick a landmark like the convenience store or the big maple tree: the wind is from there. That's enough orientation. Then, what do you notice? Temperature, velocity, texture, moisture, particulates—how is it right now? Simple, intense curiosity about how it is to live in the world brings you *here*. Are you more present now? If you try this investigation day after day, each time you leave your home, what happens with your experience of wind as *breath outside?* What more do you know? Such knowledge is the "profit" of your informal mindfulness practice: Thoreau proudly wrote in his journal that he was a "self-appointed inspector of snow-storms and rain-storms, and did my duty faithfully, *though I never received one cent for it*" (italics added).

A World of Words for the Wind (and Breath)

The ancients knew the feel of the wind on the body. They felt it inside, too. In fact, their words for wind and breath (and vital force or spirit) generate a complex and beautiful web that draws us in, not merely to intellectual and aesthetic appreciation, but, more importantly, to radical potential for expanding our own perceptions.

Maybe the words most familiar to us come from the Latin *spiritus,* pointing to wind, breath, and soul. In English, the simple drawing of a breath is *inspiration.* It can be also the involuntary filling of our faculties with a power greater than our own—a breathing into us by a god or muse.

In classical Greek, the word is *pneuma,* which for the classical dramatists and storytellers pointed to winds, particularly those of shifting fortunes, relationships, and understandings. In New Testament Greek, John 3:8 illustrates the useful ambiguity of *pneuma,* where it translates as both "wind" and "Spirit": "The wind bloweth where it listeth, and thou hearest the sound thereof, but canst not tell whence it cometh, and whither it goeth: so is every one that is born of the Spirit."

In Hebrew scripture, the word *ruach* represents the wind or breath of God, which, for example, moves upon the face of the waters and vitalizes the human in the book of Genesis.

In the Vedas, the words most parallel with those above are *atman* and *prana.* Atman (from the proto-Indo-European root *etmen,* "breath") points to the self or soul; lowercased, it's the individual's, capitalized (or enlightened) it's the world's. *Prana* (the breath of life) points to the animating force inside the body.

In ancient China, and across East Asia now, *qi* (or *chi* or *ki*) is breath as vital force. The congruence of wind in the world and breath in the body comes clear in practice. In *fengshui* (wind/water) divination, the flow of wind as vital force defines the most propitious places for living, which the diviners refer to as *xue,* meaning holes or caves from and into which the wind flows. In acupuncture, practitioners use this same term, *xue,* for the places in the body where they control the flow of *qi.* We translate *xue* as "point" rather than "opening," thus entirely missing the point of congruence.

If we can feel the wind outside us in something like the older ways, *inspired* by them, so to speak, perhaps we can do the same with the breath flowing within us. Just as the wind circles the world, in ancient views the breath fills the body, bringing power, movement, and change.

Among the Hippocratic treatises, *Airs, Waters, and Places* and *The Sacred Disease* clearly support a *pneumatic* description of bodily life— control by inner winds. In this view, roughly, the inbreath flows first to the brain, causing intelligence. Then most of the breath goes into the belly to cool it. And the remainder flows into the lungs and the veins, with the veins dispersing it for cooling and to power the movement of the limbs. Another detailed description maps two major hollow veins running from the brain to the extremities, one on each side of the body—arising and descending from the liver on the right and from the spleen on the left. Further, we're told that the breath cannot rest, it must move in and out, up and down; if it stops in any one place in the body, that part becomes paralyzed. If you're sitting or lying wrong, for example, you may block the breath's flow to an appendage, and it goes numb—proving the theory. This fifth-century-BCE view may prompt a pause in your reading: just check in as the breath enters and leaves your body. Do you sense or resonate with some or all of this conception of breathing? How far does the sensation of the breath extend? What moves or wants to move and when? How is it with you right now?

In the development of Western thought, it's interesting to note, this view was refined over centuries, moving further away from direct feeling into realms of abstraction—from the physical to the metaphysical. Aristotle's view from the end of the fourth century BCE posited that it was not direct wind/breath pneuma, but *vital* pneuma derived from the aether of space by the lungs and heart and carried in the blood to the muscles that activated the *psyche* (soul) of the muscle and facilitated movement. This view dominated until the second century CE, when Galen and his students discovered that it was nerves that delivered the signal and power to the muscles. They made sense of the link to pneuma by describing how the brain refined Aristotle's vital pneuma from the blood into psychic pneuma, which traveled in the nerves to move the muscle. This refined pneumatic view prevailed for more than 1,300 years in the West, until Descartes' corpuscular "animal spirits" theory in the seventeenth century, which was then replaced by Galvani's electrical theory in the eighteenth, carrying us into modern theorizing.[13]

Compared with the ancient Greek conceptions, the ancient Hindu and Chinese views of prana and qi, respectively, suggest much the same original sense and expanding of refinements.

As a simple statement and image, in Hindu thought, prana is the vital force, tangible as the inbreath and the outbreath. Prana flows through channels in the body, the *nadis,* and storage places, the *chakras,* a system facilitating movement, physiological processes, and activities of the mind. When flow is blocked, the result can be bodily distress, psychological instability, or even spiritual issues. In the yogic tradition, prana can be cultivated and controlled through prescribed *pranayama* breathing practices.

Qi in the East Asian traditions is the vital force, which has qualities of breath and also encompasses other sources and characterizations of energy. Qi is all-encompassing; it might be said to be "the cause, process, and outcome of all activity in the cosmos."[14] The evolution of the written character tells the story. Ancient ideograms used three strokes to symbolize cloudlike vapor—the breath visible in the cold. It may be seen in a more metabolic sense as steam over cooked rice—available energy that can move us. In Song dynasty China (960–1127 CE), the character was elaborated to four "vapor" strokes above the character for rice, which is still used in classical Chinese; in contemporary Chinese pinyin, *qi* is just the top four strokes, without the "rice" below—simple as the changing breath again.[15] As with pneuma and prana, the qi flows in the body through a system of channels, here called *meridians,* and is stored in organs that share names and functions with, but are not entirely identified with, the physiological organs as we conceive them. And, as with the other systems, when energy flow is blocked in a specific area, the healthy processes stop and disease can develop. Further, as with prana, qi can be cultivated through exercises featuring the breath—*qigong,* for example.

A study of the practices of pranayama and qigong will reveal similarities. These arise not only from a "universal" human physiological and phenomenological connection to the concept of vital energy, but also from the direct influence and exchange of insights and practices that were facilitated by the great trade routes linking India, China, and even the Mediterranean civilizations.[16] As Eastern sciences or technologies striving toward longevity or immortality, pranayama and qigong are attempts to control the flow of vital energy—particularly as breath—and thus control that major characteristic of the universe, change. Practitioners in both traditions attempt to resist the depletion of vital energy—to contain it, cultivate it, refine it, and use it to preserve themselves from aging and death. Looked at from a different angle, such practices attempt to slow or stop time, the sense of which may be derived from the longer and shorter rhythms of wind and breath, as we'll soon see. These practices may very well reveal to us sensations and conditions of body and mind that hold great interest, and may, indeed, improve our health; however, we will not present such activities, as in our projected American approach to mindfulness, our practice is to simply attend to the unimpeded flow of experience (you could say, qi), fully living in the ongoing transitions of moment to moment.

Let's give Thoreau the last word—literally—on wind and breath. On the final day of his life, his sister, Sophia, was reading to him from his revision of *A Week on the Concord and Merrimac Rivers,* the last chapter.

After the description of the two brothers in their boat sharing an apple as they crossed back into Massachusetts, Henry, with fever-bright eyes, whispered to Sophia, "Now comes the good sailing." It was the last full sentence he spoke. His reference was to the passage coming next, a passage from the book, or perhaps a passage of another kind. The book passage contains this description of the easiest and most joyful of voyages (the unfulfilled promise of Aeolus to Odysseus)—sailing home *with* the wind:

> They were great and current motions, the flowing sail, the running stream, the waving tree, the roving wind. The north wind stepped readily into the harness which we had provided, and pulled us along with good will. Sometimes we sailed as gently and steadily as the cloud overhead, watching the receding shores and the motions of our sail; the play of its pulse so like our own lives, so thin and yet so full of life, so noiseless when it labored hardest, so noisy and impatient when least effective; now bending to some generous impulse of the breeze, and then fluttering and flapping with a kind of human suspense (8:50).[17]

PASSING TIME/PRESENT MOMENT

The motion of Thoreau's sail, "the play of its pulse so like our own lives," distills the rhythms of the wind and breath that simultaneously beat out the measure of our days and capture the timeless quality of mindful presence.

Felt familiarly, wind carries a certain kind of time, spreads it among us, brushes it against us. A perceptible shift in temperature, direction, or moisture does not merely signal the advent of, say, autumn or the monsoon, it *embodies* the change: it *is* autumn; it *is* the monsoon. Wind offers a cyclical perception of time as it moves through its quarters and season succeeds season. It offers, as well, a linear progress as cycle succeeds cycle; as I type this, the winds of my fifty-seventh autumn rattle the windows. And the rattle punctuates my reverie, dropping me into the present moment in awareness, the pull of gravity on my head and shoulders tilting toward the keyboard, the breath beginning an outward motion. A slash, a comma, in the cycle or line of flowing time, this breath as I attend to it neither measures nor contains the moment, but rather full-fills it. From the wind to the breath, from flow to punctuation, from the dreariness of aging to the freshness of now.

The breath and the present moment coincide, nest within each other, for measurement and concentration across many dimensions. The geographer Yi-Fu Tuan explains that the alternating experience of tension and ease in the body gives us a sense of time—and of space.[18] Time may be marked, say, with inbreath and outbreath, the contraction and relaxation of the diaphragm like the pulsing of Thoreau's sail, opening and closing space in the chest and abdomen. Space is the experience of freedom of movement, of ease. So we tend to conflate time and space. I might say that my office is *twenty minutes* from my home or that I have *room* in my schedule to talk with you today. If I didn't have that room, I might tell you that I need some *breathing space*. I might even create that space for myself, instantly, by dropping into the pause, the punctuation, the comma, of present-moment awareness. (In fact, in Mindfulness-Based Cognitive Therapy,[19] an important short-form practice is the "three minute breathing space.") Right in the embodied experience of breathing, then, is the "meditative space" that we are said to be "in" in present-moment awareness. Tuan reminds us that because of this time-and-space conflation, architecture has been called "frozen music"—human rhythm and feeling we can walk into.[20]

The three-second cycle of tension and ease in the breath also coincides with the making of meaning. In attempting to describe the temporal/experiential boundaries of *now*, psychiatrist Daniel Stern marshals an impressive array of scientific measures of the time it takes to make meaning.[21] In music, if two tones occur in a three-second span or less, there is a sensation of forward motion; if the span is greater, the sense of motion is suspended. This sense of song applies to speaking as well. Most sentences are said in three seconds or so. Taking a turn in a dialogue requires two to three seconds. We interrupt the speaker in conversation about every three seconds to reflect our understanding. A pause of more than three seconds often signals a shift of speaker or topic. Even when we talk baby-talk to an infant, it's a two- to three-second exchange, while the nonverbal riffs of faces and gestures we use to get the infant smiling or giggling run about two to five seconds.

Comprehending meaning, *grasping* something, suggests physical action. And, indeed, the cycle of breath helps us make sense of such actions. For example, Stern notes that as we become conscious of walking, our steps often synchronize with inbreath and outbreath: two steps on the inbreath, and two or three on the outbreath.[22]

In fact, breath, music, speech, and meaning coalesce in marching songs and cadence counts: in America, examples range from the "Yankee Doodle" taunt to the British in the Revolutionary War, to "When Johnny Comes Marching Home," sung by both sides in the Civil War, to the seismic shift of African American Private Willie Duckworth's chant in World War II—"SOUND OFF: one, two; SOUND OFF: three, four; cadence count: one, two, three, four; one-two: THREE-FOUR!"—and the ensuing "Jody calls" that opened to improvisational meaning-making in the moment— "Ain't no use in going home; Jody's got your girl and gone. Ain't no use in feeling blue; Jody's got your sister, too. Ain't no use in lookin' back; Jody's got your Cadillac." Even the subtle gestures of greeting a friend compound and generate meaning and context in three to five seconds: raised eyebrows and smiles while approaching, spoken exchanges, and shared hand gestures or embraces bring us together in the *now*. In conversation, besides the turn-taking and phrase-speaking, significant shifts of posture—crossing or uncrossing legs, leaning to the other side—also take three to five seconds and signal a new present moment with a new focus or subject.

These groupings and measures, of course, expand or contract depending on physical and emotional states. Therefore, Stern suggests, it is clearest to think of a duration of from one to ten seconds for a present moment. He also notes that *now* can endure over longer periods formed by present moments refreshed in a series, as we focus our attention, or as it is caught and held by the context.

Breath, Time, and Well-Being

Inbreath and outbreath are, for most of us, easy to identify and locate. We may even assume that the two-part feeling of in-out, up-down is the basic rhythm of the breath. We may need reminding that the rhythm is far more subtle, and actually in three parts: inbreath, outbreath, and pause. And it is in the pause that the sense of time truly touches us. The feeling of "enough time" and of feeling "rushed" are hidden in that pause.

As Carola Speads describes it, the pause has a double purpose. It is both a rest from the effort of the prior inbreath and a renewing of energy for the next.[23] It's not downtime; it's pivotal in the cycle, and vital to a sense of well-being. Should you choose to shorten the pause ever so slightly, notice the sensation of time that results. Perhaps you feel pressured? Rushed? Irritable? Anxious? Notice, in contrast, how hard it is to *choose* to make the pause *right,* to expand it consciously so that you relax. The only way is to allow the breath to respond to the infinitely shifting physiological demands of the moment and measure its own pause.

If you're not used to experiencing your breath in this three-part way, the pause may not be immediately available to your perception. It may take practice to find it.

A Hebrew Perspective on the Breath

The name of G_d, YHWH, commanded never to be spoken in vain and never to be written with the vowel sounds noted, is a marvelous breath of paradox. It represents an unavoidable, inevitable practice that you may choose to recognize, if it is helpful for you.

Although it is often written as "Yahweh" (in non-Hebrew texts), the true pronunciation of the name is considered lost. However, the consonants that make up the name are the most breathlike in the Hebrew alphabet (*aleph-bet*). Philosopher and cultural ecologist David Abram notes that contemporary students of Kabbalah believe that the pronunciation of *YHWH* may have been a whispered sounding of the first syllable, "Y-H," as the breath comes in, and a sounding of the second, "W-H," as the breath goes forth. The name reverberates through the whole cycle.[24]

Following Abram's suggestion, the Franciscan retreat leader and writer Richard Rohr teaches this whispered breathing of *YHWH* as a practice that he has seen as transformative for contemplatives in many traditions around the globe. As he describes it, with supporting Biblical quotations:

> When considered in this way, God is suddenly as available and accessible as the very thing we all do constantly—breathe. Exactly as some teachers of prayer always said, "Stay with the breath, attend to your breath": the same breath that was breathed into Adam's nostrils by this Yahweh (Genesis 2:7); the very breath that Jesus handed over with trust on the cross (John 19:30) and then breathed on us as shalom, forgiveness, and the Holy Spirit all at once (John 20:21–23). And isn't it wonderful that breath, wind, spirit, and air are precisely *nothing*—and yet everything?[25]

Just knowing that the breath is forever saying this name—it's our first breath and our last—generates possibilities for new and deeper connections with others and with the world, moment by moment, breath by breath.

8

THE BREATH II

The Breeze across the Inner Landscape

Emerson's gifted harp says, "Lift the sash, lay me within, / Lend me your ears, and I begin." We can start now to listen to the music inside, identifying the notes, chords, and harmonies sustained in quiet breathing, or the rests and syncopations of sighing and yawning that announce, perhaps, the entry of a new theme.

AUTOMATIC AND INTENTIONAL

The breath is unique among ongoing body processes, because it is continuously open to both autonomic and conscious control. It flows ever on, adjusting instantaneously to the myriad changes in you and your situation, sighing out Aeolian music as background to your life. Yet you can override and intervene at any moment to accomplish your intention, and to play a tune of your own choosing on the harp for a while. As we begin to investigate some of the tensions and beauties of this double-edged control—captured in the pairs universal/unique, willful/willing, continuity/disruption—a background in the physiology of respiration will be helpful. In fact, the description that follows may prompt you to pause and investigate as you read and breathe. Please, take the time to follow any promptings or questions, as the path we're following here is not so much about science as about sensing, not so much about *thinking through* as

132

about *feeling into* what you can know of your experiences—and yourself.

In a lifetime of eighty years, a body will breathe in and out about five hundred million times, with only the tiniest of pauses or respites. Such relentlessness is no surprise, as just a few minutes without oxygen coming in and carbon dioxide going out results in irreparable brain damage. We really don't hold much oxygen, or for long. At rest, a healthy man weighing about 155 pounds will use roughly 250 milliliters of oxygen in a minute, and the body can only hold a liter at a time (about one quart). The next breath is inevitable, soon. And that's just at rest. Add a little work, like walking, and consumption more than triples, to 800 milliliters per minute. The breath adjusts to meet the demand for oxygen in and carbon dioxide out; fuel and waste for walking energy. The breath adjusts to such changes in metabolic demand. It does so immediately for variation in effort, whether physical or mental, and it does so over time for alterations in condition, such as development, disease, disability, or aging. The desired result is continual *eupnea*—from the Greek roots *eu-*, "good or well," and *pnein-*, "to breathe or blow," through which the spirit of pneuma arrives in the contemporary world of medicine and science that is more interested in dyspnea and apnea than in eupnea, which is also called "quiet breathing."[1] Let's settle into the quiet, focusing our description of breathing mainly on muscular and neurological involvement in eupnea.

The muscles most involved in quiet breathing are the muscles of the upper airways, the thoracic diaphragm, and the dorsal intercostals. They may be smooth muscles, which operate involuntarily, or skeletal muscles, which also respond to the will and are subdivided so that they can move incrementally. The accessory respiratory muscles of the neck act by pulling the entire rib cage upward. The upper airway muscles include the smooth muscles of the bronchi and the skeletal muscles of the mouth, nose, throat, tongue, and glottis. The diaphragm (at rest) is like a dome opening up into the bottom of the chest. It is attached to the lowest ribs all around and to the sternum in front and the upper lumbar vertebrae in back. One of the largest muscles in the body, it has characteristics of both smooth muscles and skeletal muscles. Psychologist and bodyworker Alan Fogel suggests that the diaphragm is like the eyelid muscles, which can both blink unconsciously and be winked expressively.[2] The intercostals, located between the ribs, raise and lower the ribs to increase or reduce lung capacity. They are skeletal muscles, yet they have nerve inputs that allow both voluntary and involuntary control.

The respiratory cycle in quiet breathing actually begins with *preactivation* of the upper airway muscles, about 200 milliseconds before the diaphragm receives its signal to begin inspiration. This ensures that the upper airways are open, and prevents a collapse that might be caused by the negative pressure of the inbreath. The diaphragm is the next muscle activated. It contracts, descending into the abdomen, expanding space in the chest and thus increasing the capacity of the lungs to draw in air. This expansion is followed by activation of the intercostals to oppose the negative pressure it creates. Almost immediately, as the inbreath ends, all the inspiratory muscles contract slightly in the transition to expiration. Then, the diaphragm passively returns upward, reducing lung capacity and pushing air out. The muscles of the upper airway narrow and create more resistance than during the inspiration, so the outbreath takes longer than the inbreath.

That's how quiet breathing, eupnea, works; respiratory muscles operate for inspiration without conscious intervention or resistance, and expiration is essentially passive, as the diaphragm and intercostals just relax naturally. However, when breathing demand and effort rise, other muscles are recruited. For a stronger inbreath, muscles of the neck and shoulder area—the sternomastoids, scalenes, and pectoralis minors—expand the top of the chest. For the outbreath, the lateral intercostals and the muscles of the abdominal wall add compressive force.

Quiet Differences in Posture (and Gender)

Gravity plays an obvious role in breathing. The contents of the abdomen—the viscera—are pulled downward, away from the diaphragm, when you're sitting or standing. As your body tilts toward lying down, the viscera press more and more against the diaphragm.

A study of quiet breathing in four postures, sequentially tilting the body from a seated posture to lying flat on the back, revealed significant differences in breathing patterns and engagement of muscles between postures.[3] As postures tilted progressively toward lying flat, there was a lower volume of air in each breath, less and less movement of the ribs, and an increase in the contribution of abdominal movement to the overall volume. There is a gender difference in this, with women showing greater rib cage contribution to quiet breathing in any position and men showing greater abdominal movement.

This study was the first to look at breathing patterns when sitting, both with and without back support. With back support, there was greater abdominal contribution. Without back support, it seems that the muscular effort to hold the body upright limits abdominal contribution and increases rib cage movement.

Perhaps there's an experiment (or two) in this for you? What do you notice about the breath in the different positions you find your body in throughout the day?

As this good, quiet, spontaneous work goes on, how does the body know—below conscious awareness—when to breathe in and out? There are many possible influences, including chemoreception, mechanoreceptor feedback, airway protective reflexes, developmental changes, neuroplasticity, and neurotransmitters and modulators such as noradrenaline, serotonin, and GABA. But, for making sense of our walking-around experience in the world, a detailed description of the role of chemoreception offers the most descriptive power and direct assistance in understanding.

Eupnea, as we've described, maintains the precise balance of oxygen coming in and carbon dioxide going out that the body requires in the moment. The exchange of gases takes place as the circulatory system brings the blood into contact with the lungs. In chemoreception, common sense and common language may suggest that oxygen is the more important gas, yet it is actually carbon dioxide buildup that ultimately signals the need to breathe. The body does have oxygen receptors, in the carotid bodies, which are located where the carotid arteries branch out. Carbon dioxide sensing takes place in the brainstem, in a variety of areas, including the pre-Bötzinger complex and the ventral medullary surface.

It's easy to illustrate the dominance of the effect of carbon dioxide sensing. Consider this classic (and dangerous) demonstration: first, the subject breathes and rebreathes the air in a closed system, and as carbon dioxide builds up, he feels the need to breathe more and more deeply. Next, the same demonstration is performed, but with the excess carbon dioxide filtered out: as his oxygen level declines, the subject has little signal of oxygen deprivation, fails to change the rhythm and depth of his breathing, and does not notice as his mental and physical functioning begin to degrade.[4] This is what happens to mountaineers at high altitudes, who may exhibit irrational behavior and even hallucinate—often feeling that another person is accompanying them. So, to answer our question, the body knows *from inside* when to take the next breath, instructed by the level of carbon dioxide, the product of its own metabolism. The quiet breath rests gently, balancing on this burning, tending this unfolding of energy.

Underneath the precision of this tending, the brainstem is generating a breathing rhythm to help maintain efficient breathing over time, without conscious intervention. Obviously, such rhythm generation is important, as its disruption is deadly. Sudden infant death syndrome (SIDS) is one example, while adult deaths from respiratory arrest are common in diseases affecting the central nervous system, such as ALS (Lou Gehrig's disease) and Parkinson's disease, and perhaps even simply in cases of advanced aging.[5] Although the science is still settling out, it seems that there may be two rhythm oscillators in the brainstem, the pre-Bötzinger complex and the retrotrapeziod nucleus, which may or may not be identical to the parafacial respiratory group. The pre-Bötzinger complex, it seems, generates inspiratory rhythm, while the retrotrapeziod nucleus/parafacial respiratory group generates expiratory rhythm. The rhythm of the pre-Bötzinger complex dominates normal quiet breathing, so that the outbreath is more passive.

We can, of course, intervene and change the rhythm consciously at any time, but as we let go of conscious control, the brain-stem rhythm reestablishes itself. It is possible that if one oscillator is damaged, a rhythm can be maintained by the other. Both active inspiration with passive expiration and active expiration with passive inspiration are sustainable, although they each have a different quality. Perhaps those qualities may be worth your while to sense into, *now*. How is it to breathe *in* deliberately and then suspend activity to simply observe? How is it to reverse the process, breathing out purposefully and watching and allowing whatever happens?

UNIVERSAL/UNIQUE

We're all breathing, all the time. Breathing along with the world—the universal movement of inbreath and outbreath. It simply happens. It ultimately controls us. Without active interference, the breath returns to the unconscious, steady, life-continuing exchange of gases. Yet the rhythm that reasserts itself in this quiet breath is not simply the universal inspiration and expiration. It is also a measurable airflow shape as unique as your fingerprints or signature.[6] Interestingly, the airflow shapes of identical twins have very high levels of similarity.[7]

Each of us seems to have such a particular, stable pattern of quiet breathing, which is revealed in the measured shape of variables such as volume breathed, length of inbreath and outbreath, and duration from inbreath to inbreath. This all can be represented as sort of a sine wave (figure 8.1A). This signature of the breath really doesn't change much over our adult lives. We even maintain this uniqueness in changes of environment—whether we are breathing at sea level or at high altitude.[8] Exercise or other such increases in metabolic demand do alter the signature, shifting it from curves to rectangular shapes (figure 8.1B). As we settle back toward quiet being, our signature breath begins to write itself again.

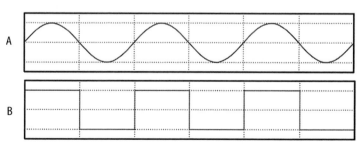

Figure 8.1. Resting-state breathing can be represented by smooth sine waves (A), whereas increased metabolic demand results in an altered signature, which can be seen in these more rectangular-shaped waves (B).

The unique signature of the breath of our embodied being is an entirely natural, empirical fact. That it asserts itself when we come to quiet, when we cease striving and give up conscious control, when we surrender to it, also is unassailable. And it's worthy of continuing experiment. Perhaps you're willing to connect these testable facts with the earlier descriptions of spirit, pneuma, prana, and qi, and to consider the ways in which your unique breath may come to rest within the universal, in which your signature may write itself on the flow of experience, in which your quietest name may be carried into silence by the breeze. Or maybe you're not willing to go so far. And it is this fact of choice, this possibility of asserting your will, that deepens any experiments you may make.

An Ideal Object of Study

Both breath and heartbeat originate in the center of the body, in the chest. Both are rhythms of life. Both respond instantly to demands that are physical or mental, that are tied to love or fear or anything in between. Yet, the breath gets all the attention! Across the contemplative traditions, there is an obvious preference for moment-by-moment concrete study of the breath, while the heart is more likely to be engaged metaphorically.

Any answer to *why* would include the fact that the breath is open to a certain level of conscious intervention and control, while the heart is uncontrollable (which is part of its metaphoric meaning). And, more concretely, only the breath is completely available to the analytic instrument that we *are*. Our comfortable capacity to process sensory stimuli reflects a rate of 20 to 30 Hz, or twenty to thirty events per second. The information from the breath falls right in this range. In fact, in the scientific study of respiration, digital sampling or recording rarely exceeds 30 Hz, as that's plenty of data to trace whatever is being studied. The heart, on the other hand, generates events at least four times faster—just consider 70 beats per minute versus 15 breaths per minute—and the waveforms are highly varied.[9] Even an electrocardiograph for amateur home use would be sampling at least at 100 Hz.[10]

Our instrument, the body, is dialed in just right for reading the breath.

WILLFUL/WILLING

So we have will, and there is spirit. The pioneering spiritual director and psychiatrist Gerald May beautifully articulates the relationship of these two interdependent dimensions.

> Sometimes it seems that will moves easily with a natural flow of spirit, and at such times, we feel grounded, centered, and responsive to the needs of the world as they are presented to us. . . . Then, at least for a moment, we are whole.
>
> There are other times when will seems to pull away from spirit, trying to chart its own course. . . . At such times, we may feel fragmented, contrived, and artificial . . . struggling against the truth of who we really are and what we are really called to do.[11]

May sees the first dimension, the conjunction of will and spirit, as saying yes to the experience of the moment, and the second dimension, division, as a speaking of no to the flow. The tendency toward conjunction he calls *willingness,* while the movement to divide he calls *willfulness.* These two can be considered with great subtlety, acknowledging that they easily change character and quality—one becoming the other as *yes* closes down or *no* opens up.

The American Revolution and the development of the American character are May's case in point. When John Paul Jones hoisted the first flag of resistance—"Don't Tread on Me"—it flew with the willing wind of individualism, courage, and self-determination, the spirit of a creative drive toward freedom. This was the spirit that breathes in the bravest passages of the Declaration of Independence and the Constitution and that inspired Emerson's articulations of everyday philosophy—transcendent and pragmatic all at once—in works that became keystones of American character, such as "The American Scholar" and "Self-Reliance." Yet willfulness was there from the start, as well, backing away from the flow of spirit, dividing meaning and intent in debates around the Declaration and Constitution. The founders threw off foreign oppression while maintaining slavery, denying women participation in their nation, and turning a blind eye to the wholesale destruction of indigenous societies. Likewise, one hundred years later, the powerful elites of the Gilded Age stripped away Emerson's spirituality and advocacy of social reform from his celebration of individual genius. They enlisted his still, strong prose to justify a rapacious capitalism that dispirited and exploited the citizens whose dignity was (and is) the true source of the country's wealth.

The continual shifting between willing and willful, yes and no, is part of what we are, as Americans and as human beings. It is present in our most sophisticated social thought and in our simplest body processes. We are facing, every moment of our lives, the question that William James posed nearly a century before May's ruminations: "Will I or won't I have it so?" Approaching this question just at the level of breath—attending to its physiological expression moment by moment—offers the possibility of encountering and learning about the ambivalence of our own way of being. If you're willing to extend the learning, such concrete explorations have the potential to blossom into insights all the way up through your most important personal relationships and widest social commitments.

The compounding of willful and willing in the breath can be seen as habits that may take on specific expressions in the contexts of our lives.[12] For example, we may have developed a personal idiosyncrasy of slightly overbreathing, so that the normal carbon dioxide level in the blood is slightly low, which amplifies the effect of any physical or mental demand, making us react more strongly. Or, in a social mode, the habit may be taught and ingrained, such as a military-style posture in which the chest is consciously expanded up and out, suggesting, if not continually encouraging, the type of breathing demanded by exercise or by anxiety. When we experiment with breathing as a mindfulness practice, such habits may become available to observation and may even abate or evaporate altogether in the present moment.

This experimenting is quite simple. It's paying attention to the breath as it is. That's it: no matter what's happening inside you or in the physical or social environment, just trusting the breath to be doing what's required and being *willing* to be present for what emerges. Studies of the effectiveness of instructed breathing to reduce stress suggest that *willful* control of breath rate or depth does not significantly impact the turn of the body and mind toward quiet breathing when compared with just paying attention to the breath without intervening.[13] The breath does what the body needs, without instruction.

What effect is reading this having on your breath in this moment? If you pause and tune in to sensations of movement in the ribs in back and the belly in front, what do you learn?

And when you come back to reading, how is it now?

Poetic Demands

Ruth Denison is a teacher in the Vipassana tradition and is credited as holding the first retreat exclusively for women. She was born in Germany in 1922 and immigrated after World War II to America. She studied in the Advaita tradition and in the Zen and Theravada Buddhist traditions. To this she added the study of Sensory Awareness with Elsa Gindler's student Charlotte Selver. Denison was friends with the integrator of Eastern and Western spirituality and philosophy, Alan Watts, who often taught workshops with Selver. In fact, Denison was in India when Watts died, and when she received that news, she found her way to a Hindu temple, where she spontaneously performed a dance to Watts's memory—and to great acclaim from the worshippers.

Denison was involved with much of the fomentation and change in personal and cultural consciousness that took place through the 1950s into the 1970s. She continues to teach in the Vipassana tradition, using many of the experimental approaches from Sensory Awareness to explore mindfulness through embodiment.

She speaks of the breath as we experience it in the willing mode, saying again and again that "breath wants you." Don wrote this poem after he met her for the first time in 2007, when she was eighty-five years old.

B.W.Y.

For Ruth Denison

Frail with a cane and attendant,
even slow walking brings fast breathing.
And that is simply the elements,
you said, "Breath wants you."

Breath: not just this poor ragged thing
in an aging body, yours or mine;
not just a lower case sibilant sssssss,
but also an upper case, indomitable Spirit.

Like the story that's entered mythology,
of you dancing against your will
in a temple in India, moved by the death,
moving in the Spirit of your friend.

That was thirty years ago. Now you still
move in the spirit. "Breath wants you,"
you said in a conversation I passed through
three thousand miles of air and back to hear.

In-breath and out-breath, head wind
and tail wind. And a larger scale still.
This Spirit, our friend, moving in us
as you said, "Breath wants you."

Breath, a gentle insistent teacher,
commands every moment, demands
your (totally fragmented) attention.
And your complete surrender.

CONTINUITY/DISRUPTION

Quiet breathing suggests a continuity, a flow. Yet, there is variation from breath to breath as situations inside and outside you shift minutely or hugely. In the flow of breath, with its easy variations, we find rest. But not for long. A sensation, an emotion, or a thought arises, and the pattern of breathing shifts—on its own or with intention and effort. Maybe you've played with this while attending to the breath in formal sitting meditation. The attention wanders. When you notice, you bring it back, taking a deliberate inbreath, starting over. Or, perhaps, you become aware of the wandering and gently find the breath again—observing without disturbing. In either case, the chances are good that there is a sigh nearby—the body-mind hitting the reset button to come into a new balance in the moment.

SIGHING

The sigh as a resetting mechanism makes a lot of sense.[14] The respiratory system is highly complex, with many different feedback mechanisms, as we've seen, such as the sensing of carbon dioxide and oxygen levels, as well as pH levels, in the blood. To add even further complexity, such feedback mechanisms interact with other systems, such as the cardio-vascular system, as well. And, of course, there is the need to respond to internal and external demands. Yet the breath has a tendency to move toward a steady state. That is, the differences in each breath are determined by the qualities of the previous breaths. In systems theory, this would be called *correlated variability*. There's a sort of short-term memory in the respiratory system that helps the variations in breath create an overall balance. This is the balance we can sense in quiet breathing. However, when that short-term memory is disturbed, say by a thought or an event, the variations in breath become more random and move away from overall balance. The sigh as a resetting mechanism fits in here, now. If the balance is out, with either too much randomness or too little variability in the breathing overall, a sigh can right the balance. A too-random breathing pattern arises when emotion dominates actual metabolic needs. An unvariable pattern arises by sustained states, such as sustained attention or mental stress. In information theory terms, in either pattern the respiratory system does not have enough information, so additional noise is required to enhance the signal-to-noise ratio and allow correlated variability to arise again. A sigh, which Vlemincx and colleagues defined for their 2010 study as a breath at least 2.5 times deeper than the prior baseline,[15] is a great source of noise. So it offers a sense of relief from emotional and mental loads.

Given this relationship of sighing to mental loads and emotion, it is surprising that sighing itself has not been a topic of empirical psychological research until the twenty-first century. About the only place sighing makes an appearance is in studies of panic disorder, where it has been shown that such patients "hit reset" about twice as frequently as control subjects—an average of 21 times versus 10.8 times over a thirty-minute period of sitting quietly in a comfortable chair.[16] Yet, there has been little interest in the interpretation of sighs generally, although there are certainly folk psychology understandings. Karl Teigen opened up this area with empirical studies of what sighs mean to the sighers and the observers of sighs.[17] His findings, while reflecting only northern European culture, are interesting, particularly in their illumination of sigher-observer differences. For sighers, the act implicitly carries two messages. First, something is not right, that is, there is a mismatch of how I wish it to be and how it actually is. Perhaps there is a situation in which I begin to see that I'm not going to get what I need, or maybe I'm working hard to reach some end or some solution to a problem, and I realize that I may not be successful. Second, the message is a movement toward acceptance, that is, there is a sense that I must "let go" of something. Even sighs of relief or pleasure could fit this basic description. Relief could be read as a letting go of negative expectations. Pleasure could be seen as a letting go of agendas and surrendering to the moment. Lover's sighs may be generated by the mismatch of longing for the one not available to us or by the presence of the beloved, to whom we give ourselves—the erotic form of letting go. So sighers most often interpreted their own sighs from this *something's wrong/need to let go* perspective. As social communication, the meaning of a sigh seems to follow self-knowledge, as the typical interpretation is that the sigher finds something or someone "hopeless" and is giving up (or letting go).

Maybe you noticed a spontaneous sigh as you read the last several paragraphs? Maybe one is due right now?

Sigh of Relief

We have found that people who report enough life stress to take a Mindfulness-Based Stress Reduction course often find benefit from sighing—on purpose. Here's how we instruct them:

> Inhaling through your nose and exhaling through your mouth, making a quiet, relaxing sigh as you exhale. Taking long, slow, gentle breaths that raise and lower your abdomen as you inhale and exhale. Focusing on the sound and feeling of the breath.
>
> You can use cues throughout your daily routine to remind yourself to take three to six relaxing sighs (red lights while driving, telephone sounds, waiting for elevators, waiting in line, etc.). You may want to place stickers in areas where you look frequently, or areas that cause you stress, as a reminder (computer, refrigerator, watch, cell phone, spouse's forehead [just joking!]).[18]

Tune in to a sense of relief, if you find one. Tune in to what happens next. Perhaps a yawn follows your sighs?

Workin' 'n' Sighin'

When folks are working on a tough task, where they have to try, try again, sighs occur. And it makes sense. Brainteasers like the nine-dots problem (see below) provoked sighs in one study by Teigen. He reports that almost 80 percent of participants sighed while working on the problems, with an average of four clearly marked sighs each, and two doubtful ones (a breath that may be a sigh, or maybe not). And here's the telltale—one participant actually said the word *sigh* at three different times, without really sighing. This paragraph in Teigen's discussion is rich in description of how we live and work with sighing.

> Sighs occurred throughout the experiment, some sighed already when they received the task, and some when they handed it in, but most sighs appeared to occur in the breaks after one or several fruitless attempts. When interviewed, 12 participants (of 36) remembered explicitly that they had sighed (but not necessarily when), whereas the majority had not been aware of sighing, but admitted it was likely, given the nature of the task. Three participants (who actually sighed) denied categorically that they had sighed, one said: "I may have felt like sighing, but I did not, because it would have been rude." When asked to give probable reasons for sighing, they explained that they may have sighed because they had to give up, they were frustrated, felt helpless, or stupid.[19]

How do you work with sighing? When does it come into your attention? What might you learn by turning toward the sighing in your life? Here's the nine-dots puzzle from the study. Try your own experiment!

The Nine Dots: A Puzzle

Instructions: Without lifting the pencil from the paper, draw four lines so that all of the dots are connected with a line passing through them. (The answer appears on page 148.)

YAWNING

Despite the fact that we yawn spontaneously five to ten times a day, and that it is a highly pleasurable event, comparatively little effort has gone into understanding why we yawn. In fact, it was not until 2010 that the first English-language textbook on yawning was published.[20] So, we don't know much about yawns, but much of what we do know is practical and can add to our practice with the breath.

Common knowledge and, indeed, common sense support the claim that yawning brings more oxygen to the brain. Essentially, that was the major "scientific" position from Hippocrates' time until the 1980s. Maybe it's what you "know" about the whys and wherefores of yawning. However, this piece of wisdom was finally tested, and roundly rejected, by R. Provine, B. Tate, and L. Geldmacher, who showed that neither reduced oxygen nor increased carbon dioxide triggered yawns in their subjects.[21] This finding brought about more serious research on the neglected yawn, which is ongoing today. One researcher, Wolter Seuntjens, has proposed a name for this new area of concentration: chasmology, from *chasm*, the Greek for "yawn."[22] Makes sense, doesn't it? A yawning mouth really does open chasm-wide.

As we feel our way through understanding them, we see that yawns certainly do bring discontinuity to the breathing pattern, yet they entail much more than just the respiratory system. They are a stereotyped behavior that seems to be a key to maintaining well-being. The movements and events are always roughly the same from person to person. In fact, yawns can be seen in developing fetuses from the end of the first trimester on. Further, yawns are in the repertoire of all vertebrates, whether warm or cold blooded, whether they live on land, in water, or in air.

You'll feel your way through this description: a gaping of the mouth with a long inbreath; a pause at the peak, or acme, of the sequence; followed by a short, full outbreath, accompanied by relaxation of all the involved muscles.[23] And that's just the outline from the breathing point of view. A comprehensive description would notice the stretching of the muscles of the jaw, cheeks, and neck (maybe obscuring hearing and seeing, and even bringing tears to the eyes); the opening of the throat; the stretching of muscles of the arms, chest, back, abdomen, and possibly elsewhere; the sensations from a cascade of hormones and neurotransmitters, such as the pleasurable feelings from oxytocin and serotonin; the sense of relaxation from activation of the parasympathetic response; and the sense of slipping away from or coming into the sense of the body (falling asleep or waking up).

It may be that yawning facilitates a transition in consciousness or attention. We yawn before sleep and upon waking. We yawn often before an intense undertaking, such as a musical performance—or a parachute jump! Fogel suggests that the yawn may be a signal for the body to "wake up to itself," for the yawner to come into embodied self-awareness.[24] Neuroscientist Andrew Newberg explains that one of the parts of the brain that is stimulated by yawning, the precuneus, is a key to consciousness, self-reflection, and memory retrieval, noting that this same structure is stimulated by yogic breathing and other forms of meditation. As he puts it, "Yawning will relax you and bring you into a state of alertness faster than any other meditation technique I know of."[25]

It's quite possible that reading these last few paragraphs about yawning has caused you to yawn. That prospect takes us to new realms of research and

---

The Nine Dots: An Answer

(Start)

Solution: The box shape made by the dots suggests that the solution is to be found inside the confines or boundaries of the dots. It is only through the discovery that lines can be drawn "outside the box" that solutions become possible. And sighing stops!

---

speculation. Yawning is highly "contagious." It gets triggered in 45–60 percent of adults when seeing, hearing, or even imagining someone else yawning.[26] This phenomenon of contagion seems to be related to our capacity for empathy, as it involves areas of the brain that help us to be aware of ourselves *and* attune to others.[27] Groups can attune to each other through a contagious yawn. And there is even an erotic dimension, as yawning is linked to sexual response and pair bonding.[28] It is revealing that yawning does not appear to be contagious among children diagnosed with autism spectrum disorders, who do not orient socially in typical ways. Further, contagious yawning only appears in humans and other primates—with the interesting possible exception of dogs, those animal companions that join with us socially.[29]

Just as the *sigh* helps to bring the respiratory system into greater balance, into a state of correlated variability in systems theory terms, so a *yawn* acts in the same way for the embodied awareness within you and within a social group. Yawning might be seen as a strange attractor, from which emerges a new and clearer way of being in the body and being together with others. And the best part is, yawning is both automatic and intentional, spontaneous and contagious. It's ambiguous, so you can be playful with it.

When a yawn arises on its own, can you notice where it's taking you? Can you get one started when alone, to help transition to a different activity? Can you get one started in a group, to bring you all together? Scientists may not know much about yawning, but the real challenge is, what can you find out?

Fake It 'Til You Make It

To get a real sense of the embodied self-awareness brought on by a yawn, all you have to do is fake one. You know how they go. Then add another. And another. Until a real one spontaneously kicks in. It may take six or seven fake ones before the real thing comes along. Then, when it does, keep on going. Don't stop until you reach a dozen.[30]

Check in then. What do you know about your attention, muscle tightness, and sense of well-being? (By the way, if you couldn't stop after twelve, that's just fine; you may just be yawn deprived!)

9

THE BREATH III

The Storms and Stillness of Subjective Experience

It may be evident by now that the breath reflects the moment, even as it offers a moment for reflection. It is a constant in the background of our lives, and can come to the foreground of our attention—and even the attention of others—to express and help us work with our ever-changing inner lives.

Contemporary research on links between breathing and emotion reveals the monolithic clinical bias of almost all biomedical research. It rarely diverges from physical and psychological pathologies, and focuses almost exclusively on hyperventilation and anxiety. Empirical studies of joyful breathing, for example, are hard to find. Yet, our mindfulness practice includes the full range of experiences, from ecstasy to agony, that Emerson's Aeolian harp suggests:

> *Many and subtle are my lays,*
> *The latest better than the first,*
> *For I can mend the happiest days*
> *And charm the anguish of the worst.*

In the nineteenth century, the word *mend* carried a sense of "improve," so the days could be happier still. And, of course, the word *charm* invokes the ability to control through spells and magic, as well as emotion and sentiment. So as we attend to *today's* lays—the creative and magical songs our own harps play—we come to see how our subjective experience shapes the breath, and the reverse, how the breath shapes our subjective experience.

REVEALING AND REGULATING

Our changing breathing patterns reveal what is happening with us. Perhaps the change is brought about by an increase in metabolic demand from exercise. Or maybe it's in psychological preparation for a challenging encounter. It could be a conditioned response, or even a learned pattern, a little of the actor's craft, to send a message to other folks: maybe, "Welcome," or, "Oh, please," or, "Jump back, Jack." We'll explore the full range, through the paradox pairs of thought/action, threat/safety, and intervention/observation.

THOUGHT/ACTION

There is a little bit of scientific information on breathing and the body-mind (or in these cases, *body/mind*) that is not related to pathology, so let's start simply, by taking a look at differences in how the breath adjusts to physical or mental tasks. A series of three studies revealed basically two contrary strategies.[1] As physical demand increased, subjects' breathing patterns adjusted, mostly by increasing the volume of each breath, and as demand increased further, by increasing the rate of breathing. In contrast, as mental demand and stress increased, subjects' breathing adjusted mostly by increasing the rate first, and by adjusting volume only during the most mentally stressful moments.

So, perhaps a rule of thumb for practitioners of mindful awareness is, *we breathe deeper from exercise, and faster from thinking.* Any explanation for the mechanisms of these differences between patterns in physical and mental tasks is speculative. Yet, it could be that metabolic demands from physical exercise are gross, and thus volume change is an efficient strategy to meet them, while metabolic demands from mental effort are subtle and shifting, and therefore rate changes more easily meet and match them.

A fourth study reported by the same researchers compared two different types of mental demands: (1) subjects took a timed math test with problems presented at a pace controlled by the computer, and (2) subjects were left alone to prepare a structured speech, which they then presented. (However, breath was monitored only during speech preparation.) This study revealed contrasting breathing patterns, in which the most obvious response to the math task was increased breath rate, as in the other studies, while the major shift in the speech preparation task was increased volume. The study's authors suggest that the differences may have to do with the fact that the math task was repetitive and controlled externally, while the speech preparation task was free-form and controlled internally by each subject. There is also the difference, we might add, between rote and creative tasks. So rote math elicits the thinking response by the breath. However, creative thought is associated closely with body sensations and motions, and the breath responds accordingly. There are tensions and releases in the passage from a blank page, an empty mind at the initiation of a project, to the fullness and flow of its completion. This difference is often literal; Einstein, for example, was known to squeeze a hard rubber ball while working on his field equations.[2] (It's interesting to note that some of his work was heavily involved with the geometric entities called *tensors!*)

So, tuning in for informal mindfulness practice, what do you notice about your breath as you're working (at your own pace) to read and understand these paragraphs? How does the breath respond as you go about the *mental* work of your day? How does it respond during your *physical* work? And, more interesting, how do you tell one from the other?

What happens when you just *think* your physical work (or play), that is, move in the mind but not the body? In a number of studies in which subjects simply *observed* or *imagined* doing physical exercises or tasks, changes in breathing patterns were found.[3] Watching someone running or walking, say, will likely increase your breathing rate—right along with the runner's rhythm. The same thing happens when you imagine yourself doing the exercise. Imagining yourself walking a path that you know will take you precisely the same amount of time as actually walking it. Further, the heart rate and breathing changes in the imaginary and in the real walks will be the same; it's just that you won't metabolically use the extra oxygen you're taking in.[4] You don't even have to be practiced at the task to get the effect. For example, folks who had never rowed a boat showed increased breathing rates when they imagined rowing in a race, and practiced rowers responded with even larger changes.[5]

How Do You See It?

Our bodily processes do indeed respond to our minds. If we imagine exercising, we'll experience increases in cardiovascular and respiratory activity. Studies going back at least to the 1930s show this relationship again and again. Yet, it took quite awhile for anyone to become curious about *how* these effects actually occur. You might presume that everyone would take an *internal* perspective in imagining themselves running or rowing—feeling it as if doing it with their own bodies. Yet, the mind being infinitely flexible (and people infinitely different), it's also possible to take up an *external* perspective and imagine *watching* one's body doing the exercise. Y. Wang and W. P. Morgan measured subjects' responses to imagining from both these perspectives and found physiological responses to both.[6]

As you might expect, the internal perspective created a greater sense of effort in the imagined exercise, with an accompanying increase in breath volume, so the response was more like actual exercise. However, the external perspective *also* resulted in significant increases in physiological measures, including respiratory rate (but not volume) and heart rate, which were equal to the response to the internal perspective.

This observation suggests just how sensitive we are. We respond physiologically to ourselves. And to others. And even to ourselves *as* others.

So, our experiences perhaps cannot quite be crisply defined as *this* happens in the body and *that* happens in the mind. There isn't as much distinction as our language and our contemporary sensibilities suggest. We respond with great sensitivity to our world and ourselves. We might be defined as a *body-mind-world* complex. To follow the wide-ranging ramifications of such a definition, it will be helpful to address one of the keys to our experience of this complex—the *autonomic nervous system* (ANS).

THREAT/SAFETY

As noted in the previous chapter, respiration is the only fundamental physiological process that is under *both* conscious, voluntary control and autonomic, involuntary control. The ANS provides the automatic control for continuing respiration, and acts as the *only* control for other systems, including cardiovascular, digestive, urinary, reproductive, and endocrine. The nerves of the ANS connect the internal organs with the brain, brainstem, and spinal cord and with all the internal organs, so that much of the ANS activity occurs prior to consciousness, and "below" the cerebral cortex of the brain itself (see figure 9.1).

The ANS responds as reflexes, without conscious thought or reflection, to threat and safety in the environment (outer *and* inner) and adjusts our energy immediately to what the bodily processes require in the moment. It does this through its two divisions: the sympathetic nervous system, which mobilizes our energy when threat is present, and the parasympathetic system, which moderates our energy when the environment is safe, engendering the so-called relaxation response. It would be easy to see these systems as in opposition, in a mechanical metaphor of accelerator and brake. Yet, the relationship, as always, is much closer and more complex. The two are at work simultaneously, continually, adjusting and balancing, *tuning the harp,* as it were, to meet the demands of the moment. As Emerson reminds us, in our own experience of the world, there is no rest, no nesting place; there is only a flowing of transition, only tuning, only change, and rebalancing. The ANS is built to keep us in harmony with that world.

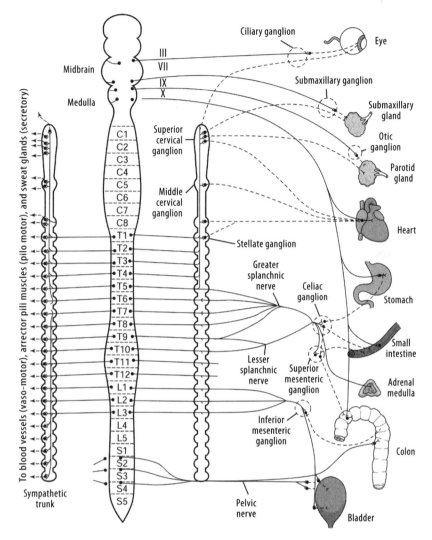

Figure 9.1. Autonomic nervous system and cranial nerves; this drawing shows the sympathetic and parasympathetic connections to organs and systems. From P. L. Williams, Gray's Anatomy, *Edinburgh: Churchill Livingstone, 1995.*

The Autonomic Nervous System

Despite the graphic representation in figure 9.1, which suggests opposing systems, the sympathetic and parasympathetic branches of the autonomic nervous system work in concert to provide us with the energy we need to meet the experience of the present moment. The breath responds continually to this tuning.

In moments of increasing stress, the sympathetic branch dominates in order to rally energy for "fight or flight," as the typical response is known. The many direct connections from the spinal cord to the organ systems suggest the high speed at which this branch can operate. In moments of increasing safety, the parasympathetic branch comes to dominate, reducing and vectoring energy into processes of "rest and repair," as the handy phrase describes the response. And in keeping with its more "laid-back" character, the connections to the organ systems are less direct and so a bit slower. Maybe we can think of them as more contemplative.

TABLE 9.1. BASIC EFFECTS OF ACTIVATION OF SYMPATHETIC AND PARASYMPATHETIC BRANCHES OF THE AUTONOMIC NERVOUS SYSTEM

Psychophysiological Response	Sympathetic Activation	Parasympathetic Activation
Blood pressure	+	−
Heart rate	+	−
Breath rate	+	−
Skeletal muscle tension	+	−
Blood clotting	+	−
Hypothalmic-pituitary-adrena l (HPA) axis (adrenaline/noradrenaline for short-term energy; glucocorticoids for long-term energy)	+	−
Digestive function	−	+
Immune function	−	+
Reproductive function	−	+
Growth and repair of tissue	−	+
Threat detection	+	−
Valence of memory	−	+
Valence of emotions	−	+

In a threat situation, the sympathetic branch of the autonomic nervous system mobilizes energy for "fight or flight" by increasing (+) or decreasing (−) activation, as shown in Table 9.1. Notice that when threat is withdrawn, the parasympathetic branch conserves energy and increases positive functions—essentially reversing the sympathetic activation.

Many of the negotiations between the sympathetic and parasympathetic branches of the ANS are available to us as sensations in the shorter or longer term. There are many folks who are quite sensitive to the immediate changes that come with an increase in what we usually call stress or anxiety—a heart that beats faster; breath that's quick and shallow; tense muscles (particularly in the neck and back); and attention, thoughts, and emotions that are preoccupied with problems. And there are those who are sensitive to the longer-term changes, too—digestive upset, pain from chronic tension, even frequent illness from reduced immune function. What stands out for you when you take this negative inventory? How do you notice stress?

Throughout his life, William James was powerfully influenced by Emerson's thought. In 1884, in an article titled "What Is an Emotion?" in the journal *Mind,* James suggested a theory that captures the Emersonian idea of a continual transition of the body-mind-world complex. This has received much empirical support over time, even by the most contemporary work on emotion and the ANS. It can be argued, in fact, that the enduring impact of James's article and its ideas is unmatched in the history of psychology to this day.[7] James continued to work on his theory, elaborating it in his 1890 masterwork, *The Principles of Psychology.* It came to be joined with a more limited theory developed during the same period, in Denmark, by the physiologist Carl Lange, and is known to history as the James-Lange theory of emotion.

The James-Lange theory is counterintuitive. It suggests that, although common sense says that we feel sad and then cry, feel angry and then yell, or feel frightened and then tremble, it is actually the reverse that is correct; we cry and so feel sad, yell and so feel angry, and tremble and so feel fear. It's the physiological response that happens first, and, in fact, there is no "emotion" apart from the response. In his own highly italicized way,

James states that *"the bodily changes follow directly the* PERCEPTION *of the exciting fact, and that our feeling of the same changes as they occur* IS *the emotion."*[8] Famously, James describes how if we bump into a bear in the woods, we don't feel fear and then run, but rather we find ourselves running and then, in the accompanying physical sensations—exaggerated facial expression, rapid movement, fast breath and heart rate—we recognize our fear.

This understanding is straight out of Darwin. Our emotions—at least what James called the "standard" ones, including fear, anger, grief, and surprise, as opposed to the more subtle, socially constructed ones—are adaptive physiological responses. It's helpful to have the tense muscles, fast breathing, and racing heart of fear when you need to flee that menacing bear. The autonomic nervous system tunes to match the demands of the environment, and this tuning *is* the emotion we recognize and experience as fear. There are specific sensations and events in the body that are associated with each of the "standard" emotions. Over more than a century, this view has been eclipsed and then brought back to light time and again. By the 1930s, the James-Lange theory had been subsumed by the position of Walter Cannon (who had been a student of James) and his student Philip Bard, who suggested that body feelings and emotions were independent, and that the ANS response was just undifferentiated activation—fight *or* flight, anger *or* fear. This kind of basic understanding supported the arrival of behaviorism in psychology during the 1930s, as well. In the 1950s, research by the psychophysiologist Albert Ax, using the new technologies that allowed recording of ANS output, showed that there were indeed differences in the tuning of emotions. He noted particularly that anger and fear were discernibly different. Then, with the rise to dominance of cognitive approaches in the 1960s and onward, the James-Lange theory was subsumed again. Rather than bodily feelings, emotions were understood as coming from cognitive appraisals of external cues, and this was supported particularly by the work of Stanley Schachter and Jerome Singer. Beginning in the 1980s with the beginning of Paul Ekman's work on basic emotions and ANS specificity, the James-Lange position came to light once more—blue light, in fact, as it found a place in television drama, in the series *Lie to Me*.

Although Ekman and other scientists today are, in a way, continuing to support and challenge James's ideas with sophisticated methods and technologies, we, as mindfulness practitioners, can investigate the same way James did, by simply bringing attention to the body-mind-world complex that we are and *noticing* how it is for us in the moment. Here's the suggestion, direct from James himself, in "What Is an Emotion?"

> The next thing to be noticed is this, that every one of the bodily changes, whatsoever it be, is felt, acutely or obscurely, the moment it occurs. If the reader has never paid attention to this matter, he will be both interested and astonished to learn how many different local bodily feelings he can detect in himself as characteristic of his various emotional moods.[9]

So, where do we start? Reflecting the logic of the ancient connection of vital energy and the breath, perhaps the easiest indicator of the changes that are emotions is breathing. As pneuma, prana, and qi, the breath is the response of the body-mind-world complex to the experience of the moment. Although James warned that each of us is different in our response, he suggested that there is enough similarity that we can recognize and parse the standard emotions. Indeed, the empirical work that followed his is demonstrating the existence of standard emotions.

Perhaps, if you choose to make attention to breathing in emotional situations part of your informal practice, you'll find it helpful to learn of some of the ways in which the correspondence of breath and emotion has been studied, as well as the findings of those studies. In researching emotional responses of the body-mind-world, whether the full complex is acknowledged or not, it's not surprising that ancient, traditional forms of purposefully potentiating emotion would be methods of choice, such as *drama and music*.

Drama and the breath are intensely related. Audiences recognize authentic emotion through what they can see and hear. As with facial expressions and body gestures, breathing patterns are easily seen and heard, although more subtly and perhaps less consciously. In actor training, from traditional theater forms, such as Japanese Noh, to contemporary experimental theater, the use of the breath not just to carry texts but also to generate and convey emotions is crucial.

In the same way, music is dependent on the breath in the realms of both technique and emotional meaning. With vocal music, this connection is directly comprehended by musician and audience alike, while with instrumental music, it may seem more abstract—to non-musicians. Wind instruments, as woodwinds and brass are known in the West (note the conflating of wind and breath, as in chapter 7), have a voice that derives from the artist's breath, while string instruments and even percussion instruments are also judged to have voices—and a musician's playing is often prized for its singing tone. Further, string and percussion players, although they produce their "voice" indirectly, perform with full awareness of the breath and its effects on expressivity. Coauthor Don McCown, a jazz drummer, notes that from first lessons to master classes, attention to breathing takes a dominant place, even in percussion pedagogy.

Impacts of Sound and Silence

The more you know (or practice) music, the more responsive the breath is to its effects. An interesting study comparing physiological responses of musicians and non-musicians involved listening to four-minute tracks of music of six different styles, speeds, and structures.[10] Investigators also randomly inserted two minutes of silence between two of the tracks and kept the measuring devices rolling then, too. What they found may be useful to you in your walking around (and sitting down) mindfulness explorations.

The first thing they found was that responses were unrelated to the subject's preference for musical style. Surprisingly, both musicians and non-musicians rated the selections in the same order of preference: (1) fast classical, (2) slow classical, (3) rap, (4) raga (for sitar), (5) techno, and (6) dodecaphonic (think of the spine-tingling music in mystery and thriller movies). However, the measures of blood pressure, heart rate, and breath rate did not respond in one way to the number-one choice and in another way to the least favorite. Rather, all the measures increased in proportion to the *tempo* of the selections—the faster the music, the higher the measures. During the slower and faster selections, subjects breathed at a rate very close to the music tempo, but there was not such a correlation of breath to speed in the midtempo pieces. The investigators had difficulty interpreting the findings clearly. It may be that the rate of the breath was pulled along—*entrained*—by the music. Or, perhaps, our sympathetic nervous system is stimulated more by faster music, and thus we breathe faster. Musicians and non-musicians differed in that musicians had lower baseline physiology measures, yet they actually breathed faster with the faster-tempo music—perhaps unconsciously (or consciously) playing and trying to keep up.

Here's something intriguing for us as mindfulness practitioners: the two-minutes of silence, the *pause,* resulted in the lowest blood pressure, heart rate, and breath rate in the study—even lower than at the end of the five minutes of relaxation used for the baseline measure. No entrainment. No sympathetic stimulation. Just rest. And since *rest* is the term musicians use for a pause, it's appropriate that they responded even more to it than the non-musicians. Maybe they put down their mental instruments.

Practices for musicians and non-musicians alike can be derived from this observation. What do you notice about the breath when you listen to a favorite "calming" musical selection? What do you notice when it's over? And that party song, what's the breathing like when you tune in, listen, and let go? What happens when the party song ends?

Outside the theater, there has been little empirical study of specific patterns of breathing and the emotions they reflect, create, or subserve. A thorough review of historical studies suggested that there are discernible differences between (and among) positive and negative feeling states and tense and relaxed states.[11] Further, given the mind-body connection, if you mimic a breathing pattern, it should precipitate the associated feeling, so you'd know if you got it right.

Pierre Philippot and colleagues used sensitive digital equipment to measure the breathing patterns of male and female subjects as they were asked to produce feelings of anger, fear, joy, and sadness.[12] The experimenters noted that it was remarkable how consistent the patterns for each emotion were. Then, they created breathing instructions for another group of subjects, who were asked to breathe using the four different patterns—under a cover story that had nothing to do with emotion.

With some embedded questions in a larger questionnaire, the researches were able to discern that just through the breathing instructions, the target emotions were, indeed, precipitated at significant levels. Of interest for us, as explorers of experience, is that they found joy and anger to be the most distinctly induced, while fear and sadness had some fluidity and blending. The result of the fear breathing pattern was sometimes interpreted as anger rather than fear, and the sadness pattern sometimes led to labeling as happiness. As the researchers drilled down into the "whys" of the fear/anger ambiguity, they found that the fear pattern could, indeed, generate a blend of fear and anger. The sadness pattern, interestingly, was the only one of the four that induced sadness. However, there were also subjects who reported positive, happy responses to it. As the researchers looked at this ambiguity, they found that the happy responders were actually breathing with shorter inbreaths and outbreaths than the sad responders. They note that it appears, therefore, that the feeling state is a direct result of the breathing pattern, rather than other reasons.

Breathing Instructions for Emotions

In the Philippot and colleagues study, the breathing for particular emotions was described in ways that could be used as instructions to the participants.

Joy: "Breathe and exhale slowly and deeply through the nose; your breathing is very regular and your rib cage relaxed."

Anger: "Breathe and exhale quickly through the nose; slightly deeper than regular breathing amplitude. Your breathing is slightly irregular with some tremors and your rib cage is very tense."

Fear: "Breathe and exhale quickly from the top of your ribc age; with a normal amplitude. Your breathing is slightly irregular with some tremors and your rib cage very tense."

Sadness: "Breathe and exhale through the nose with a normal amplitude and pace. Your rib cage is slightly tense, and there are some sighs in your expiration."[13]

The Subtle Lays of Noh Theater

The traditional Japanese theater form of Noh, which has not changed in more than six hundred years, was fascinating to the Americans who encountered it as Japan opened economically and culturally to the West in the late nineteenth century. Such Americans included Henry Adams, Lafcadio Hearn, Ernest Fenollosa, Ezra Pound, and Wallace Stevens—who wrote his own Noh plays.

Noh drama is a highly stylized form of presentation, in which, contrary to almost all other performance approaches, actors create and convey the emotion of the characters only through *interior* means, not through external expression. Actors wear masks and are restricted in their posture, gestures, attitude, and vocal qualities. External outlet for emotion is highly restricted, yet, emotion is felt by the actor and communicated powerfully to the audience, whether the audience is Japanese and knows all the subtleties of the tradition or a Western audience encountering it for the first time.

Noh training across seven centuries has put the breath at the center of the subtle emotional link of actor and audience. Recently, scientists have literally looked inside the body-minds of the actors for an empirical look at this link.[14] They measured respiratory movement and brain activity in actors (always men in Noh) performing the role of the mother in the Noh play *Sumidagawa,* in which the mother confronts her child's death, reacting in extremes of grief that help classify this play as one of the "mad mother" plays. The intolerable sadness reads out on the respiratory instruments as an increase in the breathing rhythm with a greater inflation of the chest, and on the EEG as an accompanying burst of activity in the limbic regions of the brain—particularly the right amygdala, the region most associated with fear and sadness. Underneath all the bindings and compressions of traditional rules, costumes, masks, and vocal stylizations, the actor *feels* the emotion and the breath *responds* with an immediacy that attunes the audience to the interior expression.

So far, we've been discussing breath and emotion from the actor's standpoint. It is also useful to notice how breath is affected from the audience perspective, as receivers of another's emotion. Of course, we have these experiences constantly in our media-saturated culture, bidden or unbidden. Yet, how often do we take the time or make the space for mindful observation of our physiological responses—to the news bulletin, commercial, or video loop in the supermarket that randomly assaults us, much less the play, movie, or event that we intentionally attend? There is a richness here for our practice, and we can be certain that much is available to us, much that we can access and discriminate about emotion and breath. Because we *can* discriminate, with the breath as a guide.

A recent study measured a wide range of physiological responses to fear- and sadness-inducing film clips, to parse how the two emotions differ.[15] Investigators measured cardiovascular changes, changes in skin conductance, and changes in measures of respiration for fear (clips from a horror film series), sadness (clips from melodramas), and a neutral state (clips from a nature film). While sophisticated (even abstruse) models of the variety of measures helped to distinguish the target emotions from neutral and from each other in the study, the most helpful indicators (and ones it's possible to tune in to in just your movie or concert seat) still seem to be heart rate and the breath. In preparing for the study, the investigators compared the measures of more than forty studies involving the two emotions and others. Even a cursory scan of the differences the studies revealed again and again shows that respiration rate and depth make the clearest distinction, with the rate up in fear and down in sadness, and the depth lesser and greater, respectively.

This information is not presented to limit your exploration to a few emotions, but rather to suggest the vast potential for practice. Being with your breath's response in moments of emotion, whether great or subtle, whether expressed through interior or external means, whether you are actor or audience, brings a new perspective to each discrete scene or to an entire performance.

A night at the theater or a movie at home offers an almost formal mindfulness practice: How is it to stay connected to the breath as dramatic intensity rises and falls? When do you lose touch? What brings you back?

Chances for informal practices abound: What do you find when you connect to the breath immediately as you're saying goodbye to a child, spouse, or friend? On the other side, what's hello like? Or, from a different direction, consider the dramas your stumble over every day. The contretemps ahead of you at the checkout counter—how does your breath respond? Or the meeting of friends at the booth near yours in the diner— does your breathing share the humor and joy? The news update on the car radio—what do you notice when you tune in to the breath? And when you stay tuned in to it, what happens then?

INTERVENTION/OBSERVATION

In much of contemporary scientific investigation and clinical approaches to intervention, the breath plays second fiddle to the heart. Measures of heart-rate variability, particularly respiratory sinus arrhythmia, are considered useful in assessing the health of the autonomic nervous system. Respiratory sinus arrhythmia is a measure of the variations in the heart rate—the time between beats—that naturally happen as we breathe in and out. Here's how it occurs. An important "pacemaker" for the heart is located in the brainstem, in the *nucleus ambiguous*. When we breathe out, the nucleus ambiguous provides parasympathetic (slowing and calming) input to the heart via the vagus nerve. When we breathe in, though, the nucleus ambiguous inhibits parasympathetic input, so the heart rate picks up. This variability is a sign of health, while lack of it is used to diagnose illness, even to predict mortality. Athletes in training often have a healthy, high heart-rate variability, and studies of mindfulness practitioners and other meditators and spiritual practitioners suggest that such training may increase variability as well.

So, why don't we use the heartbeat as an object for mindfulness practice, rather than the breath? The answer is probably different for each of us. So, go on, give it a try. Get quiet for a moment and feel into your heartbeat. How easy is it to find? What do you notice if you connect? What's it like if you can't—or can't always?

Empirical studies suggest that it's not a feeling that's available to everyone, and not a sensation that's necessarily neutral or comforting to be with over time. On the whole, while some people seem to connect to the heartbeat easily and accurately, others struggle and may not find it. And when you put meditators into the mix, the whole situation becomes even more variable. An intriguing study looked at meditators and non-meditators to test whether the meditators were better (or, perhaps, better trained) at sensing the heartbeat than unpracticed folks.[16] As it turns out, and as supported by a smaller, earlier study, even practiced meditators don't seem to develop or improve a skill of detecting the heartbeat.[17] They do, however, *believe* that it is easier for them to do and that they are more accurate than non-meditators. It's just that the data don't support those beliefs.

And again, even if we're in that set of folks who can detect and track the heartbeat, we can't intervene directly the way we can with the breath, which, as we've said, is open to voluntary and autonomic influence. There's no heart equivalent for the intentional relaxing sigh or fake yawn that can help us make shifts and transitions in our being, thinking, and emotions. (There is, of course, the use of technology to find and monitor the heart rate or some other ongoing process for us, which we can then use to learn to adjust and control it. Biofeedback, as it is called, emphasizes intervention, and relegates observation as simply a tool—an expensive, electronic one—in a "big fix" brought to us from outside experts.)

We're left, then, as practical practitioners in the tradition of Emerson, Thoreau, and James, with just the breath—unplugged, unadorned, and right under (and in) our noses: the breath to help us feel out and know about our emotional responses, the breath to help us express those responses, and the breath to help us work with and recover from those responses. Very often, our own impulses, and the impulses of those who want to help us, run right to the big fixes—actions to take, changes to make. Yet, if there is one take-away message from this series of chapters on the breath, it is this: *ultimately, observation is more powerful than intervention.*

In looking for ways to counteract stress and strong emotion, the ever-hopeful cadres of researchers and clinicians have tried to instruct, shape, and, yes, control our breathing. They suggest interventions for our own good, of course. They've been finding, however, that the default, the neutral position, the experimental control, may actually be what works best. In research on sighing, investigators noted how *instructed* sighs appeared to inhibit recovery from mental stress, while *spontaneous* sighs seemed to bring relief.[18] Clinicians working with a population with post-traumatic stress disorder (PTSD) found that interventions including one or more modalities such as instruction in relaxation, deep breathing, and biofeedback were no more effective than simple instructions to relax in a comfortable chair.[19] Researchers comparing the efficacy of simple breathing instructions for managing stress found that the various combinations of anti-hyperventilation breathing instructions did not move any of their measures toward relaxation, while paying attention to breathing by counting breaths did help stabilize breathing, and the baseline of relaxing in a comfy chair was as helpful or more helpful than the interventions.[20] And let's push this discussion of observation and intervention and their effects on the body-mind-world complex a little further and a little farther afield than just the breath. Other investigators looked at how subjects responded when wired up for heart-rate biofeedback and asked them (1) to intervene to stay calm by suppressing any increase in their heart rate, and (2) in another session, to just observe the heart rate by counting in tens. When intervening by suppressing, subjects reported becoming more anxious, yet, when observing, they noticed no change in emotional tone; further, physiological measures (heart-rate variability) showed the same trend, with suppression reducing the healthy variability, while noninterventive observation had no negative effect.[21]

Emerson's poem, amplifying the value of the Aeolian harp, seems to have it right. It simply asks us to lay it gently in the window and listen to the music that naturally arises. Certainly, it tells us how it is from moment to moment—the shifting, feeling tone, the varying intensity. Yet, as we listen quietly, without intervention, we begin to understand how this song has the power to change us—how we may be transformed as we fully experience the fleeting joys of our happiest days and thoroughly feel the transient anguish of the worst.

10

DISPOSITION

A Map of the Terrain of Your Immediate Experience

There is only one question that really matters, says William James. He asks it at what has been described as the peak of his two-volume masterwork, *The Principles of Psychology,* when considering *will* and *effort.* He frames it this way:

> *"Will you or will you not have it so?"* is the most probing question we are ever asked; we are asked it every hour of the day, and about the largest as well as the smallest, the most theoretical as well as the most practical, things. We answer by *consents and nonconsents* and not by words. What wonder that these dumb responses should seem our deepest organs of communication with the nature of things![1]

For James, the ultimate definition of *effort* is clear: to consent to take the world as it is in the moment, whether the experience unfolding seems wonderful or dreadful, a delight or a risk. That effort aligns us with the prophets and with the charismatic leaders to whom we turn for help. That effort makes us, in the Emersonian phrase that James quotes, "one of the masters and lords of life." In terms of this book, this effort is required in the "turning toward" that is at the center of our description of mindfulness history, theory, and practice.

This effort presents a paradox. The greater the effort we exercise, the less the consent truly registers in our being. While we may be able to force ourselves to say, "Let it be so," in such a way that we can be helpful to others, all the while, in our "deepest organs," consent eludes us. And nowhere is the lack of consent (and the pressure of effort) more obvious than in the body. The "dumb responses" that James describes are expressions in the very fiber of our being—particularly in the skeletal muscles, which, as you remember, are the kind of muscles controlled by the will, that is, by effort. Consent and nonconsent, or content and discontent, are not merely wordless, they are beyond words. They are revealed in how we hold ourselves, in whatever posture we've assumed. They are our *disposition* toward our experience.

This term, *disposition,* connotes a sense that we are set in a certain place, inclined toward a certain direction, and ready to undertake a certain action. In popular use, disposition is interpreted as an abstract description of one's general character: "She has a kindly disposition." "He's disposed to argue." In this chapter, however, we're exploring it as an embodied phenomenon. It's about body posture and condition, how we feel, and how those feelings shift from moment to moment. Disposition is the context in which we check in to the triangle of awareness, and relate to *gravity* and the *breath*.

Disposition is one more navigational instrument, a topographical chart of *three dimensions:* the quality of *space* within ourselves, the level of *vitality* available to us, and the capacity we have to *flow* with the inevitable transitions in our ongoing experience. As we explore each of these dimensions, we'll once again use paradox pairs to reveal a wide range of meaning. We'll encounter freedom/constraint, power/presence, and optimum/maximum.

Consider a thought experiment, an opportunity to explore disposition and its dimensions abstractly, at first, by imagining *someone else's* way of being. Robert D. Richardson, in his sensitive biography, *William James: In the Maelstrom of American Modernism,* quotes James's big question and adds a touching footnote. He reports, "'*Will I or will I not have it so?*' was the favorite passage of a colleague of mine . . . who had a wasting disease from which she knew she would die early"[2] How do you imagine her disposition? What about the quality of the space in which she held thoughts of her future? How might she have been sensitive to her own feelings of vitality? And what about the sense of flow through her life's transitions, which may well have seemed not simply inevitable, but inexorable? This case is extreme, meant to highlight and expand your understanding of these terms. Yet, the most important kind of understanding is, as always, what you learn from observing yourself: how is it for you in this moment?

Let's try a check-in to understand your disposition right now, as you continue to read. Just notice how it is in your body. Maybe you noticed something shifting as you read the first sentence of this paragraph. Are you aware of a "dumb response" of consent or nonconsent to this check-in? How is it showing itself to you?

Is there a tightness that goes beyond what's required to hold your posture? Is there a softness that's part of just settling in to read and feel out answers to these questions? Could you describe how it is for you in spatial terms, such as cramped, tight, roomy, open?

How is your energy level? Has there been a jolt, an arousal? Is there a continuing gentle sense of vitality—of being alive?

Are you open to how it is? Can you work with it? Are you turning toward any tension and becoming curious about it? Are you settling in more deeply? Are you feeding a feud with this authorial request? Are you resting in well-being? Is there movement from one feeling to another?

Maybe by now thinking is stirred up. Maybe there is an emotional tone or mood-state evident. How do they relate to the body's disposition? In short, what do you know, now? And what can you say about it? What do you notice as you bring experience into words?

A Religious Perspective
from William James

"Yes, I will even have it so!" This answer to the most probing question we are ever asked reveals the enormous potential tension between consent that is effortful and consent that reflects contentment. In 1890, the publication date of his *Principles,* James held that tension, seemingly without resolution. His next all-consuming work was the series of lectures that became *The Varieties of Religious Experience,* in many ways a search for resolution. The religious resolution he was looking toward is perhaps most clearly and popularly expressed in his description of the experience of Brother Lawrence, the seventeenth-century Carmelite friar who found "perfect liberty and continual joy"[3] by continually acting from his love of God—a passage found at the close of the lecture, "The Gospel of Relaxation." He sets it up with a passage that acts as an elegant description of the attitude of mindfulness practice.

> Worry means always and invariably inhibition of associations and loss of effective power. Of course the sovereign cure for worry is religious faith; and this, of course, you also know. The turbulent billows of the fretful surface leave the deep parts of the ocean undisturbed, and to him who has a hold on vaster and more permanent realities the hourly vicissitudes of his personal destiny seem relatively insignificant things. The really religious person is accordingly unshakable and full of equanimity, and calmly ready for any duty that the day may bring forth.[4]

In the monastery, Brother Lawrence was given job after job that he found unwelcome, only to realize that, as he did each one for the love of God and not for his own fulfillment, he was always pleased and satisfied. James notes, "The simple-heartedness of the good Brother Lawrence, and the relaxation of all unnecessary solicitudes and anxieties in him, is a refreshing spectacle.[5]

SPACE
And Something about a Frontier

Your disposition toward your experience in the moment is reflected in your sense of space. Certainly, one aspect of this dimension is where your body is disposed—outside or inside. There is the place that you're occupying. There is the posture you've taken—sitting, standing, reclining, walking, or anywhere on that continuum. Perhaps there's furniture involved. You might shift from nonconsent to consent (or the other way 'round) to your experience of the moment by choosing a different outside space— walking a different path, finding another place to shelter you, or even drawing your body into your armchair or stretching out beyond it. Any of these moves engage the space that's around you. However, it's the space inside you, your bodily experience, that helps you know which moves to choose. (At the end of this chapter you'll find a formal mindfulness practice that will show you how helpful this space can be, and how gravity and the breath can add to your exploration.)

We talk about this bodily space with a vocabulary associated with geography and architecture, using the same words but in a different register. The space *outside* us is quantitative and exact. We measure it in cubic "whatsits": This box will hold 5.5 cubic inches of glitter. My car trunk will hold 13.8 cubic feet of grocery bags. That mixer truck will hold 11 cubic yards of concrete. We can make comparisons and selections. We can calculate the best fit. In the other register, the space of disposition *inside* is qualitative and ambiguous. We don't measure it; rather, we "take its measure." Yet, we arrive at no less certainty about what will and won't fit! For example, in everyday speech, the statement, "Our family can make room to rescue this puppy," actually has little to do with physical floor space (or even sofa space). The geographer Yi-Fu Tuan uses the example, "Does the college have room for more students?" to illustrate this register of usage. He explains, "[A] college must have not only adequate classrooms and facilities, but it should feel commodious and liberating to students who go there to enlarge their minds."[6]

In such overtones of spaciousness and independence we speak of our "inner" disposition toward experience. In everyday speech, we may be "filled with" joy or wonder, a feeling of spaciousness, a lifting of limits. Alternatively, we may register our protest of unwanted news or events that we "can't take any more," a feeling of pressure, an imposition of boundaries over which we have no control. Two descriptions of the fullness of space, two very different dispositions. Do you feel them?

Toward the other end of the spatial continuum, in emptiness, such a disparity is also evident. When a bothersome pain is relieved, we say, "My headache's gone," an opening of space that offers freedom to move. On the flip side, when we encounter a serious loss, we may express our grief as, "I feel so empty," an opening of space that freezes us in our tracks, immobilizes us. Our sense of space in the inside register depends considerably on dispositions involving freedom or constraint. Let's explore this paradox pair further.

FREEDOM/CONSTRAINT

If we shift back to the outside register, the geographer can help us grasp the subtleties of these aspects of space.[7] He explains that in order to experience a sense of freedom, we need both the power and the space to take action. Put another way, freedom is a feeling that we can change how we are disposed.

That may mean changing things outside—moving to a different posture or place. It may also mean changing things inside—making a move toward consent and contentment. The second depends upon the first. In order to grasp the more abstract space inside, and our degrees of freedom for moving within it, we also need to be familiar with the direct sensations of bodily movement in geographical and architectural space.

Researchers have found that infants in the womb and in the early days after birth come to sense their bodies through spontaneous twitches in the muscles that take place while the infant is relaxed or asleep.[8] This *myoclonic twitching* builds the connections of the muscles with the brain and brainstem and helps to integrate the infant's awareness of the body as a whole. As the infant ages and begins to gain control, these twitches give way to the voluntary movements that continue the integration process. In older children or adults who have lost touch with the body due to damage to the brain or spinal cord, twitching can be induced via electrical stimulation to assist in rebuilding the necessary connections for body awareness—and to regain a sense of freedom.[9]

Feelings of freedom and restriction and their spatial equivalents, inside and out, are socially constructed. Consider one example, a very dominant one, in shaping consciousness in North America. The continent was settled from the east, with a frontier of unsettled space always to the west. At first, a frontier of forests and mountains presented itself, not so much as open space but as potential space, waiting to be opened, to be cleared for agriculture and settlement. Its vastness was in its unknown, unseen quality. By the nineteenth century, the frontier passed through the forests and onto the grasslands. The Great Plains presented "wide-open spaces," as we say, all the way to the western horizon. Such a prospect may be seen as terrifying Yet, in North America, it came to symbolize opportunity and freedom. In making a move westward, settlers from the East could make undreamed of changes—in spiritual and physical well-being, in financial situation, and even in social station. The potential for improvement was as expansive as the landscape.

For contrast, Tuan points us to the Russian steppes in the same time period.[10] To the peasants in the tiny villages seemingly dropped onto the vast, unpopulated, treeless plain, the sense of space was associated with oppression and despair. Humans were dwarfed by the immensity and fierceness of the landscape and climate. There was little possibility for alterations in any physical or social domain, and even less impulse to move. No wonder body and soul both seemed blunted on the wearying, unstoppable round of joyless labor.

That picture conjures up another characteristic that helps define space and reveals another paradox: the absence or presence of others. We can be lonely in a crowd and find good company in solitude, and vice versa. In solitude, there is a potential for freedom akin to that of the frontier. Thoughts and emotions may move more freely, without running in to critics, naysayers, or advocates (but they may also run into all of these, who populate our thoughts and even intrude on our solitude). Such wide-open inside spaces traditionally have been sought and cultivated by thinkers and prophets, artists and mystics. The possibilities are there for dramatic change in who and how we are. In the presence of many others, ambiguity awaits. When the group is working toward a common goal, there is a feeling of liberation, of the group itself expanded. Yet, with the inevitable hidden and mixed agendas comes a sense of crowding, frustration, and constriction that ultimately makes it harder to move.

What have been the shaping elements and events of your own inside space? Is there a disposition you can touch into in your workplace? Your home? Are there landscapes of your past that have shaped how you hold yourself, outside and in? Is solitude for you the Great Plains of America, or the steppes of Central Asia? Are there groups that sustain you? Or constrain you? Or both?

What's happening in the inside space right now?

VITALITY
Of the Parts and the Whole

As we explore disposition and the possibilities of consent and contentment, it may be easy to imagine or even sense the body beginning to collapse into "relaxation," whatever that might represent for us. We first need to be clear about our inherited, socially constructed concepts of relaxation. The facts of the body are in significant contrast to those concepts. To give consent is not to give in or give up. When our disposition shifts that way, we don't collapse—not like a tower of blocks falling, nor like a balloon deflating. We can't. We're living tissue (on a frame of bone) with vital processes continually underway. We're built on a principle of *tensegrity* (see the "Stand Up and Feel Your Tensegrity" box on page 178).

When we explore our disposition in the moment, we encounter our physical anatomy and our vital energy (pneuma, prana, qi). Through pro-prioception and interoception, we can feel into the quality of the muscles, the body's articulation, and the level of energy that is available. That is, we can sense our readiness to meet what is arising in the moment.

To be able to sense this readiness accurately is a significant chal-lenge, for at least two reasons. First, the challenge is related to something fundamental that may get in our way—our habitual response to *gravity*. For many years we've spent all day, every day, resisting gravity to present ourselves to the world with socially acceptable postures and expressions. We've built habits of tension in the smallest and the largest muscles—say, in the face and in the back. We need to identify these habits in order to better see through them. In working with gravity back in chapter 6, you may have noticed that these habits appear again and again as you turn your attention to awareness of gravity. We can notice the habits, work with them, and see that they nevertheless come right back. Consequently, in feeling our disposition, our readiness, it's helpful to know what's always there, so we can sense what's new.

Second, the challenge is related to time. As psychologist and body-worker Alan Fogel describes, because of the way our nervous system con-tinually "reports in," some information is available early and can shape our understanding and responses.[11] We may get a not-quite-right idea of our disposition, based only on what Fogel calls our *conceptual self-awareness,* our ideas and judgments in the realm of thinking. This form of self-awareness is served by nerve fibers that have a coating of myelin insulation, which increases the speed of the messages being sent. On the other hand, our *embodied self-awareness,* which we can think of as knowl-edge of our disposition, is served by nerve fibers without a myelin coating. In addition, chemical messengers (neuropeptides) are continually released from the gut (our "gut feelings") into the circulation, traveling through-out the body and persisting in the bloodstream. The powerful energy of the heart ("heartfelt") is conducted continually throughout this involun-tary muscle, influencing the energy of the entire body.

Messages from all over the body may therefore travel around continu-ally and persist for up to several minutes before they register. This means, of course, that we need to *slow down* sometimes in order to receive all the relevant information about how it is with us.

Stand Up and
Feel Your Tensegrity

Tensegrity ("tensional integrity") was developed as a concept in the late 1940s by the renowned architect Buckminster Fuller and the sculptor Kenneth Snelson.[12] Its basic premise is that many structural systems—a suspension bridge is a very clear example—are based on a balance between compression and tension. These two counteracting forces provide both form and strength.

Tensegrity is also a feature of biological systems, including the human body. The muscles and other soft tissues (such as connective tissues, joint capsules, tendons, and ligaments) act as tensional elements, while the bones resist the compression of weight bearing. By maximizing the ratio of tensional elements to compression elements, such a system enables the organism to maintain balance and move with a minimum amount of energy expenditure.

A simple experiment can help make this clear. Just bring your attention to the awareness of your body's posture as you're reading this. Now shift your weight: sit up, stand up, or even lie down. Do you sense new tensions and oppositions? Do you feel yourself becoming a different sculpture or building of a new design?

POWER/PRESENCE

In the West, we have an anatomical understanding of the body. "What's happening in my muscles?" tends to be a touchstone for how we are. A gym class or two, a season on a sports team—it doesn't take long to learn some names and terms and to learn what might get hurt and what might need some care. We've been culturally conditioned for many centuries to perceive the body this way.

Throughout history and across the world, a view of the body as component parts, especially the muscles, is an anomaly that very likely relates to the Western fascination with dissection and distinction.[13] In contrast, the medical understandings of people in Middle and East Asia, from early Greek, to Indian ayurvedic, to Chinese medicine, have not relied on actually opening up the body (most often a dead one) and peering inside. Rather, they took the route of observation, of seeing what the living body can tell, for example, through watching the climate and weather as it affects people's health and ways of being, or through the great technologies of yoga and meditation, or through attending to diet and digestion, the pulses, even bodily wastes. These more contemplative approaches also privilege the observation of vital energy, in living bodies, through physiological systems that cannot be located by the anatomical dissection of dead ones (see figure 10.1). The chakras and nadis of ayurveda, and the channels, meridians, points, and "organs" of Chinese medicine can all can be found, felt, and mapped (in different ways), and none are available to the knife (see chapter 7 and figures 10.2 and 10.3).

The West's long rapprochement with the East has brought these new possibilities into the way we might sense our disposition in the moment. These contemplative, energy-watching traditions have been known to our culture since the eighteenth century.

Now, widespread use in the West of health interventions derived from these traditions (perhaps the term complementary and alternative medicine [CAM] fits not too uncomfortably here) has blossomed. The U.S. Center for Health Statistics and the Centers for Disease Control and Prevention, in the best surveys that have been done on CAM usage, show that in the early twenty-first century, the majority of Americans have tried one or more of these modalities. Most people who try CAM continue to use it.

It's no longer a stretch to ask someone today, "How's your energy?" and to expect an appropriate answer. But it's likely to be secondary to answers involving parts—especially muscles.

The explanation for our anatomical understanding is double-faced; it was shaped by the ancient Greek focus on power as revealed in action, and

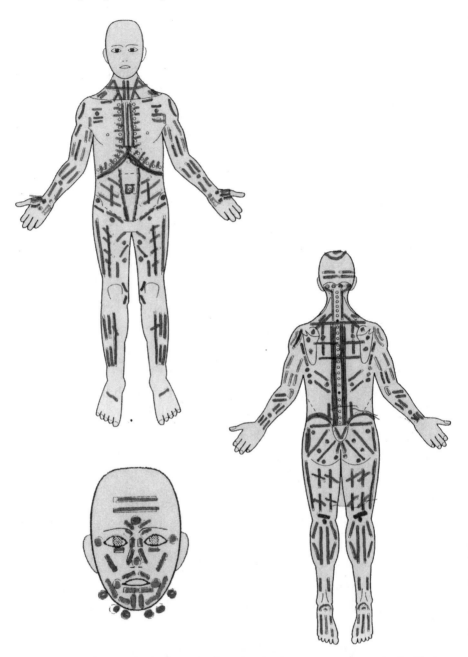

Figure 10.1. Bodymap of a Biodynamic client showing human musculature. In the West, the action of energy in the muscular body came to represent individual choice and effort. The impulse to define this capacity led to a focus on individual parts that could be controlled by the self and identified through dissection and analysis. Image provided by Bodynamic Institute USA.

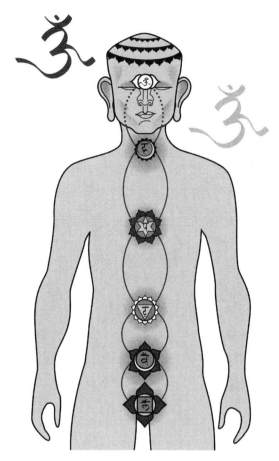

Figure 10.2. Yoga's psychic anatomy. In greater India, the motions of energy in the world and its movements in the body came to indicate a transcendent unity. Investigation of this employed contemplative observation through tools such as yoga, meditation, and ayurvedic medicine practice.

on will or effort as a laudable, measurable characteristic of a person.[14] In Homeric times, about the seventh century BCE, humans were thought to be moved (both bodily motion and emotion) from without, by inspiration from the gods. In the fifth century BCE, Hippocrates and his contemporaries were very much interested in the capacity of humans to choose action and to make articulated movements. One's capacity to use the will spoke to one's character. Heroes, therefore, had well-articulated bodies in which movement and effort were easy to detect. This is the reason and

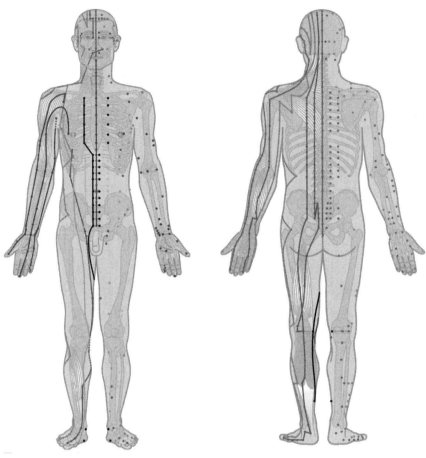

Front view of the 12 principal
acupuncture meridans

Back view of the 12 principal
acupuncture meridans

Figure 10.3. Chinese meridians. In greater China, a view of the world simply as energy flowing resulted in the identification of patterns and potentials that are applicable to government, war, art, and medicine—macrocosm and microcosm. The focus of inquiry was (and is) on natural processes in their fullest contexts—noticing and working with relationships within the whole.

meaning behind the rippling muscles in Greek art; the bulges denote willed action, a sense of distinctiveness, which could confer social distinction. By Galen's time, in the second century CE, muscles had come to be called the organs of voluntary motion, and dissection was a way of investigating how the will worked. Westerners were well on the way to seeing in parts (Galen wrote a treatise, "On the Usefulness of the Parts," a detailed anatomy) and to distinguishing themselves from others—the weaker, less defined and decisive, less individualistic others. This tendency toward seeing in parts gathered cultural momentum. Defined parts became smaller, distinctions became finer, and the ability to anatomize became a compulsion to atomize.

It is instructive to trace the Western characterization of vital energy across time, as the concept of the individual as actor, as agent, as hero, and as self-directed force came into the foreground of what it means to be human. Vital energy began as the wind/breath, becoming the pneuma of Hippocrates, which was seen to power the muscles directly through hollow veins, linking human action and the outside energy of the natural world. Aristotle's *vital pneuma* was an inner power that traveled in the blood, acting on the psyche, or soul, of the muscle for movement, thereby detaching such motion from outside forces, and locating the will inside. Galen's *psychic pneuma,* moving through nerves to affect the muscles, refines the energy, connecting it more closely still to the animating soul of the individual. As pneuma was refined to a spiritual power over time—becoming *spiritus* in Christianity, for example— the muscles and other body parts gained definition and lost mystery. Descartes' inheritance of these understandings and the valorization of will and effort made his splitting of body and mind a simple, logical move. Anatomy and agency define one side of how we experience "how it is."

Eastern understandings of energy provide a clear counterweight to the sense of effort and control that underpins our Western concept of an independent self. Prana and qi, in the associated spiritual and medical traditions that have entered our culture, are ongoing processes that are part of a larger whole, of nature. This energy cannot be mastered through effort, although it can be known through observation—and knowledge opens possibilities of influencing, cultivating, and accepting the way it is.

A simple check-in to sense your disposition in the moment is likely to be an exercise in summing the parts before it's about feeling the whole.

If you'd care to, notice how you're disposed right now. And notice how you start the process. Where is your attention directed in the body? What sensations are most vivid? Are they sensations of effort or consent? What happens as you notice either one? Proceed as you need to, gaining a comprehensive view of the body.

Do you have an awareness of your energy level now? (Or was this a prompt to get in touch?) Is the breath available? The heartbeat?

What's happening with thinking? Don't attend to the content of your thoughts, but rather, sense the quality of the process. Speeding, crowded, slow, foggy—what's it like?

Is there an emotion, a mood state that you can identify?

Resting now with the knowing you have. Resting with how it is in this moment.

Perhaps you noticed that this short practice engaged both Western and Eastern modes of knowing about your energy. We might shorten the practice to its essentials: *In this moment, can you contact your personal power? And can you be aware of your full presence as a body-mind-world complex?*

FLOW
And the Influence of Inclination

Consents and nonconsents are the core motions of disposition. We are *inclined* in one way or another. This inclination is not revealed to us in thought. Rather, as James says in the quote that opens this chapter, it is revealed in "dumb responses." We are *already ready* for the present moment, and that knowledge is resident in the body.

James, in his famous chapter on "The Stream of Thought," and at other moments in *The Principles of Psychology,* keeps returning to his understanding that the body's inclinations and responses underlie and underline the activity and contents of thinking. He notes:

Our own bodily position, attitude, condition, is one of those things of which *some* awareness, however inattentive, invariably accompanies the knowledge of whatever else we know. We think; and as we think we feel our bodily selves as the seat of the thinking. If the thinking be *our* thinking, it must be suffused through all its parts with that peculiar warmth and intimacy that make it come as ours.[15]

There is a homely sense of thinking with the body, a flowing along with experience in the moment.

There are moments, however, in which the thinking and relationship with the body are perhaps less warm and intimate and more like a discussion or negotiation. In his next chapter in *Principles,* "The Consciousness of Self," James gives up speaking in the abstract and speaks of his personal experience: "I am aware of a constant play of furtherances and hindrances in my thinking, of checks and releases, tendencies which run with desire, and tendencies which run the other way." He is aware, further, of his reactions to his thinking, "welcoming or opposing, appropriating or disowning, striving with or against, saying yes or no."[16]

Yet, James says, when he is able to catch himself in one of these reactions, all he can sense is some movement in the body. He feels smaller reactions of welcoming or rejecting in the muscles of his face and in his breathing, while he feels the stronger reactions in either direction, not only in the face and breath, but adds that "a set of feelings pour in from many bodily parts, all 'expressive' of my emotion."[17] These are one (extra) ordinary man's subtleties of disposition, and he acknowledges how challenging it is to turn toward whatever experience may be available in the moment.

This kind of sensing is central to the art of acting, and the millennia of experiencing by theater practitioners has identified much that can be of value for mindfulness practice. The work of the visionary theater practitioner Jerzy Grotowski, and his American collaborator and heir, Thomas Richards, is closely linked to the most archaic and visionary understandings of performance.[18] The work points to the inherent possibilities for the personal transformation of the performer. Grotowski's work moved from experimental theater works aimed outward to the audience to become finally "theater as vehicle"—work that is aimed inward at the development of the practitioners.

Among many powerful ideas, the Grotowski work proposes two terms that can be quite useful to us in being aware of the disposition in the moment. The first term is *impulse,* which reveals its definition in this typographic treatment: *in/pulse.* It refers to a subtly felt pulse or push from inside that precedes an action. Grotowski suggests that working just with impulses is a profound way of training—rooting the actor's actions firmly in the body.

As with all experiential concepts, it's better to try it than read about it, so imagine that you are coming to a standing posture right now. What do you notice as you run that image or scenario in your imagination without moving the body? Do you feel the pulse inside, the push toward bodily movement?

The second term is *intention,* which can be typed to reveal: *in/tension.* This follows on impulse, moving from a sort of action prompt inside to a search for the exact muscular tensions required to bring it about. The sense of exactness is important. Living is a process of alternations in tension and relaxation, like breathing in and breathing out, like rising up and settling down, like muscular contraction and release. To bring back some of James's words, it's a process of consent and nonconsent, welcoming and opposing, saying yes and no. Richards quotes Grotowski using the words *contraction* and *decontraction,* making the point that both are necessary. What's most helpful is "to find this river, this flow, in which *what is needed* is contracted and *what is not needed* is relaxed."[19]

That is art, and mindfulness practice, at a high level—sensing in to what's needed in the moment and letting go of what's extra. Grotowski's image for this balance illuminates the sense of flow. An experienced craftsperson does not work in fits and starts, but continuously, slowly, because to continue in an effort requires much less energy than to start up over and over. Imagine, for example, a knitter who is quietly, deliberately letting out an even length of a scarf each hour. Or, in terms of your mindfulness practice, staying present with what's in your awareness over time, noticing your inclination toward consent and nonconsent, and choosing the level of energy you really need to bring into each moment.

William James Goes Bowling

Impulse and intention come together in the present moment, the moment of action. When we act, we are *already* ready, inclined, and aligned. William James, considering effort in the chapter on "Will" in *Principles,* describes it in a way that must have been drawn from his own direct experience.

> Whenever a movement is difficult and precise, we become, as a matter of fact, acutely aware *in advance* of the amount and direction of energy which it is to involve. One has only to play tenpins or billiards, or throw a ball, to catch his will in the act, as it were, of balancing tentatively its possible efforts, and ideally rehearsing various muscular contractions nearly correct, until it gets just the right one before it, when it says, "Now go!"[20]

OPTIMUM/MAXIMUM

The distinction we might make is between the optimum and the maximum. That is information that you, alone, are able to access. How much effort is required? Which energies must be engaged, and which might be conserved? It takes practice to work with this balance, and practice can affect both your inclination and actions.

It is heartening to find that the great director Constantin Stanislavski used an exercise that directly parallels an exercise that we've been using for a number of years in teaching mindfulness. He asks the actor to sit in a chair in a particular way and then to explore what is optimum for that posture.[21] *Perhaps you'll choose to try this practice now or at some other time when you're seated. Check in with how it is in the moment, with particular emphasis on your posture. Notice how you're sitting, then check in to muscle tension and let go of any extra effort. Try sitting with only what's required.*

Learning to work in this way, in the body, is a helpful skill in harboring your energy—saving what you don't yet need. As well, it's a transferable skill, since you can notice when you're bringing extra effort into emotional responses or interpersonal situations and can engage only when and at the exact level that the specific situation requires. Of course, this is not just a formal exercise for sitting; it's actually a casual way of living. And finding your optimum energy flow.

Consider a case: a graduate student was troubled by a very high level of anxiety about his work in the classroom and the field. He couldn't focus on his studies, and his presence actually unsettled fellow students, his clients, and his field supervisor. Logically, for him, it was difficult to build formal mindfulness practice into his schedule. Although he did manage to do formal practice several times a week, we concentrated on moments of awareness, coming into contact with his disposition in the moment. By checking in to how it was with him, with the consents and (many) nonconsents reflected in the subtle (and not so subtle) feelings in the body, he found ways to move away from the maximum energy output of his anxious disposition and toward a more optimum flow.

In less than two months of approaching his life in this way, he noticed changes in his anxiety level, and more impressive (and more important for him), his fellow students, clients, and faculty members began noticing a change as well. Here's how he responded, after almost a year of working with mindfulness, when asked what his current practice was like:

I'm really not doing the formal practice very much right now. I like it, but I still can't find the time. Mostly what I do is check-in—about twenty or thirty times a day. I'm not kidding. It really helps just to get an idea of how I'm feeling. Then I sense gravity, letting my muscles go the way they want. Sometimes I go to my breath, you know, if I'm really tense and anxious. I might sigh or yawn a few times, but I don't do it that often. Then I'm ready. I just go on, until I feel like it's time to check in again. . . . Oh, I absolutely know when it's time.

Noticing. Knowing when it is time. Moving toward the optimum energy. And continuing to notice. The principle is clear: flow now, like a river, like a stream, like a scarf knit just for you.

A FORMAL DISPOSITION

We have been emphasizing *informal* mindfulness explorations based on disposition. There is, of course, an equally broad and instructive use of disposition in *formal* practice. If you're drawn to that mode, perhaps you'd like to set aside the time to try this meditation, which is usually done in a reclining posture. We'll keep the instructions simple, so that you can practice without propping the book open.

Bringing the body into a comfortable reclining posture. You may wish to be on your back, although a comfortable posture on the side or prone is fine, as well.

Begin by checking in: noticing what's available in your awareness, in the realm of thinking, in emotion, and in the body. What do you notice about consent and nonconsent, about welcoming and opposing?

There is a fork in the road here. If you find that you're disposed toward nonconsent in the body, that is, that there is distress or discomfort of some kind, you can follow step A below. If you notice nonconsent—struggle or disquiet—in the mind or emotions, you can follow step B.

A. *Locate the area of the body where you feel the distress or discomfort most plainly. Then turn your attention toward it—with kindness and curiosity. Skip to step C.*

B. *As you connect to the thought or emotion, what do you notice in the body? Bringing your attention to what you find. Is there an area that definitely reflects or responds to your thinking or emotion? Now, with kindness and curiosity, begin to explore that area in the body. Move on to C.*

C. *Perhaps you can name or describe the sensation that you're experiencing. This could be a traditional sensation word, such as dull, sharp, pulsing, insistent, or the like. It may simply be whatever word comes to mind, such as fizzy, grabbing, bubbly, gnawing. If words don't come, you might try getting a sense of the size and shape of the area, or an associated color, texture, or image. In either case, don't struggle for exactitude; an OK fit is fine. When you have a representation, just hold it lightly. Move to D.*

D. *Turning toward what is there, and making space for it to simply be there. This is the inner space dimension of disposition. Perhaps you can use attention to gravity to help expand the space, letting the body respond to the pull, helping you to soften around the area of distress. Or you may use attention on the breath in much the same way, breathing into the area of distress to expand the space and to leave it open as the breath goes out.*

E. *Just staying with this process. Feeling gravity. Breathing. Attending to sensations. Spending time; nowhere to go but here, nothing to do but this.*

F. *After a while, checking in again to how it is with you. Trying on your original description. Does it still fit? Or is there a different word, size, color, or location? That is—what's your disposition, now?*

PART 3

PUTTING DOWN
THE GUIDEBOOK

11

IN SEARCH OF
THE SPRINGS OF LIFE

And now we come to practice: to bringing attention to what is in aware-ness, whether you're sitting down in formal meditation, rushing out the door to work, or pulling yourself together for another trip to the doctor. The formal and informal practice of mindfulness is useful and beneficial to you at any moment, at any stage of life, in any condition in which you find yourself—young or old, settled or struggling, robust or fragile. That's why we've made this book in just this way.

We've simply presented a description of basic elements of practice that you can begin to apply whenever and wherever it seems right to you. Mindfulness is not something odd or added onto a normal Western life. It's already here—in our particularity and potential as humans and in our shared history and culture, developed through centuries of East and West cross-fertilization of ways of thinking and being. You don't need a new identity as a meditator, or a yogi, or a Buddhist because this is a prac-tice of being who you are. You don't need to be repaired (or replaced!) through mindfulness, because the present moment is complete—and you fit it perfectly.

The sole purpose of this book is to help you to be present to *how it is,* knowing all that you can about your immediate experience. What you do with that knowledge is entirely your choice. We're not offering prescrip-tions, because only you can decide what's right for you. In fact, one of the most important and transformational aspects of mindfulness is that it makes you *aware* that you indeed have choices. When you bring friendly, curious attention to how it is, you can choose, for example, to eat the donut, argue with your partner, accept the status quo in business, politics, or culture—or choose something very different. This is not a low-stakes pastime for self-help; it is high-stakes living for self-understanding.

Thoreau, as always, is a solid guide here. He took his meditative practice—walking—seriously, in just the way you might frame your own practice as you begin. Whatever you choose to undertake, it is not a means to an end, rather, it is an end in itself.

> [T]he walking of which I speak has nothing in it akin to taking exercise, as it is called, as the sick take medicine at stated hours—as the swinging of dumb-bells or chairs; but is itself the enterprise and adventure of the day. If you would get exercise, go in search of the springs of life. Think of a man's swinging dumbbells for his health, when those springs are bubbling up in far-off pastures unsought by him![1]

In this chapter, you'll find ways to search for the springs of life that, we trust, will suit the way you're living now, and the many ways of living that you may choose or find as your practice unfolds.

Learning and leaving it alone: Previous chapters have offered definitions and details of concepts and tools that can help infuse each moment, each movement, with mindfulness. There's the three-part definition of mindfulness, highlighting (1) the *intention* and effort (not too much!) required in turning toward your experience; (2) the kinds of *attention* that turning toward experience can comprise, whether sharply focused or opening and flowing; and (3) the *attitude* that characterizes your intention and attention, based on nonjudging, and known by names like *kindness* and *friendliness.* There's the triangle of *awareness,* a scheme for quickly and comprehensively checking in to the totality of awareness and noting what stands out in the experiential realms of body sensation, thought, and emotion. And there are the *navigational* instruments we've provided—a compass of gravity and breath, and a chart that unrolls to reveal your disposition in each moment.

We've presented history, concepts, theories, scientific evidence—even poetry and philosophy. If you've read this far, we trust that you've been pushed and prodded, shaped and changed in some small (or larger) ways, even if it has all been struggle and argument. Every experience brings change. You know things now that you didn't know before. You're not who you were when you first picked up this book.

After ten chapters, it is time to let go of "book learning" and experiment more extensively with your own experience. If we distilled the words and practice of Ralph Waldo Emerson, William James, and Alan Watts, their advice for now would be: *let go of what others think and take hold of what you know.*

Emerson's transcendent concern (so to speak) is the continual flow of experience. Transition, to use his universal term for this flow, never stops. He admonishes us to be open to the certainty of change, again and again. A journal entry for 1847 notes, "We dive & reappear in new places."

In the essay "Self-Reliance," he describes the energy inherent in change: "Power ceases in the instant of repose; it resides in the moment of transition from past to a new state, in the shooting of a gulf, in the darting of an aim." In "Fate," he pithily describes how thinking that you know something for certain actually impedes further learning: "Every spirit makes its house; but afterwards the house confines the spirit." To put a finer, sharper point on it, we've proposed this bold statement from "Circles" to you as a motto: "I unsettle all things. No facts are to me sacred; none are profane; I simply experiment, an endless seeker, with no Past at my back."

James, in "The Gospel of Relaxation," proposes a way of being and working of which he became ever more sure as his own life unfolded. When you've finished with the book learning and the conceptualizing, he suggests, "Dismiss absolutely all responsibility and care about the outcome. *Unclamp,* in a word, your intellectual and practical machinery, and let it run free; and the service it will do you will be twice as good."

That word, *unclamp,* conveys the spirit of our informal practice. A bit further on in his "Gospel," James puts it in the affective register as he advises people to "forget their scruples and take the brakes off their hearts." Free and friendly—that's the approach to mindfulness that we're cultivating, which is nothing more or less than living in the now.

Watts was a source, a container, an overflowing spring of the integration of Eastern and Western approaches to the practice of meditation and daily life throughout the 1950s and '60s. His engagement with Zen Buddhism supported and encouraged his sense of freedom in practice, art, and his incredibly popular lectures and writing. Without notes or preparation, he could *unclamp* and speak for an evening, enrapturing audiences with detail, depth, wit, and clarity.

In what were his all-too-early last years (he died at fifty-eight), Watts shifted his scholarly interest and practice from the Buddhist tradition into an intense study of early Taoism in China. This early Toaism (like Shintoism) is the Taoism emerging from the contemplation of nature and stressing flowing with experience, not the later Taoism that attempts to leverage its insights in order to prescribe practices for longevity and immortality. Watts seemed to have found at last a *Tao* (a way) that perfectly suited his freedom-seeking character. His writing, according to his friend and collaborator Al Chung-liang Huang, was no longer an intellectual undertaking; with his mind and body in the flow, it just happened. The closing paragraph of his last, unfinished, book, *Tao: The Watercourse Way* might stand as a description of the possibilities of freedom in mindfulness practice that can carry you into your day—not as a Buddhist, not as a Taoist, not even as a meditator, but simply as one in search of these springs of life, in search of everyday mindfulness:

> Taoism is not a philosophy of compelling oneself to be calm and dignified under all circumstances. The real and astonishing calm of people like Lao-tzu comes from the fact that they are ready and willing, without shame, to do what comes naturally in all circumstances. The unbelievable result is that they are far more sociable and civilized than those who try to live rigorously by laws and watchwords.[2]

THE FOUR DIGNITIES

In the Buddhist and Taoist literatures, four postures are identified to illustrate the whole range of possible postures of the human body, which is traditionally said to number eighty thousand. Often called the *four dignities of man,* these ideal postures are usually translated as *walking, standing, sitting,* and *lying down.* Wonderfully, standing is sometimes called *stopping,* which highlights what is true of all the postures—they are transitional. While formal practice investigates the precision and definition of each of the four dignities, informal practice experiments with the other twenty thousand postures that surround each one, with all the liberty and luxury of the expansive transitional surface that that makes available. The point behind this exercise in taxonomy and arithmetic is that wherever and however the body is placed, we can use it to turn toward our moment-to-moment experience with a friendly and attuned attention.

Within the discipline of formal meditation practice, certain postures are favored for particular types of meditation. A lying-down posture allows the greatest relaxation and is favored for practices of care and healing, whereas the sitting posture is more conducive to concentration and clarity, for example. Within informal mindfulness practice, every transitory posture is a gateway to the now, and a treasury of possibilities.

We'll follow the dignities through transitions from reclining to sitting, standing, and at last to walking. If that's not an evolution, it's at least an elevation. As we investigate each posture, we will provide instructions for an appropriate formal practice. This will be useful as a repeatable experiment, which you may wish to adopt as part of an ongoing commitment to formal practice. Also, the instructions may generate patterns for informal practices that can reveal specific dimensions of experience. We will also describe major features of the transitional postures, as well as particular modes of inquiry that may be especially apt for awakening attention—approaches to gravity, breath, or disposition that can be applied narrowly, and perhaps broadly too, as the transitional surface expands.

No Right. No Wrong.
Nobody's Practice but Yours

Please, please, keep in mind, as you begin to bring these body-based mindfulness occasions and inquiries into your everyday life, that you are creating this practice for yourself. You don't need to do what we suggest. Indeed, you may or may not be able to do the things described here.

If you have physical limitations, know that you can investigate how it is for you to *do what you can*. And know that doing what you can is *exactly* equal to doing what we suggest. In fact, it is marvelously mindful to be aware of what you can do, want to do, and will do. It might be that you must investigate standing with a concentrated imagination while you are seated or lying down—feeling into posture and context as if you were standing. As long as you are paying attention to what you are engaged with, in the present moment, with friendly curiosity, you are doing *your* practice. Perfectly.

12

RECLINING

There Is a Place Past Sleepiness

The posture of lying down is not always open for exploration. We assume the posture and then are held in it by gravity, and by sleep, for long periods of time, regularly. Reclining is only *sometimes* voluntary. It's associated with exhaustion, illness, incapacity, death, and the stigma of laziness on the one hand, while, on the other, it's linked with relaxation, healing, restoration, procreation, and the creative power of dreams and visions.

Importantly, the ambiguities of reclining revolve around sleepiness and wakefulness, and around strong experiences all along the continuum of emotions. Of all the postures of meditation, it is the one most likely to carry the meditator away from rather than toward an awakened state. It is also the one that all but guarantees the polar experiences of bliss in falling asleep instantly and distress when sleep eludes us.

We can, of course, work mindfully with these ambiguities. There is a formal mindfulness practice that is an opportunity to turn toward any possibility. Known as the *body scan,* it is the first formal practice taught and assigned in the Mindfulness-Based Stress Reduction curriculum. It is scheduled first because it assists participants in making closer and more regular contact with bodily experience. It allows time for embodied self-awareness to arise. Importantly, it has the potential to provide deep relaxation—positive reinforcement right at the start! The body scan practice involves focusing on sensations in the body as the attention moves from head to toe (or toe to head, or any other journey you care to take), so it may quiet the activity of thought, rather than rev it up—often a much needed respite for ill and highly stressed participants.

Experience is always more helpful than verbal description (however articulate). If you care to, you can try the body scan that is outlined simply here. Don't worry too much about getting it right; the specific map of the body or the order you follow is entirely arbitrary. The key, as we've noted so often, is to proceed with authentic curiosity and genuine friendliness toward your experience as it unfolds.

A Body Scan

Because this is a formal practice of exploring the body in a reclining posture, it is helpful to bring your body under a little bit of discipline, as described in step A. Please keep in mind that you may choose to make small or large adjustments to your posture at any time during the practice. Simply notice the prompting to move, make a conscious decision to do so with intention, and stay connected to the movement until the body settles to stillness.

A. *Come to lying on your back on the floor, ground, or even a bed, with your arms and hands at your sides and legs outstretched. You may wish to bend your knees and place the soles of the feet on the surface beneath, if that is more comfortable. (Remember, for future reference, that you can do the body scan [or any formal meditation] in any of the eighty thousand postures, so there are many opportunities for bringing the kinds of attention explored in the body scan into your everyday experience.)*

B. *Checking into your disposition toward this experience. What is already ready, already here in the body-mind-world complex?*

C. *Noticing the relationship with gravity. If it might be useful, explore coming to rest using the microyoga technique. (See the "Microyoga for Exploring Disposition and Gravity" box on page 202 for details.)*

D. *Beginning gently to notice the breath. Actually feeling the sensations as the breath enters and leaves the body of its own accord. Noticing any impulses to control or* change it or to breathe "right." If it's possible, just watching without responding to those impulses.

E. If you would like to, you might use the palms and fingers of your hands, lightly, gently, to explore the motions of the breath. (See the "Handfuls of Breath" box on page 202 for details.)

F. Taking your hands away, and allowing the arms to come to rest at your sides. Moving your attention to the top of your head, and noticing that sensations may arise when you bring your attention to a particular part of the body. Or perhaps there's no sensation; that's OK, it's simply your experience in the moment.

G. And when you're ready, moving your attention to your forehead. Dwelling with how it is until you're ready to move on. Then continue to dwell, notice, and move on at your own pace. Perhaps moving slowly enough to ensure that all the information comes in from the body as well as from thinking.

H. Visiting the areas of the eyes, the cheeks, the jaw, the lips, and the mouth (inside and outside), and sensing the entire face and head, resting. When thinking, sounds, distracting sensations, or emotions come to dominate your attention, just see if it is possible for them to move to the background again. As much as possible, keeping the larger part of your attention on body sensations. Toggling back and forth as you notice your attention being drawn away again and again.

I. Then moving from the face and head to the body and its members, noticing sensation, and if you care to, using the breath to explore: How far does it go in the body? Does it reach to where you're attending? And onward to the neck and throat, the shoulders, the discrete parts of the arms and hands on both sides—either simultaneously or one at a time. And tuning in to the upper back, the middle back, and the lower back, in turn.

J. Moving attention to the chest, perhaps to heartbeat (if you can sense it) and breath. Extending attention into the abdomen, to "gut feelings." Then attending to the pelvic region, the groin, the genitals, the lower abdomen—tuning in to the sense of the breath: how far does it reach?

K. Shifting the focus into the upper legs, then extending to the lower legs—the relationship to gravity, the sense of the breath, any sense of vitality. And exploring onward to the feet.

L. Now expanding the attention to include the entire body, from the soles of the feet *to the top of the head, being present to the totality of the experience of the body reclining—dwelling in what it knows.*

SLEEPINESS AND BEYOND

Bringing attention to the body in reclining may often lead to repose, relaxation, rest, and sleepiness if not outright sleep. This is not at all unusual. Consider: how often during your day are you both relaxed and awake? For many of us the answer is once—the moment before we fall asleep. Reclining meditations take us to that point, and habit tips us over. We're embedded in that moment in bed, and it is difficult to shift that habit. It would, however, be helpful (and healthy) if we could spend more time awake and relaxed. So, we can work in subtle ways to bring the habit into consciousness and make choices.

Clinical experience in working with meditations such as the body scan has suggested three approaches to sleepiness:

1. **Use it.** You may simply be tired enough to require the sleep, so be kind and nonjudgmental and give yourself permission to snooze. Many people even use the body scan as a way of inducing sleep when their disposition is more toward wakefulness or anxiety.
2. **Explore it.** Sleepiness is just another state of *how it is,* and our practice is to attend to that. When you turn toward your experience of sleepiness in a curious and friendly way, what happens? What do you notice in body, thinking, and emotion as you fall asleep?
3. **Change it.** When we notice *how it is,* we often have choices. We can accept how it is in the moment and work to change the next moment. Perhaps it can be as simple as opening your eyes when sleepiness descends or choosing a different time of day for practice.

   There is no better or lesser strategy, no answer that you can make *yours* and apply whenever sleepiness arises. There is simply the next experiment, extending the transitional surface to find out about now.

Microyoga for Exploring Disposition and Gravity

This is a practice for any time, anywhere. You can try it for a minute during a quick check-in during your busy day. You could choose to make it the core of a longer, leisurely, informal investigation of how it is. And you might use it, as we've suggested in the body scan, as an early exploration in a formal practice.

The principle is all you need to get. Once it literally *makes sense,* you'll find countless ways to bring it into your ongoing mindfulness practice.

You'll get it, naturally, by trying it. So, right now, notice how your body is disposed. Perhaps an arm or leg is at rest, or at least resting on some surface. Maybe you're reading while reclining, and your head is down. Make a choice of some resting body part, and bring your attention to it. Notice disposition; notice the effect of gravity; notice the possibility of habit at work. How is it, really?

Now, put some "lift" into the body part you've chosen. Recall our discussion of impulse and intention (in/pulse, in/tension), and raise it up just enough to experience its full weight, to feel the negotiation you must make with gravity. Perhaps take a moment to notice the quality of the breath (be sure you *are* breathing!). Now, lower what you've raised while sensing as much of the ongoing change as you can. When does it come to *rest* at last? How is it now—disposition, gravity, habit? Are you more, or less, present to your experience? In other words, does this kind of exploration do what yoga (no matter how small) does? That is, does it bring you into the now?

Handfuls of Breath

Reclining postures provide an additional free and easy mode of exploration of breathing. The hands are not only unengaged, they can rest on the body with very little energy or tension required to keep them in place. That means that the hands can be very sensitive instruments for tracking responses of breathing to the qualities of the moment.

The exploration process is simple and infinitely variable. You can place your hands as intuition suggests, on throat, chest, belly, back, or sides to tune in to movement. You might choose to place a hand on the lower part of the face, fingers beneath the nostrils, to register the flow of breath. Hands can be used together—two sides of the belly—assuming symmetry, or resting on different areas. Research can, of course, be done with one hand, as well.

With hands in place, simply notice what the breath is doing *right there* in *this moment*. Then bring the hands away, and notice how the breath responds without touch. And place the hands again, and notice what you find now. You can work with this on-off method to explore all around the domain of the breath. It may highlight for you just how responsive and expansive the body-mind complex is.

UNDERNEATH AND OVERTOP

Informal practice in reclining is, most commonly, about sleeping and waking, and checking-in on disposition, gravity, and breath can make you more present to either state. Whether there is struggle or ease around finding sleep, or tightness or luxuriousness about waking, turning—gently—toward the experience can bring new information and a new situation.

Possibilities for experiments abound: working with disposition when sleep won't come is a start. Is it possible to check in to space, vitality, and flow with kindness and without judgment or investment in the outcome? The same exploration is, of course, also available as we awaken (athough it's easy to pass by it). Gravity experiments can highlight the surface and coverings. Your bed may be full of habits, such as, "This is the right posture," or "The pillow needs to go here." But a bed is really an unstable surface. When bedclothes are new and different or merely askew, or when pillows and other "visitors" move to unaccustomed places, lying down can be new. How is it to have a pillow in a different place or at a different angle as you allow gravity to take the body where it will? How is it when, after a time, you remove the pillow? How is it when you shift the pillow to another place? How will you respond to gravity then? The contours of what lies beneath your lying down can prompt experimenting.

Likewise, the material that you draw over you offers possibilities for relating, knowing, and transitioning. What is your disposition toward your covers? Is there a yes or a no, or an adjustment that needs to be made? Do you feel gravity at work as the covers come to rest on you? How does that pressure affect your breathing? Your disposition—those impulses toward movement or stillness?

Such experimenting is not just for bedtime or naptime. You can explore reclining in the warmth of the sun at a pool or the beach, in cozy company on a lawn for a picnic with friends, or in the chill and glaring examining room at the doctor's office. How do you want to be when lying down presents itself? And how are you when you get there—breath, gravity, and desire?

The transitions of the reclining posture can lead up to the next dignity—to sitting. There are three explorations inherent in the motions toward sitting. First, consider the energy available. Perhaps it is tied up in a preference for reclining or a resistance to change? Maybe you are already ready to come to sitting? Second, feel in to gravity's effects. Is it possible to notice effort and ease as you move the trunk toward vertical? How about the movement of the lower legs if you are on raised seating? How does reclining differ from sitting, and when does slouching become lying down? Third, bring attention to the breath. Does getting ready to sit up bring change? How does the breath respond to the posture change? Do transitional events like sighs and yawns attend the shift? Do shifts in the process of thought or the quality of mood state become evident? Are you more present, or less?

13
SITTING

Where Stillness and Change Meet

This dignity plops us down right into a paradox of contemporary life. It is a posture of reflection, of stillness in the midst of ongoing change. Consider the impulse, when we are overwhelmed by action, confusion, emotion, to *sit down* at the first opportunity and *sort things out*. Yet, sitting is also the posture in which many of us do our jobs. (There are certainly more seated jobs now than at earlier times in our history.) Which means that sitting also is an opportunity to get worked up—to meet action, confusion, emotion within us. How do we sit down from that?

Sitting, then, is a posture that reveals context. You sit down in the *middle* of something—a life, a world, a transitional surface—that may well seem more expansive the more you survey it. Formal mindfulness practice in sitting posture is a container for this context. It may sound strange, yet, within the discipline of the posture and the time commitment, you may find that it is possible to hold all that gets worked up in you and all the transitional surface on which it moves. Sitting may be a way of holding what is present, in an engaged and friendly way, in the present.

Perhaps an analogy may be helpful here. It may be that you've had this experience: a terrible tangle. A hank of rope, a ball of string, a skein of yarn, a spool of fishing line—some supple stuff is in disarray, and it falls to you to bring it into order. The first moments of facing such a challenge are often fraught with time pressure ("This is holding me up"), muscle tension (fingers, neck, shoulders, face, and more), and negative predictions ("I can't possibly undo this"). This all may result in pulling the tangle tighter. The strategy that most often resolves the situation is to first *sit down,* which makes it possible to allow the churning in the body-mind to subside and to turn the attention to the task at hand without tracking or predicting the outcome. Then, through kind and curious attention, the loops and snarls—in the body-mind as well as the tangle—begin to loosen, and in the greater liberty the way becomes clear and reachable. It is the sitting down that allows it to happen. Perhaps this analogy will entwine itself with the instructions for formal sitting meditation given below.

The formal practice of *expanding awareness* is the sitting meditation that is taught in Mindfulness-Based Stress Reduction classes. It moves through a number of objects of attention, beginning with the breath and body, and eventually opening to the total experience of the body-mind-world complex, with a focus that is chosen not by the practitioner, but by what is most insistent in awareness at the moment. This free moving of the attention is known as *choiceless awareness.* As it is presented here, expanding awareness is a single, continuous practice. Yet, as in all that we're presenting in this book, each facet suggests a whole range of possibilities for formal and informal experiences and experiments.

A Formal Sitting Meditation

The image conjured by the term sitting meditation *may be of a yogi or a Buddha figure seated on the floor with legs like twisted ribbons. People in Eastern cultures grow up with sitting on the floor as a cultural norm. That norm means that in and out of meditation practice, they have a continuity in posture. Their formal practice is not removed from everyday life. For us in the West, sitting on the floor may seem exotic and a bit uncomfortable. If we sit on the floor for meditation, it puts a boundary between formal and informal practice. Our Western cultural norm is to sit on a chair. And so we can, with all good sense and the best intentions, practice formal meditation in a chair. That way, our formal and informal practice may benefit from the continuity—expanding the transitional surface.*

A. *Beginning formal practice by sitting down, right in the middle of your life. Feeling gravity holding you in the chair, the earth receiving your weight. Perhaps you can find a point of balance where gravity is holding you comfortably upright, without strain. (See the "Exploring Sitting from Three Perspectives" box on page 209.) Is it possible to allow gravity to have its way with the muscles throughout your body? As much as possible, giving the full weight of arms and shoulders, legs and feet, even facial muscles, to the insistent pull toward the center of the earth.*

B. *And bringing your attention now to the sense of your body **breathing,** the breath entering and leaving the body. Noticing any major or tiny adjustments required in posture to allow the breath to flow with ease and without effort. Allowing the breath to breathe itself. Not changing it in any way. Attending to the entirety of an inbreath from beginning to end. Attending to an outbreath from beginning to end. Noticing that there is a cycle with three parts—inbreath, outbreath, pause—that is worth investigating. (See the "Exploring Breathing from Three Perspectives" box on page 212 for one mode of investigation.)*

C. *As you attend to the breath, you may find that your attention moves off to follow some other interest—say, a sound, a sensation, a thought, or an emotion. If that is clear to you, you have received grace, you are awake, you are mindful. So, in the present moment of this realization, there is a choice—to pursue the distraction or to return the attention to the breath. In the formal practice, we favor the choice to return. You may find that the attention can be a bit wayward, and that you can be faced repeatedly with the choice of returning. This is simply the process of the practice. Each choice you face is a moment of mindfulness, so it is not a problem to have a lot of them. You're learning what it is to wake up and pay attention.*

D. *And now, when you are ready, expanding your attention beyond the breath to include the entire body. Becoming aware of sensations of contact with the chair or cushion. Perhaps of the touch of clothes on your body. Or how your hands feel in the moment. Sensations of temperature. Being present with any sensations as they come into awareness. They sometimes stay for just a short while, and at other times they linger. They change in intensity, shift, and pass away as new sensations arise.*

If the attention meets distraction, just noticing, and making a choice to return to sensations.

E. *Sometimes, sensations that are very intense may enter awareness, making it difficult to attend. There are two ways to be with this. You may choose to move the body to relieve them, attending to each intention and motion as you move. Or you may choose to bring your attention right into the intensity of the sensation. Exploring it with a friendly curiosity. As a practice of context, sitting meditation is an opportunity and a container in which to explore the nuances of strong sensation. Being aware of both your transitory disposition—the space, vitality, and flow available—and the continual shifting of sensation.*

F. *Allowing your attention to shift from sensations in the body to sounds—the sense of hearing. Noticing that you are receiving sounds from the environment and perhaps from within the body. Noticing that sounds come and go. Even noticing the spaces between sounds—the silences. Be aware of how you are disposed toward sound. Be aware of sitting in the middle of sounds. Practicing context by attending to sound as an event in the larger container of sitting, of awareness. And if the attention veers away from sound, making the choice to bring it back, as often as required.*

G. *Shifting now from sound to thoughts. Experiencing thoughts not as distractions, but rather as an ongoing process—an infinitely expanding transitional surface. Noticing how thoughts (much like sounds!) enter awareness, stay briefly or for a more extended period of time, and then dissolve. Not getting lost in the content of the thoughts. Allowing them to simply be events, in context, in the foreground of awareness, with the breath, body sensations, sounds—the experience of the moment—in the background. If you get carried away in the current of thinking, coming back to observe thoughts as discrete events that come and go.*

H. *Noticing also that emotions arise in the body-mind-world complex. Perhaps frustration, restlessness, peacefulness, sadness, joy, or fear appears. Noticing disposition. Noticing how some emotions are wanted, some are unwanted. How there may be a tendency to hold on to some emotions, maybe love or anger, and to struggle with others, maybe sadness or fear. Noticing whatever emotions arise moment to moment, holding them in the context of sitting. What happens as you stay with an emotion, regardless of your disposition toward it? (If at any time emotions or sensations become too uncomfortable, remember that you can always return to a focused attention on the breath and find a safe harbor there until you're ready to venture out again.)*

I. *Moving now into choiceless awareness. Not choosing to bring your attention to anything in particular, but simply sitting, fully aware of whatever is presenting itself to you in each moment. If sound arises, allowing it to be the center of attention. If body sensation arises, letting that be the center of your attention. Just dwelling with what is, until the next arising, which may be anything at all—say, another body sensation, a thought about a body sensation, or an emotion. Sitting in stillness as experience comes and goes (See the "Stillness and Change" section on page 213 for the contextual value of bodily stillness.) Be present in the context of now as it shifts and changes.*

J. *Then, when you are ready to bring the formal practice to a close, returning your focus of attention to the breath. Coming to a tight focus, to an intimacy with the breath. Staying fully present with the breath as you sit. As you end your formal session, not "snapping out of it," but rather, realizing that you have gained knowledge of how it is for you in the moment and bringing that knowledge with you into your ongoing life.*

Exploring Sitting from Three Perspectives

Just as the four dignities represent the eighty thousand postures between them, three sitting postures in a chair may help us to learn about the extensive transitional surface of sitting. The philosophy that educators, parents, employers, and even spiritual authorities promote with the command (maybe it even feels like a *commandment*), "Sit up straight," might suggest that one of the three postures we'll investigate is superior to the other two. Please see if you can set aside whatever immediate reactions you may have—whether for or against authority—and see if you can simply experiment with all three postures. None is intrinsically right or wrong, none essentially healthy or harmful; there is simply what best meets the requirements of the context. The only valid question is, "How is it with you, right now?"

You may choose to do these three experiments in your favorite piece of furniture for sitting. A meditation chair, a corner of a couch, an easy chair, a desk chair, a bench in the park are all as suitable as well-appointed laboratories. Even student desks, meeting room chairs, or congregational seating could be research sites for compiling data.

1. **Forward.** Sitting on the chair with your center of gravity forward. One way to achieve this is to imagine that the chair may collapse at any moment. Your back is away from the back, feet are on the floor and carrying weight, head and arms forward as well. Then check in. How is the inner disposition of space, vitality, and flow reflected? How might you react if a friend came up and offered you a gift? Or a grievance? How is the breath responding? What is the relationship to gravity? That is, how much effort? How much ease? Then making any large or small adjustments to your posture to be sure that you're in comfort. Noticing the shifts you've made.

2. **Backward.** Letting the body go—all the way. Moving the center of gravity way to the back. Imagining the chair as a chaise lounge (if it's not already!). Finding comfort and luxury for your limbs and head, support for the back. And checking in. How are you disposed to respond in this moment? What if that friend offered the gift...or the grievance? Do you feel gravity holding you? How does the breath move? Making whatever adjustments are required to find and maintain comfort. Now, what's changed?

3. **Centered.** Bringing the sit-bones to the seat. To investigate, perhaps place the right hand under the right buttock, palm up, and sense the bone; bring the left hand under the left buttock, and sense again. Bringing the two sides into balance—after removing the hands. With your back near the back of the seat, feel into a way of sitting in which gravity holds you up with the least effort. How is it for you? How would you receive a gift of grievance? Then lean back and give weight to the back of the chair. How is that?

How would you receive that gift? Continuing to explore with the breath and with gravity. What do you know? And, finally, allow any changes that need to happen. How is it now?

SITTING AROUND

Some of us, it's true, may just sit around all day. And it truly is a-*round*. We move from sitting on the edge of the bed, even momentarily, as we awaken, to sitting at breakfast, to sitting in the car, train, bus, truck, plane, to get to a work place, where, if we don't sit to do our job, we nevertheless sit to rest. We mostly take our meals sitting (if we're lucky!), and we rid ourselves of the final waste in a sitting posture, too. We sit for travel home. And sit again to eat, to talk, to entertain and be entertained. At last, we return to that transitory seat on the edge of the bed, for the round to begin again.

That's a lot of sitting and a lot of different contexts, each worthy of exploration and experimentation. If we get in touch with our disposition as we encounter each context in turn, we become more present to the unfolding of our days and of our lives. Knowing how it is with us when we're sitting is a simple practice that can be enriched by bits and pieces of the formal expanding awareness.

Consider some of the myriad possibilities: Relying on gravity and the breath (A and B) to be always available as you consciously take a seat. Maintaining attention (C) and tuning in to body sensations (D) when you're feeling challenged—and perhaps choosing to work with them in a friendly way (E). Allowing sound (F) to help you find the size and center of awareness (and to help you feel centered) in the moment. Checking-in to the process of thought (G); not to change it, but to know its qualities, as you sit down in a quiet place (maybe the bathroom!) in a hectic time. Likewise, bringing attention to the ongoing mood-state or emotion (H); can it just be there, in the context of now? Maybe there's a chance to touch down in the formal practice of choiceless awareness (I), to open to receive what life is offering—whether gift or grievance.

Exploring Breathing from Three Perspectives

Attending to breathing is a facet of a great many formal meditations across traditions and around the world because it links the practitioner to the present moment and, as we've seen, offers a bonus possibility of turning on the parasympathetic response and precipitating relaxation. Any time, anywhere, you can attend. There is a basic structure to the breath that can help you to experiment (and experience). It's three transitory phases: inbreath, outbreath, and a pause. It is therefore logical, and sensible, to investigate this structure. And the sitting posture provides a context.

1. **Inbreath.** This is the working phase, as the diaphragm contracts and travels into the abdomen to create space for the expanding lungs. Control of the process is, as we know, two-sided—voluntary and involuntary. So the question, in the context of sitting, is, "Which side are you on?" Noticing the impulses and pushes that may break in when you're attempting to attend. What disposition is apparent when the inbreath comes in on its own volition?

2. **Outbreath.** This is the returning phase, as the diaphragm expands and retracts into the chest, pushing the air from the lungs, with no effort required. (For the unfortunate person with emphysema, things are reversed, requiring active efforts to breathe out and expel the air, while the lungs fill up again automatically). How is the disposition toward not working? Noticing urges to add power, to adjust speed, to ensure efficiency or perfection. Is it possible to allow the relaxation and expansiveness that the outbreath implies? (Remember, the outbreath is the physiological signal to the body to move away from fight or flight and toward rest and repair.)

3. **Pause.** This is the resting phase, which is for both recovery and preparation. How is the disposition toward rest? Is it already ready to begin the inbreath, or is it in that mode we call waiting? Is it possible to truly rest? To trust the inbreath to begin—on its own schedule and not one that can be known or created in advance?

One way to use this scheme is to feature each phase in a different experiment. When you're sitting in a meeting, what do you learn about the inbreath? Sitting in the car at a stoplight, what do you know about the outbreath? Sitting and watching a movie or other performance, what do you know about the pause? Sitting is context, and context is constantly changing, so opportunities for investigation are infinite: choose a few.

STILLNESS AND CHANGE

Sitting can offer a paradoxical comfort. If you impose relative stillness on the body as you sit, you may experience some discomfort. Yet, simultaneously, you may find that a still body can contain and perhaps alleviate such discomfort—and much more. To put it another way, an attitude of not moving can highlight the fact that experience changes from moment to moment. Or to be Emersonian, stillness is a means of optimizing the transitional surface available to us.

You may choose to investigate this facet of sitting practice in a formal session or in an extended informal experiment. A time period of five minutes or more of stillness should be enough to show you the paradox.

Begin by bringing care and curiosity to your sitting posture. Permit any changes or adjustments required. Gently allow the body to settle in to gravity (and even to be touched and adjusted by the breath); with each outbreath you might see if there is a little more settling that can happen. When you've settled, turn the attention to the breath. Being present for the process of breathing, just as it is, without interference. You may abide this way for some time.

Then, when it feels like the right time, *decide* that you will hold the body in relative stillness. Certainly, the breath is moving however and whatever it moves, and heartbeat and pulse may be part of the background. Yet, you are refraining from adjusting the body; you're holding still.

Allowing the stillness to be at the foreground of your attention.

Notice what happens in the body—impulses to move, perhaps, or itching, tingling, discomforts, pleasant sensations—and meet the experience in a friendly way, holding it in the context of the body's stillness. How is it to *not* react in movement to the sensations, thoughts, or emotions that come to visit? What happens with them as you simply offer a container, a space for them to be?

When you feel that your experiment is complete, allow whatever adjustments—large or small—the body requires, and return your attention to the breath. An easy resting state. And, when it seems right, carrying any newfound knowledge into your next posture, your next present moment.

14
STANDING

Opening to the World

"Taking a stand." "Standing up for what's right." It's obvious in our language that standing is the posture of courage. Feeling in to it may reveal why. Standing hides nothing. The entire body is exposed and vulnerable. The other three dignities offer some protection. Reclining and sitting conceal broad surfaces, and walking makes us a moving target. Except for the soles of the feet, standing opens us completely to the world. Making a choice to be so available, in many situations, requires courage.

Standing is also the posture of wakefulness. Again, it's inherent. An upright bipedal stance is very difficult to maintain. Any sway from side to side or front to back is destabilizing; gravity stops holding us up and starts to pull us down. This tendency happens on both a macroscale and a microscale. Not only must we make larger adjustments when we're disturbed (from inside or out), but we also must make continuous smaller adjustments as we get feedback on our relationship to gravity and the vertical from our eyes, our inner ears, and the proprioceptors and graviceptors distributed throughout the body (as described in chapter 6). We must be awake to respond.

As we noted in chapter 11, standing is also called *stopping,* and that throws the transitional qualities of standing into relief. It's a momentary stillness that's not all that still. In this posture, we are *on the way* to another posture—walking, sitting, reclining. This all means that the

215

possibilities of openness, wakefulness, and being "in the flow" come together for us in the moment. Standing is when we know where we are and how it is with us. It's the moment in which we can precisely feel the wind and the breath, and we can begin to make sense of the body-mind-world complex.

The Ball and the Foot

The soles of our feet contain and link to arrays of proprioceptors that help to keep us upright. These sensitive instruments deserve care and attention, and certainly function better when treated well.

There's a small experiment that offers attention, care, and an opportunity to learn more about these body parts that we mostly hide and protect—that is, ignore. If you choose to work this way, you may awaken your soles to their greater potential, learn more about how your feet contribute to the process of standing, and find that you've shifted your disposition. All you need is a golf ball or any small, relatively hard ball—tennis, baseball, handball, squash, stickball, all might contribute.

Let your feet out of your shoes! Then, barefoot or in socks or stockings, sitting or standing, begin to explore the topology of one sole—the plantar surface, as they say in medical circles. And maybe you can actually make circles, pressing down and moving your leg so that the ball travels around the sole. Explore everywhere: heel, outside and inside the arch, the ball of the foot, the toes, and all the nooks and crannies that suggest themselves. Stop when it feels like a good time, and bring the busy foot to the floor, to supporting half your weight. Rising on it if you've been sitting. What do you notice? How is this foot compared to its opposite? And then, working on that one, allowing the ball to meet the foot with curiosity and friendliness. When you've finished, bring both feet to standing and check in. How is it for you now—disposition, breath, and, especially, your relationship with gravity?

A Standing Meditation

This meditation is an opportunity to practice respect for the experience of the body-mind-world complex—being present for what is in awareness from moment to moment. If your disposition is one of taking a stand against what is arising, you might consider it a form of "dis-respect." Respect, at the root, means "to look back at, to look at again" (re-spect), that is, to not judge but to remain open. Such a posture will allow flexibility of response—to choose what is really required in the moment. You could say that it is about your capacity to be "response-able."

A. *Ideally, this practice is done standing. There is potential to notice the flow across the transitional surface, if you stand long enough to experience some physical challenge in remaining standing. Please feel free to begin standing in front of a chair, and to take a seat when the time feels right to you—showing self-respect and being "response-able" to your own experience.*

B. *Beginning by taking a stand—not against anything, but in your life in this moment. You can choose to explore one of the four foot positions described in the "Getting Your Feet under You" box on page 218. Feeling in to uprightness—in to standing. Opening to the range of sensations. Being willing to look again, to make the small adjustments required for ease and balance.*

C. *Standing with eyes closed. Sensing your feet on the floor. Noticing any tension in the ankles or lower legs, knees, thighs, hips, lower back. Feeling the spine rising up and sensing into the feeling of being open or closed. How is it for you? Is there a sense of shoulders and chest opening, perhaps a feeling of the heart opening, of some vulnerability to the full potential of the beauty, fearfulness, and sadness of moment-by-moment experience? See if it is possible to find ease and openness in standing aware of how this posture complements or conflicts with thoughts or emotions in this moment.*

D. *Being open, as is possible, to the experience of the space of the environment. Is it limited to what is in front of you? Human perceptual organs are pitched forward. The mind leans into the future. There may be physical and habitual limits you can feel. Yet, you may be able to bring yourself into 360 degrees of connection with what surrounds you. Can you sense the space behind as well as before you—being open to it all—expanding your "response-ability"?*

E. *When you're ready, adding a focus on sounds to your experience. Allowing whatever sounds arise to come to you, without judgment or preference. Noticing that the sounds arise from all quarters, and allowing them to help you remain open to the full 360-degree experience of standing.*

F. *Noticing what closes you down, what shuts the valve of your experience—thought, emotion, body sensations. As much as possible, working to reopen the valve when you find it closing; finding a way to respect your experience—to look again.*

G. *Now getting in touch with your eyes behind the eyelids. What are they doing? Are they still? Or are they trying to look? And getting in touch with the eyelids—feeling their weight, and maintaining contact with the sensation of their weight as you raise them. Opening the eyes in this indirect way, so the visible world enters your experience gently. How does this affect posture? How does it affect breathing?*

H. *When it feels right to you, slowly raising your gaze. Opening to the sense of the full environment—seeing or sensing peripherally the 360 degrees in which you stand.*

I. *Aware of moments of shutting down, aware of thoughts and feelings that arise that make openness difficult. Accepting any pleasure or struggle as just transitional experience; showing respect by being willing to stay with it: looking again.*

J. *As you choose to end this standing meditation, making a choice, to end your practice entirely, or to continue with a sitting or reclining meditation—maintaining a sense of openness and respect.*

Getting Your Feet under You

Yoshi Oida, a Japanese actor and director who has spent most of his career in the West, has evolved a method for investigating the standing posture, by placing the feet at four measured distances from each other.[1] The measures are easily derived from your individual body structure, so any investigation you choose will fit you perfectly. The four positions actually become eight, because you may choose to place the feet parallel or at forty-five degrees to each other.

1. **The feet touching one another.** Notice the quality of standing in this way: the body's relationship to gravity conveyed by sway and feedback from vision, muscular impulses, and the vestibular sense; the process of thinking, that is, the weather in the thought space; the emotional tone or mood state.

2. **The feet directly under the hips.** We often overestimate this space. The measure is made down from the hip sockets, and is not drawn from the wider top of the pelvis. Feel into the difference. And when the thighs are dropping straight down from the hip joints, notice the qualities of this moment via the triangle of awareness.

3. **The feet shoulder-width apart.** Oida notes that this squares your body in its space. How is it to be squared? Are there urges toward stillness or movement?

4. **The feet farther than shoulder-width apart.** How are sway and feedback here? Are there urges toward stillness or movement? What feeling tones go with this placement?

In your standing throughout your day, you may choose to bring attention to the body and find your feet on the continuum of these placements.

Casual *Contrapposto*

In the formal practice of standing meditation, we may give precedence and priority to postures with evenly distributed weight. Yet, many of us prefer or default to another distribution entirely. This posture bears exploration. It is very human, very sensuous, and, in fact, very utilitarian. It is the way of standing with the body's weight on one leg and the other leg essentially free. In art circles it's known as *contrapposto,* which refers to the oppositions in the posture; the hips rise in one direction, the shoulders in another. There is a sinuous curve to the body that you can see (and feel) in Michaelangelo's statue of *David*. How is it to stand that way? As your attention to contrapposto brings you into the moment, what's it like in your discursive mind and your mood state?

There is power in this stance, a disposition that includes a readiness to take a step—the next one needed. There is also utility in this way of holding yourself, because it's perfect for bearing loads while standing. Children go right onto that higher hip when we pick them up to hold them. And we hold cargo, as well as little passengers, on that hip—books, boxes, and bags. During your day, do you note and know when your standing is *contrapposto?*

GETTING TO VERTICAL

Standing is transitory. How do you know when you're there? And how can you tell when you've left? There are two basic routes into standing: coming up from hanging over and rising up from squatting (or, more formally, sitting). This is familiar geography that you traverse often during the day. You sit down, and you come to standing. You bend over, and you rise up. Maybe those movements can help bring you into the present moment as you attend to the process of getting to vertical.

You can try a formal, extended investigation of the flow from sitting to standing, to bring the movements and sensations into focus. Begin by standing and feel gravity pulling you down, right along and through the center of the body. When you feel the pull is really centered, begin allowing ankles, knees, and hips to "accordion fold" the body down into squatting. If that destination is too challenging, you might try standing with a chair behind you and folding down onto the chair seat. Checking in, as you come toward stillness, with disposition and the breath. Then, in touch with gravity and the choices you make as you move, coming up to standing. And checking in again, just to know how it is with you in the moment. You may decide to repeat these transitions in order to increase your focus.

Formal research on the motion through bending and standing might look like this: Bringing the head forward—chin toward the chest—and following the tendency to fold forward, arms loose at your sides so they swing to reach toward the floor. Bringing the body to stillness when it feels like the right degree of bending. Noticing the disposition and the breath. How is it, then, not to crank the back and head upward mechanically, but to find the impulse to arise and follow it to vertical.

In both these experiments, as you reach vertical, sense in to that dimension: do you feel your full stature? Standing starts at the soles of the feet, but where does it end? It's good to know just how you fit into the space you're in. When you've reached standing, bring a hand up and gently place the palm and fingers on the top of your head. Tune in. Does that touch affect the sense of your stature? Stay with these sensations for a while; get to know how it is between the floor and the palm of your hand. Remove your hand and sense again. Where are you now? And as you replace the hand again, what comes into focus?

UP AGAINST THE WALL

The upright posture highlights limitations of strength and balance. You are on your own, isolated and constrained by the 360 degrees of empty space around you.

That situation changes, however, when you meet a wall. Such solid support highlights the potential for transcending your limits. You are held, perhaps you could say buoyed up, by this relationship. A wall makes it possible to stand in attitudes that are far outside your independent vocabulary. Suddenly the body-mind-world comes into focus, even when you're just waiting around.

You might find an occasion for some extended explorations of standing and its neighboring postures with support. How is it to back into the wall and give it your weight? Noticing your disposition. Noticing how the breath responds. If the wall is smooth, can you investigate moving the feet farther away? Or folding down and rising up—what's in that movement for you with support? Exploring with your side against the wall: bending, rising, leaning with the arm up overhead or hanging down—shoulder to the wall.

It's possible to meet the wall face-to-face, if you would like. Maybe beginning by standing with your toes six inches or so away from the wall. Then leaning forward to bring your forehead against the surface. How is it to do this with eyes open? How is it with eyes closed? What happens in disposition and breathing? What do you come to know about your disposition—and the sense of anticipation? You can work further by placing the hands against the wall and exploring with the arms—up, out to the side, describing an arc. Moving in this way to complete the investigation of support in 360 degrees.

Informally, when you're presented with a wall, you can loiter with intent—to live in the present moment.

A Note on Pain

There will be pain. It will show up in movement and posture. In our mindfulness practice, we notice it as sensation and make what conscious choices we can, with curiosity and kindness, to work with it in ways that support our well-being.

As we notice these sensations, and their locations, we come to a new level of awareness. We find that we cannot move or stop in our habitual ways, but must create new ones. Is it possible to allow the little aches and pains of being a body-mind-world complex to bring you into the present moment?

15

WALKING

Practice at the Speed of Life

A sort of prelude: we could argue that walking is the dignity that most belongs to the West. We can trace it in the same way that we traced the arrival and absorption of Eastern meditative and contemplative influences, as well as the simultaneous discoveries of homegrown modes and practices. To go to the extreme, the fourteenth-century Italian poet Petrarch, who provides one of the first Western descriptions of Eastern practices, is often credited as the first to walk in the mountains and climb to a summit purely for the experience and the view. Again, he foreshadows the arc of development of the Romantic movement in Europe and North America.

The eighteenth century drew to its close with the resounding footsteps of solitary walkers. Jean-Jacques Rousseau, enlightenment philosopher of nature and democracy, and prodigious pedestrian, titled his last (unfinished) work *Reveries of a Solitary Walker.* His philosophical writings helped to ground the American Revolution. In England, the poet William Wordsworth, influenced in part by Rousseau, walked everywhere, both to experience his continuity with the natural world and to establish solidarity with the common people. Eighteenth- and nineteenth-century America absorbed the sense of freedom, democracy, and the value of walking. Emerson, for example, knew much of Wordsworth's poetry by heart—including long sections of *The Prelude,* a spiritual epic that is dense with stories and descriptions of journeys by foot—and knew the man as well, visiting him on trips across the Atlantic. So, Continental, English, and American thinkers made walking their way of being in the world. Perhaps none was as committed as Thoreau, whose practice was, indeed, walking.

Thoreau's essay "Walking" provides an image and some language that may be useful in exploring the practice of walking. It opens with the idea of *sauntering*. Thoreau fancifully derives the word from the French Sainte-Terre, the "Holy Land," suggesting that those walking on pilgrimage to Jerusalem, and other holy shrines, were called Saint-Terrers. All those who walk can go to the Holy Land that Thoreau has in mind, the land in which our experience is clear and authentic, provided they are prepared to be on the walk and nowhere else, to be in the moment and not in the past or future. Thoreau puts it in prophetic, Biblical language.

> We should go forth on the shortest walk, perchance, in the spirit of undying adventure, never to return,—prepared to send back our embalmed hearts only as relics to our desolate kingdoms. If you are ready to leave father and mother, brother and sister, and wife and child and friends, and never see them again,—if you have paid your debts, and made your will, and settled all your affairs, and are a free man, then you are ready for a walk.[1]

Whether the walk is down the hall to the bathroom or a backpacking trip in the mountains, it's only Thoreau's walking if you're *walking into now.*

Discipline and diversity: This walking posture of meditation is much bigger than putting one foot in front of the other. In its twenty thousand transitions, it is all the moving that we do through the world—and then some. It may be that we walk barefoot or in boots, with an ice axe or a walker. It may be that our walking is sitting and rolling, or reclining and imagining. However we travel through our lives, we can bring curious and friendly attention to our movement, and that can bring us into the present.

As we choose to turn toward our experience, the world is available to us in a new way—always new. We more clearly perceive the world we're moving through, including what is outside and inside us. We can experience our own thought processes and emotional states with less reactivity. We can create a portable container for contemplation—making room for the philosophy and poetry of everyday life.

Ultimately, any movement can be walking. It's the discipline of attending to awareness that makes it so.

A Walking Meditation

This formal practice also provides a list of hints and approaches for moment-to-moment informal improvisation. You may find that the way you're moving in a given moment connects to something we've described and that you've practiced formally. Or it may be that you take a principle revealed here and meet the experience of the moment with it to bring you to structure and to the present moment.

A. *One definition of walking would involve the shifting of the weight of the body from one leg to the other. You must do that in order to free the feet to stride forward, back, or to the side. While standing with feet hip- or shoulder-width apart, feel the body responding to gravity in a centered posture. Then slowly shift the body's full weight onto one leg. Sense into it, then allow the weight to slowly shift back. In all but motion away from center, this is walking.*

B. *When one leg is free because the weight is on its opposite, lift the free foot and step slowly forward. Feel the foot as it touches down and as the weight shifts forward. When the trailing leg is free, lift that foot and step forward, maintaining attention on the shifting of weight. Moving and attending in this way at a slow pace. If balance seems difficult, be certain that you are stepping slightly outward—away from the centerline of the walking—so the feet are more than hip-width apart to create stability.*

C. *You may choose to walk at a slightly quicker pace, approaching your everyday walking. At this speed, you may find it difficult to stay with the shifting of weight. You might try attending to the contact of the soles of the feet with the* floor. *Noticing the sense of pressure and lack of pressure on the feet, perhaps even the swing of the legs as they go forward. Do you feel the floor beneath you?*

D. *As you investigate different speeds of walking, you may choose to attend to the relationship of the breath to your walking. How does the rhythm of breathing coincide with your steps? What brings a sense of ease in walking and breathing?*

E. *You may choose to attend to the motions of walking in the body—other than the legs. Perhaps maintaining contact with the arms, held loose at the sides. When do they move with your steps? Is there a steady motion?*

F. *If you choose quick paces, the visual sense is something easy to connect to and stay with over time. You may keep the attention unfocused, so to speak, on what is in your peripheral vision. Just noticing the environment as you pass through—not sightseeing, but attending to visual motion.*

G. *At any time, you may choose to stop walking, drop into the sense of the body standing, and connect with the triangle of awareness—your disposition, your relationship to gravity, and the breath. This is also a moment in which you can open to the world—sound, sight, and the full 360 degrees of awareness.*

H. *When you stop, you can also choose to turn the body. It can be useful discipline to walk in one straight path and, when you've reached what you decide is the path's end, to turn and walk over the same ground again—as new. This turn can be a powerful feature in your formal (and informal) practice. When you've come to a stop, coming to stillness and dropping in to gravity and the breath. Raising the gaze and looking, listening, and feeling the larger space around you. Then, when you're ready, turning the body while maintaining your connection to your sense of the space. When you meet the impulse to move, beginning the journey.*

Tiny Spaces

In the formal practice, we're not walking toward a destination, we're not walking for speed or distance, we're simply attending to movement in this moment. This posture means that formal walking meditation practice is possible in any space where you can stand up and take at least one step.

A tiny office at lunchtime, a back porch in a rainstorm, a hotel room away from home—all are perfect venues. In the little path you choose to bring your feet to, any speed of walking is workable. Turning is everything. The connection with gravity, breath, and environment, and the awareness of thought and emotion can make the fullness of your life available to you, wherever you are.

When Prompted, Walk Differently

The Jerzy Grotowski "theater as vehicle" work has something to offer in working with thought and emotion in walking meditation. An American disciple, Stephen Wangh, describes a useful warm-up exercise in his book *An Acrobat of the Heart*.

An adaptation for mindfulness practice would look like this:

1. Just begin walking, without a destination or agenda, while staying with the space you've chosen.
2. Tune in to the sense of motion in a way that works for you, and keeping that as your focus of attention for a while.
3. Then, when you feel ready, expand your awareness to include what is happening in your mind as you walk. You might even speak your stream of thought out loud if you're alone (or whisper it, if others are nearby).
4. You may often be connected to what is happening with the body, yet your mind may also wander. When you notice that the mind has wandered, change the way you are walking—change direction, speed, stride, the relationship to the breath, whatever seems right at the moment. The important thing is to notice the shift in your attention, and to mark it with an outward change.
5. Then, when you've got the hang of it, let the change you make in walking reflect the quality of your shift in attention. If you notice anxious thoughts or emotions, walk anxiously. If you notice sadness,

walk slowly with the head down. If you notice rumination, perhaps walk in circles.

6. When you choose to end the exploration, come to standing and to stillness, and give yourself time to check in to how it is with you. What do you know?[2]

Trips and slips along the way: Our everyday walking takes place on very real surfaces. Inside or outside, in the natural or built environment, these surfaces have textures (smooth, rough, irregular) and consistencies (soft, hard, unstable). Because of the possibilities of mishaps (trips or slips), walking is a practice of being aware and taking care—a practice of mindfulness.

Anthropologist Jo Lee Vergunst makes some very useful distinctions between trips and slips—the mishaps that bring us into now.[3] They are a study in contrasts.

Trips are caused by not enough movement. That is, the rhythm of your movement is halted. The foot that is raised and moving encounters something that rises above the surface. You may attempt to recover by lifting the moving foot even higher to clear the obstruction; if that fails, you may move as the planted foot is moved. And if you can't reach stability, you will fall forward, carried by momentum.

Slips are caused by too much movement. That is, you can't stop yourself. This movement involves the foot that's down, which for some reason slides away—often forward. To recover, you may bring the moving foot down quickly, seeking purchase, a secure grip. If the moving foot is too slow or starts to slip as well, it's very likely you'll fall backward.

In either case, the recourse for safety is to be aware and to take care. This recourse can carry you into informal mindfulness practice. To be aware is not simply to see the surface clearly; it is to engage all that's around you, to be present to what's arising in the body-mind-world. To take care is likewise more than just heeding threats or warnings; it is to walk with intimate contact with the surface in each individual step, to cultivate a "beginner's foot," so to speak. And in both cases, the most important component is attention to the rhythm of walking, which, like breath and heartbeat, is best when infinitely variable by making immediate adjustments. A rhythm of awareness and care is built on responsiveness.

This little story told by the Sensory Awareness leader Louise Boedeker about a walk with her teacher, Charlotte Selver, vividly illustrates the nature of walking mishaps and the benefits of awareness, care, and sensitivity to rhythm:

> Charlotte and I were walking through Cathedral Woods on Monhegan Island in Maine. The majestically tall trees had roots that were knotted and gnarled above ground. I offered my arm to help support her walking—she was about 90 years old at the time.
>
> At some point Charlotte tripped and was pitching forward and going downward . . . something in me responded smoothly going with her . . . we both landed amidst roots, leaves and grasses. We looked at each other and she smiled and said something like, "What a surprise. Thank goodness you didn't try to interfere with my journey, but joined me instead."[4]

CODA

A WALK ON MOUNT MISERY, A GLIMPSE OF MOUNT JOY

Just a few cars at the trailhead, empty. Could be hikers on the trail. Could be they went another way. From here, it looks and sounds like solitude.

Disposition: reluctantly leaving the car radio and society's descent into who knows what—fire, ice, mud, rockslide—to walk up this trail. The breath, too conditioned (or *un*conditioned) to desk and reading chairs, is working hard. Moves through nose and mouth: a little ache in the chest, sharpness in the nostrils in this just-above-freezing early afternoon air.

Clear, white sunlight, well-defined shadows, breeze over my left shoulder from behind—southwest. Sensing a spring as the knees come all the way back, the stretch and pressure in calves and ankles on this steep incline. Little mud patches tarnish the frozen ground.

Trail levels out at the first bend; stop and stand to take in the full prospect of Mount Joy, its dome arc of gray trees with a hovering tone of red budding shyly. A buoyant little smile in looking out over the creek and the road. Two gray tracks through late winter trees—dull asphalt and a ruffled shimmer—the only traveler, up here.

Revolutionaries and Real Estate Developers

These mountains are low and worn, the oldest mountains in the world, part of a quartzite ridge running through the limestone-rich Great Valley in southeastern Pennsylvania. Mount Despair and Mount Joy were key to General George Washington's choice of encampment for his revolutionary army in the winter of 1777. The mountains' high ground provided a strategic geographic anchor, meeting with the Schuylkill River to form a strong defensive position.

Today, the border of Valley Forge National Park runs through Mount Misery. The developed residential area outside the park bears the name Valley Forge Mountain. It would seem that homes on Mount Misery are a hard sell.

Turning back to the trail (noticing tight thighs, calves, and shins), looking up this long grade to see the trail turn and go on up, and up. The idea of your life as a journey, of watching your mind as a journey, is so well worn as to be banal, so well worn as to be a public path—with blazes, perhaps, or even signs on posts. There are two modes to understand this reality. First, Hebbian learning, a neuroscience mode that says as we do things over and over again in the same way, we wear paths in the brain— "What fires together, wires together." Certainly some useful insight there.

I'm thinking about what we don't see, can't see, from these pathways. What's left, way away, off to the sides? In a narrative like this one, what gets lost, what do I record and not use? What do I put into the outline only to leave it behind because it does not fit the sentence structures, doesn't fit my ever-narrowing "vision" of the narrative?

How does this inflect our lives and our learning? What do we leave behind, and what chances do we have to recapture it? Can we walk a path again with ever-opening eyes, a beginner's mind? Do we lace our way differently through the rocks and over the logs? Do we walk nearer to the creek? Or so far away that it disappears from sight and its sound recedes into the background of the breath? Do we venture forth to investigate dead ground as we cross a familiar meadow? And see that edge that hides we know not what? An army? A memory?

A second mode of understanding is perhaps (a big perhaps) that this journey we're on is metaphor, as Lakoff and Johnson tell us, deriving from our embodiment. What else would it derive from? I am nothing but this body that feels the friction of passing through life. I *am* the journey: constantly in flux, fluid. Experiencing each walk, each step, each moment, as different—a transitional surface created to support my next step and the next—the patterns of the shrinking patches of snow behind me on the switchback path different this walk than the last.

An attempt at a poem on the upward incline of the trail—the upclimb:

> *Too early in the year, too late in the day*
> *for birds singing.*
> *The sound in my ears is singing, though,*
> *high pitch of effort and breath and blood—*
> *and tripping*
> *into a groove,*
> *a habitual step that tumbles me*
> *to a Ted Hughes line that's wired in:*
> *"Sit on my finger, sing in my ear, O little blood."*
> *Because this singing is of blood,*
> *of mortality,*
> *and of flux.*
> *Little poetry here; interloping habit steals*
> *any sparkle,*
> *silences and overshadows*
> *any possibilities. I return to feeling my feet,*
> *out of the groove, just in time.*

Crossing an ice patch. Reaching the creek, with its sheens of ice backed up by foam, leaves and twigs, and stones. And crossing the creek on a single log: thirty-six degrees, two miles from the car. What is this frisson in chest and skin—anxiety, fear, fun? Mount Joy obscured by the edge of Misery.

The "we're halfway there" of A. Alvarez's climber friend is always useful, not just in climbing or hiking, but in how we practice. We might keep such a scene in mind, making sure that our attention on the down side, the back side, is as focused as on the front: as present for the rappel as for the climb, for the walk back as the walk there.

Food for Thought from *Feeding the Rat*

In A. Alvarez's portrait of his friend and climbing partner, the mountaineer Mo Anthoine, there is a moment at the summit of Cima Grande in the Italian Alps that puzzled Alvarez at first. It's worth puzzling over.

> When we got to the summit we lay for a while in the sun and watched our wet clothes steam. I felt exhausted beyond exhaustion and slightly light-headed—surprised, I suppose, to be alive. As we set off down the easy south side of the mountain, Mo said, "Right. We're halfway there."
>
> "Pardon?"
>
> "This is when accidents happen," he said, "when you've got to the top and start relaxing."[1]

It is a fact that more accidents and fatalities have occurred while descending Mount Everest than while climbing it.

Standing and looking out over a little rivulet, a trickle of snowmelt down the steep. Caught, tripped by a memory, and dropped into a hundred walks straight up this mountain, no trail, just hard scrambling. Forty years ago, that would be. What were these ankles, these legs and lungs, then? How were those fresh springs? Where are they now? Sliding into the psalms: "The singers and the dancers will say, 'All my fresh springs are in you.'" No trails for me then, just free walking.

And now, what is this that I do? Just watch from the trail as the world passes. Two tiny cairns built just off to the left. Puzzling at this impulse—Druid, Buddhist—for stacking stones on a walk. Should I investigate how the sun shines through them on this month before the equinox?

The down climb and the stones on the trail are more important, now. Stepping on them instead of stepping around. Underfoot, these stones, last fall's leaves, a glistening where ice patches the mud. As I brake, with feet pressing stones on the downclimb, all my fresh springs are in you. How much heavier the body seems. The force of gravity on the side of Mount Misery.

Dancing down the steepest descent. Body laid back, heavy. Feeling contact: *"Contact!"* as Thoreau shouted on Mount Katahdin. Feeling the left ankle shored against the descent, and the giving away, and further descent, and all my best springs are in you. Sing in my finger, roar in my ear, little knowing, flowing blood. Mount Joy entirely eclipsed in this turn, I find within me its arc, its dome, its transcendence—the relaxing outbreath curve of my diaphragm.

Sharing Common Sense

Thoreau's 1846 hike up Mount Katahdin (he used the Native American spelling, Ktaadn), as described in *The Maine Woods*, brought him face to face with untamed nature, in beauty, awe, and danger. He finds this wildness and strangeness in himself, too, in his body. All is mystery to him, and he is reduced to italics and exclamations to *try* to express what we all share.

> Think of our life in nature,—daily to be shown matter, to come in contact with it,—rocks, trees, wind on our cheeks! The *solid* earth! The *actual* world! The *common sense! Contact! Contact!* Who are we? *Where* are we?[2]

Downclimb, to the trailhead. What I carried: keys, wallet, this recorder and two apple flavor Jolly Ranchers that I just found in my jacket pocket. Suck one during these last steps. Smell, taste, and saliva so welcome now.

Back in the car, out of the wind, warm seat, moist green apple scent on the settling breath. The ruin of culture and country is no longer of interest. I start the drive home in a silence of engine noise and the clicking of a turn signal—sharp left out of the lot.

SUGGESTED READING FOR LEARNING AND PRACTICE

HISTORICAL "HEROES" OF WESTERN PRACTICE

Because the works of many of these figures are in the public domain, there are many editions available. In fact, many of these texts are available free on the Internet. To make it easy to locate the quotations we've used from these works, we've provided chapter and paragraph numbers. Have fun with these resources. Find the editions that suit you and support your practice.

Ralph Waldo Emerson

Books
Listed below are Emerson's books, as originally published. There are many collected and combined editions. For the poetry, there are plenty of print and online collections.

Nature: Addresses and Lectures
Essays: First Series
Essays: Second Series
Representative Men
English Traits
The Conduct of Life

Essays and Lectures
We recommend these individual essays and lectures as starting points:

"Nature"
"Circles"
"The Poet"
"Experience"
"The Method of Nature"

Recommended Biography
Richardson, R. D. *Emerson: The Mind on Fire.* Berkeley: University of
California Press, 1995.

Henry David Thoreau
Books
Thoreau published only two books in his lifetime:
A Week on the Concord and Merrimack Rivers
Walden

Posthumous Book-Length Works
Cape Cod
The Maine Woods
Excursions
A Yankee in Canada, with Anti-Slavery and Reform Papers

Thoreau's journals were a vast resource for him, and are so for us all, as well.
There are many volumes of selections available. What will appeal to you?

Thoreau's late writing has been, perhaps, unfairly neglected, and is
beginning to see the light of readership and scholarship.

Wild Fruits: Thoreau's Rediscovered Last Manuscript. Edited by Bradley P.
Dean, New York: Norton, 2000.
*Faith in a Seed: The Dispersion of Seeds and Other Late Natural History
Writings.* Edited by Bradley P. Dean, Washington, D.C.: Island Press/
Shearwater Books, 1993.

Recommended Starting Points
Walden
"Walking"

"A Winter Walk"

"Autumn Tints"

The Heart of Thoreau's Journals. (Very sensitively edited by Odell Shepard and originally published in 1927. Still in print in a Dover Press edition.)

Recommended Biography

Richardson, R. D. *Henry Thoreau: A Life of the Mind.* Berkeley: University of California Press, 1986.

William James

Books

The Principles of Psychology, 2 vols.

Psychology: Briefer Course

The Will to Believe and Other Essays in Popular Philosophy

Talks to Teachers on Psychology and to Students on Some of Life's Ideals

The Varieties of Religious Experience: A Study in Human Nature

Pragmatism: A New Name for Some Old Ways of Thinking

A Pluralistic Universe

The Meaning of Truth: A Sequel to "Pragmatism"

Some Problems of Philosophy: A Beginning of an Introduction to Philosophy

Memories and Studies

Essays in Radical Empiricism

Recommended Starting Points

"What Is an Emotion?"

The Principles of Psychology, chapter 9: "The Stream of Thought"

"The Gospel of Relaxation"

Recommended Biography

Richardson, R. D. *William James: In the Maelstrom of American Modernism.* Boston: Houghton Mifflin, 2006.

Alan Watts

This list is just a selection from Watts's amazingly prolific writing and publishing career. The books listed here give the original publisher and date. All are still in print, some with other publishers.

The Spirit of Zen: A Way of Life, Work, and Art in the Far East. London: J. Murray, 1936.

The Meaning of Happiness; The Quest for Freedom of the Spirit in Modern Psychology and the Wisdom of the East. New York and London: Harper & Brothers, 1940.

The Wisdom of Insecurity. New York: Vintage Books, 1951.

The Way of Zen. New York: Vintage Books, 1957.

Nature, Man, and Woman. New York: Pantheon, 1958.

This Is It: And Other Essays on Zen and Spiritual Experience. New York: Pantheon, 1960.

Psychotherapy, East and West. New York: Pantheon, 1961.

The Book: On the Taboo Against Knowing Who You Are. New York: Pantheon, 1966.

In My Own Way: An Autobiography. New York: Pantheon, 1972.

Tao: The Watercourse Way, with the collaboration of Al Chung-liang Huang. New York: Pantheon, 1975.

Recommended Starting Points
"Beat Zen, Square Zen, and Zen"
The Wisdom of Insecurity
The Book: On the Taboo Against Knowing Who You Are

Recommended Biography
Furlong, M. *Zen Effects: The Life of Alan Watts.* Boston: Houghton Mifflin, 1986.

Jon Kabat-Zinn
Books
Wherever You Go, There You Are. New York: Hyperion, 1994.

Coming to Our Senses: Healing Ourselves and the World through Mindfulness. New York: Hyperion, 2005.

Full Catastrophe Living: Using the Wisdom of Your Body and Mind to Face Stress, Pain, and Illness, 15th anniversary ed. New York: Bantam Dell, 2005.

Kabat-Zinn, J., and M. Kabat-Zinn. *Everyday Blessings: The Inner Work of Mindful Parenting.* New York: Hyperion, 1997.

Recommended Starting Point
Wherever You Go, There You Are

CLINICAL APPLICATIONS OF MINDFULNESS

Baer, R. A., ed. *Mindfulness-Based Treatment Approaches: Clinician's Guide to Evidence Base and Applications.* San Diego, Calif.: Elsevier Academic Press, 2006.

Brach, T. *Radical Acceptance: Embracing Your Life with the Heart of a Buddha.* New York: Bantam Dell, 2003.

Brantley, J. *Calming Your Anxious Mind: How Mindfulness and Compassion Can Free You from Anxiety, Fear and Panic.* Oakland, Calif.: New Harbinger, 2003.

Cole, D., and C. Lades-Gaskin. *Mindfulness-Centered Therapies: An Integrative Approach.* San Diego, Calif.: Silver Birch Press, 2007.

Didonna, F. *Clinical Handbook of Mindfulness.* New York, Springer, 2009.

Fishman, B. M. *Emotional Healing through Mindfulness Meditation.* Rochester, Vt.: Inner Traditions, 2002.

Germer, C. K., R. D. Siegel, and P. R. Fulton, eds. *Mindfulness and Psychotherapy.* New York: Guilford Press, 2005.

Goleman, D. *Destructive Emotions: A Scientific Dialogue with the Dalai Lama.* New York: Bantam Dell, 2003.

Hayes, S. C., V. M. Follette, and M. M. Linehan, eds. *Mindfulness and Acceptance: Expanding the Cognitive-Behavioral Tradition.* New York: Guilford Press, 2004.

McBee, L. *Mindfulness-Based Elder Care: A CAM Model for Frail Elders and Their Caregivers.* New York: Springer, 2008.

Miller, A. L., J. H. Rathus, and M. M. Linehan. *Dialectical Behavior Therapy with Suicidal Adolescents.* New York: Guilford Press, 2007.

Orsillo, S. M., and L. Roemer, eds. *Acceptance and Mindfulness-Based Approaches to Anxiety.* New York: Springer, 2005.

Rosenbaum, E. *Here for Now: Living Well with Cancer through Mindfulness.* Hardwick, Mass.: Satya House, 2005.

Santorelli, S. *Heal Thy Self: Lessons on Mindfulness in Medicine.* New York: Random House, 1999.

Segal, Z. V., J. M. G. Williams, and J. D. Teasdale. *Mindfulness-Based*

Cognitive Therapy for Depression: A New Approach to Preventing Relapse. New York: Guilford Press, 2002.

Siegel, D. J. *The Mindful Brain: Reflection and Attunement in the Cultivation of Well-Being.* New York: Norton, 2007.

Williams, M., J. Teasdale, Z. Segal, and J. Kabat-Zinn. *The Mindful Way through Depression: Freeing Yourself from Chronic Unhappiness.* New York: Guilford Press, 2007.

Research Articles

An extensive bibliography, including ongoing updates of research articles, can be found on the website of the Mindful Awareness Research Center at the University of California, Los Angeles (UCLA): http://marc.ucla .edu/workfiles/pdfs/MARC_biblio_0808.pdf.

SENSORY AWARENESS AND OTHER EMBODIMENT PRACTICES

Overview of the Territory

Johnson, D. H. *Bone, Breath and Gesture: Practices of Embodiment.* Berkeley: North Atlantic Books; San Francisco: California Institute of Integral Studies, 1995.

Books by and about Charlotte Selver

Brooks, C. V. W., and C. Selver. *Sensory Awareness: Reclaiming Vitality and Presence: A Collection of Writings.* R. Lowe and S. Laeng-Gilliatt, eds. Berkeley: North Atlantic, 2007.

Selver, C. *Waking Up: The Work of Charlotte Selver.* Littlewood, W. C., and M.A. Roche, eds. Bloomington, Ind.: AuthorHouse, 2004.

Workshop Recordings and Other Publications

The webpage of the Sensory Awareness Foundation is a gateway to exclusive publications and recordings of workshops by Charlotte Selver and to records of other figures in the elaboration of the "Work" begun by Elsa Gindler: www.sensoryawareness.org.

MINDFULNESS IN
WORLD SPIRITUAL TRADITIONS

Judaism

Boorstein, S. *That's Funny, You Don't Look Buddhist: On Being a Faithful Jew and a Passionate Buddhist.* New York: HarperCollins, 1997.

Cooper, D. *The Heart of Stillness: A Complete Guide to Learning the Art of Meditation.* Woodstock, Vt.: Skylight Paths, 1999.

———. *Silence, Simplicity and Solitude: A Complete Guide to Spiritual Retreat.* Woodstock, Vt.: Skylight Paths, 1999.

———. *Three Gates to Meditation Practice: A Personal Journey into Sufism, Buddhism and Judaism.* Woodstock, Vt.: Skylight Paths, 2000.

Fischer, N. *The Buddhist Path to Truly Growing Up.* New York: HarperCollins, 2003.

———. *Opening to You: Zen-Inspired Translations of the Psalms.* New York: Penquin Putnam, 2003.

———. *Sailing Home: Using the Wisdom of Homer's* Odyssey *to Navigate Life's Perils and Pitfalls.* New York: Simon and Shuster, 2008.

Lew, A. *Be Still and Get Going: A Jewish Meditation Practice for Real Life.* New York: Time Warner, 2005.

Lew, A., and S. Jaffe *One God Clapping: The Spiritual Path of a Zen Rabbi.* Woodstock, Vt.: Jewish Lights Publishing, 2001.

Slater, J. P. *Mindful Jewish Living: Compassionate Practice.* New York: Aviv Press, 2004.

Sufism

Barks, C., and J. Moyne *The Essential Rumi.* Edison, N.J.: Castle Books, 1997.

Helminiski, K. *Living Presence: Sufi Way to Mindfulness and the Unfolding of the Essential Self.* New York: Tarcher/Putnam, 1992.

Christianity

Bourgeault, C. *Mystical Hope: Trusting in the Mercy of God.* Cambridge, Mass.: Cowley, 2001.

———. *Centering Prayer and Inner Awakening.* Cambridge, Mass.: Cowley, 2004.

Keating, T. *The Human Condition: Contemplation and Transformation.* New York: Paulist Press, 1999.

———. *Invitation to Love: The Way of Christian Contemplation.* New York: Continuum, 1999.

May, G. *Will and Spirit: A Contemplative Psychology.* New York: HarperCollins, 1982.

———. *The Dark Night of the Soul.* New York: HarperSanFrancisco, 2004.

———. *The Wisdom of Wilderness.* New York: HarperSanFrancisco, 2006.

Merton, T. *No Man Is an Island.* New York: Harcourt Brace Jovanovich, 1955.

———. *Spiritual Direction and Meditation.* Collegeville, Minn.: Liturgical Press, 1960.

———. *New Seeds of Contemplation.* Norfolk, Conn.: New Directions, 1962.

———. *Mystics and Zen Masters.* New York: Farrar, Strauss and Giroux, 1967.

———. *Zen and the Birds of Appetite.* New York: New Directions, 1968.

———. *Contemplative Prayer.* New York: Herder and Herder, 1969.

Pennington, M. B. *Centering Prayer: Renewing an Ancient Christian Prayer Tradition.* New York: Image Books, 1980.

Rohr, R. *Everything Belongs: The Gift of Contemplative Prayer.* New York: Crossroad, 1999.

———. *The Naked Now.* New York: Crossroad, 2009.

Buddhism

Analayo. *Satipatthana: The Direct Path to Realization.* Cambridge, UK: Windhorse, 2003.

Batchelor, S. *Alone with Others: An Existential Approach to Buddhism.* New York: Grove Press, 1983.

———. *The Awakening of the West.* Berkeley: Parallax, 1994.

———. *Buddhism without Beliefs: A Contemporary Guide to Awakening.* New York: Riverhead Books, 1997.

Gethin, R. *The Foundations of Buddhism.* New York: Oxford University Press, 1998.

Suzuki, S. *Zen Mind, Beginner's Mind.* New York: Weatherhill, 1970.

Trungpa, C. *Cutting through Spiritual Materialism.* Berkeley: Shambhala, 1973.

NOTES

FOREWORD

1. Tolle, *The Power of Now: A Guide to Spiritual Enlightenment,* 39.
2. Selver, *Reclaiming Vitality and Presence,* 25.
3. Rinpoche, *The Tibetan Book of Living and Dying,* 62.

CHAPTER 1. MINDFULNESS IN EARLY AMERICA

1. Watts and Selver, "Alan Watts on the Work of Charlotte Selver and Charlotte Selver about Herself."
2. Hodder, "Ex Oriente Lux."
3. Versluis, *American Transcendentalism.*
4. Hodder, "Ex Oriente Lux"; Versluis, *American Transcendentalism.*
5. Versluis, *American Transcendentalism,* 18.
6. Ibid., 29.
7. Said, *Orientalism.*
8. Jackson, *Oriental Religions and American Thought;* Tweed, "An American Pioneer."
9. Versluis, *American Transcendentalism.*
10. Brooks, *Flowering of New England;* Versluis, *American Transcendentalism;* Hodder, "Ex Oriente Lux."
11. Emerson, *Nature,* chapter 1, paragraph 4.
12. Versluis, *American Transcendentalism,* 63.
13. Hodder, "Ex Oriente Lux," 412.
14. Thoreau, *Walden,* "Sounds," paragraph 2.
15. Hodder, "Ex Oriente Lux," 434.
16. Bevis, *Mind of Winter;* Brooks, *Fenollosa and His Circle.*
17. Brooks, *Fenollosa and His Circle,* 50.
18. Bevis, *Mind of Winter.*
19. Stevens, *Palm at the End,* 54.

244

20. Bevis, *Mind of Winter.*
21. Stevens, *Palm at the End,* 212.
22. Richardson, *William James.*
23. Quoted in Scott, "William James and Buddhism," paragraph 23.
24. Tweed, *American Encounter with Buddhism;* Versluis, *American Transcendentalism.*
25. Scott, "William James and Buddhism."
26. Tweed, *American Encounter with Buddhism.*
27. McMahan, "Repackaging Zen," 220.
28. Tweed, *American Encounter with Buddhism;* McMahan, "Repackaging Zen."
29. Scott, "William James and Buddhism."
30. Tweed, *The American Encounter with Buddhism;* Obadia, "Buddha in the Promised Land."
31. Tweed, *American Encounter with Buddhism.*
32. Ibid.
33. Ibid., 157.
34. Seager, "American Buddhism in the Making."
35. Dryden and Still, "Historical Aspects of Mindfulness"; Morita, *Morita Therapy and the True Nature of Anxiety Based Disorders (Shinkeishitsu).*
36. Morita, *Morita Therapy;* Reynolds, *Plunging through the Clouds.*
37. Morita, *Morita Therapy.*
38. Morita, *Morita Therapy,* see Introduction by P. LeVine.
39. Reynolds, *Plunging through the Clouds;* Reynolds, *The Quiet Therapies.*
40. Morita, *Morita Therapy,* see Introduction by P. LeVine.
41. Merton, *Zen and the Birds of Appetite;* Pennington, *Centering Prayer.*
42. Mott, *Seven Mountains,* 326.
43. Mott, *Seven Mountains;* Merton, *Contemplative Prayer;* Pennington, *Centering Prayer.*
44. Mott, *Seven Mountains,* 399.
45. Duckworth, *Talking Music,* 21.
46. Cage, *Silence,* 12.
47. Ibid., 40.
48. Fromm, Suzuki, and DeMartino, *Zen Buddhism and Psychoanalysis.*
49. Ibid., 86.
50. Ibid.
51. Ibid., 90.
52. Ibid., 126.
53. Watts, *In My Own Way.*
54. Fromm, Suzuki, and DeMartino, *Zen Buddhism and Psychoanalysis,* 15.
55. Suzuki, *Mysticism,* 8.

CHAPTER 2. MINDFULNESS IN LATE AMERICA

1. Watts, *In My Own Way,* 152–53.
2. Watts and Selver, "Alan Watts on the Work of Charlotte Selver and Charlotte Selver about Herself."
3. Selver and Brooks, *Reclaiming Vitality and Presence;* Lavietes, "Charlotte Selver Dies"; Watts, *In My Own Way.*
4. Watts, *The Wisdom of Insecurity,* 96.
5. Ibid., 97–99.
6. Watts, "Beat Zen," 90.
7. Watts, *In My Own Way,* 358.
8. Roszak, *The Making of a Counter Culture,* xi.
9. Kantner, "Won't You Try/Saturday Afternoon."
10. Watts, *In My Own Way,* 402.
11. Mahesh Yogi, *Transcendental Meditation;* Johnston, "Marketing Social Movement."
12. Watts, *In My Own Way,* 399.
13. Wallace, "Physiological Effects of Transcendental Meditation"; Seeman, Nidich, and Banta, "Influence of Transcendental Meditation."
14. Benson, *Relaxation Response.*
15. Carrington, *Book of Meditation.*
16. Johnston, "Marketing Social Movement."
17. Watts, *In My Own Way,* 359.

CHAPTER 3. AMERICA WENT FAR TO FIND WHAT IT LEFT AT HOME

1. Vanier, *Befriending the Stranger,* 63–64.
2. Rohr, *Everything Belongs.*
3. Barks, *Essential Rumi,* 109.
4. Prebish, *Luminous Passage.*
5. Coleman, *New Buddhism;* Nattier, "Who Is a Buddhist?"
6. Prebish, *Luminous Passage.*
7. Nattier, "Who Is a Buddhist?"
8. Coleman, *New Buddhism,* 71.
9. Prebish, *Luminous Passage;* Queen, "Engaged Buddhism."
10. Coleman, *New Buddhism;* McMahan, "Repackaging Zen for the West."
11. Coleman, *New Buddhism;* Prebish, *Luminous Passage.*
12. Coleman, *New Buddhism;* Suzuki, *Zen Mind, Beginner's Mind.*
13. Coleman, *New Buddhism;* Seager, "American Buddhism in the Making."
14. Trungpa, *Cutting through Spiritual Materialism,* 3.
15. Coleman, *New Buddhism,* 109.

16. Coleman, *New Buddhism;* Fronsdal, "Virtues without Rules"; Prebish, *Luminous Passage.*

17. Ibid.

18. Batchelor, *The Awakening of the West,* 344.

19. Downing, *Shoes outside the Door,* 70.

20. Bell, "Scandals in Emerging Western Buddhism."

21. Bell, "Scandals in Emerging Western Buddhism," 236; Downing, *Shoes outside the Door.*

22. Clark, *Great Naropa Poetry Wars.*

23. Bell, "Scandals in Emerging Western Buddhism."

24. Schwartz, *What Really Matters,* 334.

25. Coleman, *New Buddhism,* 193.

26. Cupitt, *New Religion of Life,* 21.

27. Wuthnow, *After Heaven.*

CHAPTER 4. ARE YOU WAITING FOR AN INVITATION?

1. Thoreau, *Walden,* "Economy," paragraph 36.

2. Kaiser-Greenland, *The Mindful Child;* Krasner, Epstein, Beckman, et al., "Association of an Educational Program in Mindful Communication with Burnout, Empathy and Attitudes among Primary Care Physicians"; McCown, "Problems of Passionate Chess"; Riskin, "Contemplative Lawyer."

3. Shapiro and Carlson, *The Art and Science of Mindfulness: Integrating Mindfulness into Psychology and the Helping Professions.*

4. James, *Talks to Teachers on Psychology and to Students on Some of Life's Ideals,* "The Gospel of Relaxation," paragraph 4.

5. Kabat-Zinn et al., "Clinical Use of Mindfulness."

6. Kabat-Zinn et al., "Effectiveness of Meditation-Based Stress Reduction."

7. Kabat-Zinn et al., "Four Year Follow-up"; Miller et al., "Three-Year Follow-up."

8. Salmon, Santorelli, and Kabat-Zinn, "Intervention Elements."

9. Kalb, "Faith and Healing"; Stein, "Just Say OM."

10. Dryden and Still, "Historical Aspects of Mindfulness."

11. Segal, Williams, and Teasdale, *Mindfulness-based Cognitive Therapy for Depression.*

12. Kabat-Zinn, "An Outpatient Program in Behavioral Medicine for Chronic Pain Patients Based on the Practice of Mindfulness Meditation: Theoretical Considerations and Preliminary Results."

13. Segal, Williams, and Teasdale, *Mindfulness-based Cognitive Therapy for Depression.*

14. Marlatt and Gordon. *Relapse Prevention.*

15. Kristeller and Hallett, "Exploratory Study."

16. Monti et al., "Mindfulness-based Art Therapy."

17. Carson et al., "Mindfulness-based Relationship Enhancement."

18. Duncan and Bardacke, "Mindfulness-based Childbirth and Parenting Education."

19. Linehan, *Cognitive-Behavioral Treatment of Borderline Personality Disorder.*

20. Robins, Schmidt, and Linehan, "Dialectical Behavior Therapy," 37.

21. Hayes et al., *Acceptance and Commitment Therapy;* Hayes and Strosahl, *Practical Guide.*

22. Grossman, Niemann, Schmidt, and Walach, "Mindfulness-based Stress Reduction and Health Benefits."

23. Davidson et al., "Alterations."

24. Hölzel et al., "Mindfulness Practice."

25. Hölzel et al., "Stress Reduction."

26. Emerson, "The Transcendentalist," paragraph 21.

27. Coleman, *New Buddhism.*

28. Carmody and Baer, "Relationships."

29. Chang, Palesh, Caldwell, et al., "The Effects of a Mindfulness-based Stress Reduction Program on Stress, Mindfulness Self-efficacy, and Positive States of Mind"; Reibel, Greeson, Brainard, et al., "Mindfulness-based Stress Reduction and Health Related Quality of Life in a Heterogeneous Patient Population"; Jain, Shapiro, Swanick, et al., "A Randomized Controlled Trial of Mindfulness Meditation Versus Relaxation Training"; Rosenzweig, Reibel, Greeson, et al., "Mindfulness-based Stress Reduction Lowers Psychological Distress in Medical Students"; Roth and Calle-Mesa, "Mindfulness-based Stress Reduction with Spanish- and English-speaking Inner-city Medical Patients."

30. Astin, "Stress Reduction through Mindfulness Meditation"; Carmody, Reed, Kristeller, et al., "Mindfulness, Spirituality, and Health-related Symptoms"; Davidson et al., "Alterations."

31. Speca, Carlson, Goodey, and Angen, "A Randomized, Wait-list Controlled Clinical Trial"; Carmody and Baer, "Relationships."

32. Batchelor, *Alone with Others;* Fromm, *To Have or to Be?;* Marcel, *Being and Having.*

CHAPTER 5. YOU'RE NEVER LOST IN THE PRESENT MOMENT

1. Emerson, "The Method of Nature," paragraph 9.

2. Ibid., paragraph 10.

3. Thoreau, *Walden,* "Where I Lived, and What I Lived For," paragraph 21.

4. Thoreau, *Walden,* "Economy," paragraph 23.

5. Goddard, *A Buddhist Bible.*

6. Batchelor, *Buddhism without Beliefs.*

7. Ibid.; Batchelor, *Awakening of the West.*

8. Ibid.

9. Analayo, *Satipatthana;* Dryden and Still, "Historical Aspects of Mindfulness"; Thera, *Heart of Buddhist Meditation;* Batchelor, *Notes from the Path to the Deathless Retreat.*

10. Thera, *Heart of Buddhist Meditation,* 32.

11. Kabat-Zinn, *Wherever You Go,* 4.

12. Kabat-Zinn, "Mindfulness Meditation."

13. Shapiro et al., "Mechanisms of Mindfulness."

14. Deikman, "De-automatization."

15. Linden, "Practicing of Meditation"; Pelletier, "Influence of Transcendental Meditation."

16. Kasamatsu and Hirai, "Electroencephalographic Study."

17. Deikman, *Observing Self.*

18. Safran and Segal, *Interpersonal Process in Cognitive Therapy.*

19. Kabat-Zinn, *Coming to Our Senses,* 350.

20. Shapiro et al., "Mechanisms of Mindfulness."

21. Thoreau, "Walking," paragraph 13.

22. Emerson, "Circles," paragraph 30.

23. Ibid., paragraph 26.

24. Thoreau, "The Natural History of Massachusetts," paragraph 55.

CHAPTER 6. GRAVITY: NORTH AND SOUTH ON YOUR COMPASS

1. Nicogossian and Parker, *Space Physiology and Medicine;* "Physiological Effects of Weightlessness."

2. Wakayama, Kawahara, Li, et al., "Detrimental Effects of Microgravity on Mouse Preimplantation Development In Vitro."

3. Berthoz, *Brain's Sense of Movement.*

4. Cook, *Hua-Yen Buddhism,* 2.

5. Ibid.

6. Adapted from Singh, Wahler, Adkins, and Myers, "Soles of the Feet."

7. Wagoner, Collected Poems (1956–1976).

8. Geurts, *Culture and the Senses.*

9. Lakoff and Johnson, *Metaphors We Live By.*

10. Ibid.

11. Johnson, *The Meaning of the Body;* Lakoff and Johnson, *Metaphors We Live By;* Tuan, *Space and Place.*

12. Gindler, "Gymnastik for Busy People," 40.

13. Goldstein, *Sensation and Perception;* Wolfe et al., *Sensation and Perception.*

14. "Statistics," Vestibular Disorders Association.

15. Clement and Reschke, *Neuroscience in Space.*

16. Goodenough, "History of Field Dependence."

17. Murphy and Donovan, *The Physical and Psychological Effects of Meditation.*

18. Berthoz, *Brain's Sense of Movement.*

19. Mittlestaedt, "Postural Information"; Trousselard et al., "Tactile and Interoceptive Cues."

20. Clement and Reschke, *Neuroscience in Space,* 109.

CHAPTER 7. THE BREATH I:
EAST AND WEST, INSIDE AND OUTSIDE

1. Thoreau, journal entry, June 21, 1851.

2. Ibid., September 12, 1851.

3. Ibid., September 22, 1851.

4. Ibid., November 3, 1861.

5. Harding, *The Days of Henry Thoreau.*

6. Dubos and Dubos, *The White Plague: Tuberculosis, Man, and Society,* 55.

7. Hippocrates, *Airs, Waters, and Places.*

8. Kuriyama, *The Expressiveness of the Body and the Divergence of Greek and Chinese Medicine,* 235.

9. Hippocrates, *The Sacred Disease,* 172–73.

10. Ramanathan, "Contribution to 'Weather Science in Ancient India,' III."

11. Muller, *Vedic Hymns,* 451.

12. Kuriyama, *The Expressiveness of the Body and the Divergence of Greek and Chinese Medicine.*

13. Bennett, "The Early History of the Synapse: From Plato to Sherrington."

14. Kaptchuk, *The Web That Has No Weaver,* 45.

15. Micozzi with McCown, *Vital Healing.*

16. Ibid.

17. Thoreau, *A Week on the Concord and Merrimac Rivers,* chapter 8, paragraph 50.

18. Tuan, *Space and Place.*

19. Segal et al., *Cognitive Therapy for Depression.*

20. Tuan, *Space and Place.*

21. Stern, *The Present Moment in Psychotherapy and Everyday Life.*

22. Ibid.

23. Speads, *Ways to Better Breathing.*

24. Abram, *The Spell of the Sensuous.*

25. Rohr, *The Naked Now,* 26.

CHAPTER 8. THE BREATH II:
THE BREEZE ACROSS THE INNER LANDSCAPE

1. Feldman and Del Negro, "Looking for Inspiration"; Fogel, *The Psychophysiology of Self-awareness;* Lyon, "Emotion and Embodiment."

2. Fogel, *The Psychophysiology of Self-awareness.*

3. Romei, Mauro, D'Angelo, et al. "Effects of Gender and Posture on Thoraco-abdominal Kinematics During Quiet Breathing in Healthy Adults."

4. Miller, *The Body in Question*.

5. Feldman and Del Negro, "Looking for Inspiration."

6. Benchetrit, "Breathing Patterns in Humans"; Eisele, Wuyam, Savourey, et al. "Individuality of Breathing Pattern during Hypoxia and Exercise."

7. Shea, "The Breathing Patterns of Identical Twins"; Shea, Dinh, Hamilton, et al. "Breathing Patterns of Monozygous Twins during Behavior Tasks."

8. Eisele, Wuyam, Savourey, et al. "Individuality of Breathing Pattern during Hypoxia and Exercise."

9. Grossman, "Mindfulness for Psychologists: Paying Kind Attention to the Perceptible."

10. Carlson, "Home Is Where the ECG Is."

11. May, *Will and Spirit*, 3.

12. Lyon, "Emotion and Embodiment"; Van den Bergh, Stegen, and Van de Woestijne, "Learning to Have Psychosomatic Complaints."

13. Conrad et al., "Breathing Instructions."

14. Vlemincx, Van Diest, De Peuter, et al. "Why Do You Sigh?"; Vlemincx et al., "Take a Deep Breath"; Vlemincx, Taelman, De Peuter, et al., "Sigh Rate and Respiratory Variability during Mental Load and Sustained Attention"; Vlemincx, Van Diest, Lehrer, et al., "Respiratory Variability Preceding and Following Sighs."

15. Vlemincx et al., "Take a Deep Breath."

16. Wilhelm, Trabert, and Roth, "Characteristics of Sighing in Panic Disorder."

17. Teigen, "Is a Sigh 'Just a Sigh'?"

18. McCown, Reibel, and Micozzi, *Teaching Mindfulness*, 110.

19. Teigen, "Is a Sigh 'Just a Sigh'?"

20. Walusinski, "Historical Perspectives."

21. Provine, Tate, and Gelmacher, "Yawning."

22. Seuntjens, "The Hidden Sexuality of the Yawn and Future of Chasmology."

23. Collins and Eguibar, "Neuropharmacology of Yawning."

24. Fogel, *The Psychophysiology of Self-awareness*.

25. Newberg and Waldman, *How God Changes Your Brain*, 157.

26. Senju, "Developmental and Comparative Perspectives of Contagious Yawning."

27. Siegel, *The Mindful Therapist*; Senju, "Developmental and Comparative Perspectives of Contagious Yawning."

28. Seuntjens, "The Hidden Sexuality of the Yawn and Future of Chasmology."

29. Senju, "Developmental and Comparative Perspectives of Contagious Yawning."

30. Adapted from Newberg and Waldman, *How God Changes Your Brain*, 182–83.

CHAPTER 9. THE BREATH III:
THE STORMS AND STILLNESS OF SUBJECTIVE EXPERIENCE

1. Grossman and Wientjes, "How Breathing Adjusts to Mental and Physical Demands."
2. Peat, *The Blackwinged Night.*
3. Calabrese, Perrault, Dinh, et al. "Cardiorespiratory Interactions during Resistive Load Breathing"; Decety et al., "Vegetative Response"; Mulder, de Vries, and Zijlstra, "Observation, Imagination and Execution of an Effortful Movement."
4. Decety et al., "Vegetative Response."
5. Calabrese, Perrault, Dinh, et al. "Cardiorespiratory Interactions during Resistive Load Breathing."
6. Wang and Morgan, "The Effect of Imagery Perspectives on the Psychophysiological Responses to Imagined Exercise."
7. Friedman, "Feelings and the Body."
8. James, "What Is an Emotion?" *Mind,* 1884, paragraph 4.
9. Ibid., paragraph 11.
10. Bernardi, Wdowczyk-Szulc, Valenti, et al. "Effects of Controlled Breathing, Mental Activity and Mental Stress With or Without Verbalization on Heart Rate Variability."
11. Boiten, Frijda, and Wientjes, "Emotions and Respiratory Patterns."
12. Philippot, Chapelle, and Blairy, "Respiratory Feedback in the Generation of Emotion."
13. Ibid., 619–60.
14. Homma, Masaoka, and Umewaka, "Breathing Mind in 'Noh'"; Homma and Masaoka, "Breathing Rhythms and Emotions."
15. Kreibig, Wilhelm, Roth, et al., "Cardiovascular, Electrodermal, and Respiratory Response Patterns to Fear- and Sadness-inducing Films."
16. Khalsa, Rudrauf, Damasio, et al. "Interoceptive Awareness in Experienced Meditators."
17. Nielsen and Kaszniak, "Awareness of Subtle Emotional Feelings."
18. Vlemincx et al., "Take a Deep Breath."
19. Watson et al., "Treatment of PTSD."
20. Conrad et al., "Breathing Instructions."
21. Murakami et al., "Influence of Attention."

CHAPTER 10. DISPOSITION:
A MAP OF THE TERRAIN OF YOUR IMMEDIATE SITUATION

1. James, *Principles of Psychology,* chapter XXVI, paragraph 149.
2. Richardson, *William James,* 563.

3. James, *The Varieties of Religious Experience*, paragraph 27.

4. Ibid., paragraph 26.

5. Ibid., paragraph 33.

6. Tuan, *Space and Place,* 51–52.

7. Tuan, *Space and Place.*

8. Fogel, *The Psychophysiology of Self-awareness.*

9. Ibid.

10. Tuan, *Space and Place.*

11. Fogel, *The Psychophysiology of Self-awareness.*

12. Buckminster Fuller Institute, http://bfi.org.

13. Kuriyama, *The Expressiveness of the Body and the Divergence of Greek and Chinese Medicine.*

14. Ibid.

15. James, *Principles of Psychology,* paragraph 34.

16. Ibid., paragraph 19.

17. Ibid., paragraphs 20–24.

18. Richards, *At Work with Grotowski on Physical Actions.*

19. Ibid., 97.

20. James, *Principles of Psychology,* paragraph 18.

21. Richards, *At Work with Grotowski on Physical Actions.*

CHAPTER 11.
IN SEARCH OF THE SPRINGS OF LIFE

1. Thoreau, *Walking,* paragraph 10.

2. Watts and Huang, *Tao: The Watercourse Way,* 122.

CHAPTER 14.
STANDING: OPENING TO THE WORLD

1. Oida and Marshall, *The Invisible Actor.*

CHAPTER 15. WALKING:
PRACTICE AT THE SPEED OF LIFE

1. Thoreau, *Walking,* paragraph 3.

2. Wangh, *Acrobat of the Heart.*

3. Vergunst, "Taking a Trip."

4. Boedeker, personal communication to D. McCown, 2011.

CODA: A WALK ON MOUNT MISERY,
A GLIMPSE OF MOUNT JOY

1. Alvarez, *Feeding the Rat,* 32.

2. Thoreau, *The Maine Woods,* paragraph 33.

BIBLIOGRAPHY

Allen, N. B., G. Blashki, and E. Gullone. "Mindfulness-Based Psychotherapies: A Review of Conceptual Foundations, Empirical Evidence and Practical Considerations." *Australian and New Zealand Journal of Psychiatry* 40, no. 4 (2006): 285–94.

Alvarez, A. *Feeding the Rat.* Boston: Atlantic Montly Press, 1988.

Analayo. *Satipatthana: The Direct Path to Realization.* Cambridge, U.K.: Windhorse, 2003.

———. *Mindfulness-Based Treatment Approaches: Clinician's Guide to Evidence Base and Applications.* Burlington, Mass.: Academic Press, 2006.

Astin, J. "Stress Reduction through Mindfulness Meditation: Effects on Psychological Symptomatology, Sense of Control, and Spiritual Experience." *Psychotherapy and Psychosomatics* 66 (1997): 97–106.

Baer, R. "Mindfulness Training as a Clinical Intervention: A Conceptual and Empirical Review." *Clinical Psychology: Science and Practice* 10, no. 2 (2003): 125–48.

Barks, C. *The Essential Rumi.* San Francisco: Harper, 1995.

Batchelor, S. *The Awakening of the West.* Berkeley: Parallax, 1994.

———. *Buddhism without Beliefs: A Contemporary Guide to Awakening.* New York: Riverhead Books, 1997.

———. Handouts and personal notes from retreat, "The Path to the Deathless," Barre Center for Buddhist Studies, Barre, Vt. September, 12–17, 2004.

———. *Alone with Others: An Existential Approach to Buddhism.* New York: Grove Press, 1983.

Bell, S. "Scandals in Emerging Western Buddhism." In Prebish, C. S., and M. Baumann, eds. *Westward Dharma: Buddhism beyond Asia.* Berkeley: University of California Press, 2002.

Benson, H. *The Relaxation Response.* New York: Morrow, 1975.

Bernardi, L., J. Wdowczyk-Szulc, C. Valenti, et al. "Effects of Controlled Breathing,

Mental Activity and Mental Stress with or without Verbalization on Heart Rate Variability." *Journal of the American College of Cardiology* 35, no. 6 (2000): 1462–69.

Berthoz, A. *The Brain's Sense of Movement: Perspectives in Cognitive Neuroscience.* Cambridge, Mass.: Harvard University Press, 2000.

Bevis, W. W. *Mind of Winter: Wallace Stevens, Meditation, and Literature.* Pittsburgh, Pa.: University of Pittsburgh Press, 1988.

Bishop, S., M. Lau, S. Shapiro, et al. "Mindfulness: A Proposed Operational Definition." *Clinical Psychology: Science and Practice* 11, no. 3 (2004): 230–41.

Block, S., and E. Crouch. *Therapeutic Factors in Group Psychotherapy.* New York: Oxford, 1985.

Boiten, F. A., N. H. Frijda, and C. J. E. Wientjes. "Emotions and Respiratory Patterns: Review and Critical Analysis." *International Journal of Psychophysiology* 17 (1994): 103–28.

Brooks, V. W. *Fenollosa and His Circle, with Other Essays in Biography.* New York: Dutton, 1962.

———. *The Flowering of New England, 1815–1865.* New York: E. P. Dutton & Co., 1936.

Cage, J. *Silence: Lectures and Writings.* Cambridge, Mass.: The M.I.T. Press, 1966.

Calabrese, P., H. Perrault, T. P. Dinh, et al. "Cardiorespiratory Interactions during Resistive Load Breathing." *American Journal of Physiology—Regulatory, Integrative, and Comparative* 279 (2000): R2208–R2213.

Carlson, S. "Home Is Where the ECG Is." *Scientific American,* June 2000.

Carmody, J., and R. A. Baer. "Relationships between Mindfulness Practice and Levels of Mindfulness, Medical and Psychological Symptoms and Well-Being in a Mindfulness-Based Stress Reduction Program." *Journal of Behavioral Medicine* 31 (2008): 23–33.

Carmody, J., G. Reed, J. Kristeller, et al. "Mindfulness, Spirituality, and Health-related Symptoms." *Journal of Psychosomatic Research* 64 (2008): 393–403.

Carrington, P. *The Book of Meditation: The Complete Guide to Modern Meditation.* Boston: Element, 1998. Revised edition of *Freedom in Meditation.* East Millstone, N.J.: Pace Educational Systems, 1975.

Carson, J. W., K. M. Carson, K. M. Gil, et al. "Mindfulness-based Relationship Enhancement (MBRE) for Couples." In Baer, R., ed. *Mindfulness-Based Treatment Approaches: Clinician's Guide to Evidence Base and Applications.* Burlington, Mass.: Academic Press, 2006.

———. "Mindfulness-based Relationship Enhancement." *Behavior Therapy* 35 (2004): 471–94.

Chang, V. Y., O. Palesh, R. Caldwell, et al. "The Effects of a Mindfulness-based Stress Reduction Program on Stress, Mindfulness Self-efficacy, and Positive

States of Mind." *Stress and Health: Journal of the International Society for the Investigation of Stress 20* (2004): 141–47.

Clark, T. *The Great Naropa Poetry Wars.* Santa Barbara, Calif.: Cadmus Editions, 1980.

Clement, G., and M. E. Reschke. *Neuroscience in Space.* New York: Springer, 2008.

Coleman, W. *The New Buddhism: The Western Transformation of an Ancient Tradition.* New York: Oxford, 2001.

Collins, G. T., and J. R. Eguibar. "Neuropharmacology of Yawning." In Walusinski, O., ed. "The Mystery of Yawning in Physiology and Disease." *Frontiers of Neurological Neuroscience* 28 (2010): 90–106.

Conrad, A., A. Muller, S. Doberenz, et al. "Psychophysiological Effects of Breathing Instructions for Stress Management." *Applied Psychophysiology and Biofeedback* 32 (2007): 89–98.

Cook, F. *Hua-Yen Buddhism: The Jewel Net of Indra.* University Park, Pa.: Pennsylvania State University Press, 1977.

Cupitt, D. *The New Religion of Life in Everyday Speech.* London: SCM Press, 1999.

Davidson, R., J. Kabat-Zinn, J. Schumacher, et al. "Alterations in Brain and Immune Function Produced by Mindfulness Meditation." *Psychosomatic Medicine* 65, no. 4 (2003): 564–70.

Davidson, R., G. Schwartz, and L. Rothman. "Attentional Style and the Regulation of Mode-Specific Attention: An Electroencephalographic Study." *Journal of Abnormal Psychology* 8, no. 6 (1976): 611–21.

de Bary, W. *The Buddhist Tradition in India, China, and Japan.* New York: Modern Library, 1969.

Decety, J., M. Jeannerod, M. Germain, et al. "Vegetative Response during Imagined Movement Is Proportional to Mental Effort." *Behavioural Brain Research* 42 (1991): 1–5.

Deikman, A. "De-automatization and the Mystic Experience." *Psychiatry* 29 (1966): 324–38.

———. *The Observing Self: Mysticism and Psychotherapy.* Boston: Beacon Press, 1982.

Dimidjian, S., and M. M. Linehan. "Defining an Agenda for Future Research on the Clinical Application of Mindfulness Practice." *Clinical Psychology: Science and Practice* 10, no. 2 (2003): 166–71.

Downing, M. *Shoes outside the Door: Desire, Devotion, and Excess at San Francisco Zen Center.* Washington, D.C.: Counterpoint, 2001.

Dryden, W., and A. Still. "Historical Aspects of Mindfulness and Self-Acceptance in Psychotherapy." *Journal of Rational-Emotive & Cognitive-Behavior Therapy* 24, no. 1 (2006): 3–28.

Dubos, R., and J. Dubos. *The White Plague: Tuberculosis, Man, and Society.* Boston: Little, Brown, 1952.

Duckworth, W. *Talking Music: Conversations with John Cage, Philip Glass, Laurie Anderson, and Five Generations of American Experimental Composers.* Cambridge, Mass.: Da Capo Press, 1999.

Duncan, L. G., and N. Bardacke. "Mindfulness-based Childbirth and Parenting Education: Promoting Family Mindfulness during the Perinatal Period." *Journal of Child and Family Studies* 19 (2010): 190–202.

Freud, S. *Civilization and Its Discontents.* Edited by J. Strachey. *The Standard Edition of the Complete Psychological Works of Sigmund Freud.* Vol. XXI, 1927–1931. London: Hogarth Press, 1961.

———. *Recommendations to Physicians Practicing Psycho-analysis.* Edited by J. Strachey. *The Standard Edition of the Complete Psychological Works of Sigmund Freud.* Vol. XII, 1911–1913. London: Hogarth Press, 1958.

Friedman, B. H. "Feelings and the Body: The Jamesian Perspective on Autonomic Specificity of Emotion." *Biological Psychology* 84 (2010): 283–93.

Fromm, E. *To Have or to Be?* New York: Harper & Row, 1976.

Fromm, E., D. T. Suzuki, and R. DeMartino. *Zen Buddhism and Psychoanalysis.* New York: Harper & Row, 1970. First published 1960 by Harper.

Fronsdal, G. "Virtues without Rules: Ethics in the Insight Meditation Movement." In Prebish, C. S., and M. Baumann, eds. *Westward Dharma: Buddhism beyond Asia.* Berkeley: University of California Press, 2002.

Furlong, M. *Genuine Fake: A Biography of Alan Watts.* London: Heinemann, 1986.

Geurts, K. L. *Culture and the Senses: Bodily Ways of Knowing in an African Community.* Berkeley: University of California Press, 2002.

Gindler, E. "*Gymnastik* for Busy People." *Bulletin of the Charlotte Selver Foundation* 10, no. 1: 36–40. Originally published in 1926.

Goddard, D. *A Buddhist Bible.* Thetford, Vt.: Dwight Goddard, 1938.

Goldstein, E. B. *Sensation and Perception.* 4th ed. Fifth and sixth editions published 2006 and 2008. Belmont, Calif.: Wadsworth Publishing, 1996.

Goodenough, D. "History of the Field Dependence Construct." In Bertini, M., L. Pizzamiglio, and S. Wapner, eds. *Field Dependence in Psychological Theory, Research, and Application.* Hillsdale, N.J.: Lawrence Erlbaum, 1986.

Grossman, P., L. Niemann, S. Schmidt, et al. "Mindfulness-based Stress Reduction and Health Benefits: A Meta-analysis." *Journal of Psychosomatic Research* 57 (2004): 35–43.

Grossman, P., and C. J. Wientjes. "How Breathing Adjusts to Mental and Physical Demands." In Haruki, Y., I. Homma, A. Umezawa, and Y. Masaoka, eds. *Respiration and Emotion.* New York: Springer, 2001.

Harding, W. *The Days of Henry Thoreau.* New York: Knopf, 1966.

Hayes, A., and G. Feldman. "Clarifying the Construct of Mindfulness in the Context of Emotion Regulation and the Process of Change in Therapy." *Clinical Psychology: Science and Practice* 11, no. 3 (2004): 255–62.

Hayes, S., and C. Shenk. "Operationalizing Mindfulness without Unnecessary Attachments." *Clinical Psychology: Science and Practice* 11, no. 3 (2004): 249–54.

Hayes, S. C., V. M. Follette, and M. M. Linehan. *Mindfulness and Acceptance: Expanding the Cognitive-Behavioral Tradition.* New York: Guilford, 2004.

Hayes, S. C., and K. D. Strosahl, eds. *A Practical Guide to Acceptance and Commitment Therapy.* New York: Springer, 2004.

Hayes, S. C., K. Strosahl, and K. G. Wilson. *Acceptance and Commitment Therapy.* New York: Guilford, 1999.

Hippocrates. *Airs, Waters, and Places.* Volume I. W. H. S. Jones, trans. Loeb Classical Library. Cambridge: Harvard University Press, 1923.

Hippocrates. *The Sacred Disease.* Volume II. W. H. S. Jones, trans. Loeb Classical Library. Cambridge: Harvard University Press, 1923.

Hodder, A. D. "'Ex Oriente Lux': Thoreau's Ecstasies and the Hindu Texts." *The Harvard Theological Review* 86, no. 4 (1993): 403–38.

Hölzel, B. K., J. Carmody, K. C. Evans, et al. "Stress Reduction Correlates with Structural Changes in the Amygdala." *Social Cognitive and Affective Neuroscience* 5, no. 1 (2010): 11–17.

Hölzel, B. K., J. Carmody, M. Vangel, et al. "Mindfulness Practice Leads to Increases in Regional Brain Gray Matter Density." *Psychiatry Research* 191, no. 1 (2011): 36–43.

Homma, I., Y. Masaoka, and N. Umewaka. "Breathing Mind in 'Noh.'" In Homma, I., and S. Shioda, eds. *Breathing, Feeding, and Neuroprotection.* Tokyo: Springer-Verlag, 2006.

Homma, I., and Y. Masaoka. "Breathing Rhythms and Emotions." *Experimental Physiology* 93, no. 9 (2008): 1011–21.

Isanon, A. *Spirituality and the Autism Spectrum.* London: Jessica Kingsley, 2001.

Jackson, C. T. *The Oriental Religions and American Thought: Nineteenth Century Explorations.* Westport, Conn.: Greenwood Press, 1981.

Jain, S., S. Shapiro, S. Swanick, et al. "A Randomized Controlled Trial of Mindfulness Meditation Versus Relaxation Training: Effects on Distress, Positive States of Mind, Rumination, and Distraction." *Annals of Behavioral Medicine* 3 (2007): 11–21.

Johnson, M. *The Meaning of the Body: Aesthetics of Human Understanding.* Chicago: University of Chicago Press, 2007.

Johnston, H. "The Marketing Social Movement: A Case Study of the Rapid Growth of TM." In Richardson, J. T., ed. *Money and Power in the New Religions.* Lewiston, N.Y.: The Edwin Mellen Press, 1988.

Kabat-Zinn, J. *Coming to Our Senses: Healing Ourselves and the World through Mindfulness.* New York: Hyperion, 2005.

———. "Mindfulness Meditation: What It Is, What It Isn't, and Its Role in Health

Care and Medicine." In Haruki, Y., Y. Ishii, and M. Suzuki, eds. *Comparative and Psychological Study on Meditation.* Delft, The Netherlands: Eburon, 1996.

———. "An Outpatient Program in Behavioral Medicine for Chronic Pain Patients Based on the Practice of Mindfulness Meditation: Theoretical Considerations and Preliminary Results." *General Hospital Psychiatry* 4, no. 1 (1982): 33–47.

———. *Wherever You Go, There You Are.* New York: Hyperion, 1994.

Kabat-Zinn, J., L. Lipworth, and R. Burney. "The Clinical Use of Mindfulness Meditation for the Self-Regulation of Chronic Pain." *Journal of Behavioral Medicine* 8 (1985): 163–90.

Kabat-Zinn, J., L. Lipworth, R. Burney, et al. "Four Year Follow-up of a Meditation-Based Program for the Self-Regulation of Chronic Pain: Treatment Outcomes and Compliance." *Clinical Journal of Pain* 2 (1986): 159–73.

Kabat-Zinn, J., A. O. Massion, J. Kristeller, et al. "Effectiveness of a Meditation-Based Stress Reduction Program in the Treatment of Anxiety Disorders." *American Journal of Psychiatry* 149 (1992): 936–43.

Kaiser-Greenland, S. *The Mindful Child: How to Help Your Kid Manage Stress and Become Happier, Kinder, and More Compassionate.* New York: Free Press, 2010.

Kalb, C. "Faith and Healing." *Newsweek,* November 10, 2003.

Kantner, P. "Won't You Try" and "Saturday Afternoon." Recorded by Jefferson Airplane on *After Bathing at Baxter's.* New York: RCA Victor, 1967.

Kasamatsu, A., and T. Hirai. "An Electroencephalographic Study of the Zen Meditation (Zazen)." In Shapiro, D. H., and R. N. Walsh, eds. *Meditation, Classic and Contemporary Perspectives.* New York: Aldine, 1973.

Khalsa, S. S., D. Rudrauf, A. R. Damasio, et al. "Interoceptive Awareness in Experienced Meditators." *Psychophysiology* 45 (2008): 671–677.

Krasner, M. S., R. M. Epstein, H. Beckman, et al. "Association of an Educational Program in Mindful Communication with Burnout, Empathy and Attitudes among Primary Care Physicians." *JAMA* 302, no. 12 (2009): 1284–93.

Kreibig, S. D., F. H. Wilhelm, W. T. Roth, et al. "Cardiovascular, Electrodermal, and Respiratory Response Patterns to Fear- and Sadness-inducing Films." *Psychophysiology* 44 (2007): 787–806.

Kristeller, J. L., and C. B. Hallett. "An Exploratory Study of a Meditation-Based Intervention for Binge Eating Disorder." *Journal of Health Psychology* 4 (1999): 357–63.

Kuriyama, S. *The Expressiveness of the Body and the Divergence of Greek and Chinese Medicine.* New York: Zone Books, 2002.

Lavietes, S. "Charlotte Selver, 102, a Guide to Sensory Awareness, Dies." *New York Times,* September 6, 2003.

Lakoff, G., and M. Johnson. *Metaphors We Live By.* Chicago: University of Chicago Press, 1980.

Linden, W. "Practicing of Meditation by School Children and Their Levels of Field

Dependence, Test Anxiety, and Reading Achievement." *Journal of Consulting and Clinical Psychology* 41, no. 1 (1973): 139–43.

Linehan, M. M. *Cognitive-Behavioral Treatment of Borderline Personality Disorder.* New York: Guilford, 1993.

———. Keynote address, sixth annual conference, Integrating Mindfulness-Based Interventions into Medicine, Health Care, and Society, Worcester, Mass., April 10–12, 2008.

———. *Skills Training Manual for Treating Borderline Personality Disorder.* New York: Guilford, 1993.

Maharishi Mahesh Yogi, *Transcendental Meditation.* New York: New American Library, 1968.

Marcel, G. *Being and Having: An Existentialist Diary.* Westminster: Dacre Press, 1949.

Marlatt, G. A., and J. R. Gordon. *Relapse Prevention: Maintenance Strategies in the Treatment of Addictive Behaviors.* New York: Guilford Press, 1985.

McCown, D. "The Problems of Passionate Chess: Helping Business Strategists Change the Rules of the Game through Applied Meditation." In Gopalkrishnan, S., ed. *Organizational Wisdom: Proceedings of the Eastern Academy of Management 41st Annual Meeting.* Eastern Academy of Management, 2004.

McCown, D., D. Reibel, and M. S. Micozzi. *Teaching Mindfulness: A Practical Guide for Clinicians and Educators.* New York: Springer, 2010.

McMahan, D. L. "Repackaging Zen for the West." In Prebish, C. S., and M. Baumann, eds. *Westward Dharma: Buddhism beyond Asia.* Berkeley: University of California Press, 2002.

Meckel, D. J., and R. L. Moore. *Self and Liberation: The Jung/Buddhism Dialogue.* New York: Paulist Press, 1992.

Merton, T. *Zen and the Birds of Appetite.* New York: New Directions, 1968.

———. *Contemplative Prayer.* New York: Herder and Herder, 1969.

Metcalf, F. A. "The Encounter of Buddhism and Psychology. In Prebish, C. S., and M. Baumann, eds. *Westward Dharma: Buddhism beyond Asia.* Berkeley: University of California Press, 2002.

Micozzi, M. S. *Fundamentals of Complementary and Alternative Medicine.* 4th ed. St. Louis, Mo.: Elsevier Health Sciences, 2010.

Miller, J. J., K. Fletcher, and J. Kabat-Zinn. "Three-Year Follow-up and Clinical Implications of a Mindfulness Meditation-Based Stress Reduction Intervention in the Treatment of Anxiety Disorders." *General Hospital Psychiatry* 17 (1995): 192–200.

Mittelstaedt, H. "Origin and Processing of Postural Information." *Neuroscience and Biobehavioral Reviews* 22, no. 4 (1998): 473–78.

Monti, D. A., C. Peterson, E. J. Kunkel, et al. "A Randomized, Controlled Trial of

Mindfulness-Based Art Therapy (MBAT) for Women with Cancer." *Psycho-Oncology* 15, no. 5 (2006): 363–73.

Morita, S. *Morita Therapy and the True Nature of Anxiety Based Disorders (Shinkeishitsu).* Translated by Akihisa Kondo. Edited by Peg LeVine. Albany, N.Y.: State University of New York Press, 1998; Japanese publication, 1928.

Mott, M. *The Seven Mountains of Thomas Merton.* Boston: Houghton Mifflin, 1984.

Murakami, H., H. Ohira, M. Matsunaga, et al. "Influence of Attention to Somatic Information on Emotional and Autonomic Responses." *Perceptual and Motor Skills* 108 (2009): 531–39.

Mulder, T., S. de Vries, and S. Zijlstra. "Observation, Imagination and Execution of an Effortful Movement: More Evidence for a Central Explanation of Motor Imagery." *Experimental Brain Research* 163 (2005): 344–51.

Muller, F. M., trans. *Vedic Hymns.* Oxford: Clarendon Press, 1891.

Murphy, M., and S. Donovan. *The Physical and Psychological Effects of Meditation: A Review of Contemporary Research with a Comprehensive Bibliography 1931–1996.* With an annotated update, September 2002. Petaluma, Calif.: Institute of Noetic Sciences, 1996, 2002.

Narada, M. *The Buddha and His Teachings.* Singapore: s.n., 1980.

Nattier, J. "Who Is a Buddhist? Charting the Landscape of Buddhist America." In Prebish, C. S., and K. K. Tanaka, eds. *The Faces of Buddhism in America.* Berkeley: University of California Press, 1998.

Nielsen, L., and A. W. Kaszniak. "Awareness of Subtle Emotional Feelings: A Comparison of Long-term Meditators and Nonmeditators." *Emotion* 6 (2006): 392–405.

Newberg, A., and M. R. Waldman. *How God Changes Your Brain.* New York: Ballantine, 2009.

Nicogossian, A., and J. Parker. *Space Physiology and Medicine.* Washington: NASA, 1983.

Obadia, L. "Buddha in the Promised Land: Outlines of the Buddhist Settlement in Israel." In Prebish, C. S., and M. Baumann, eds. *Westward Dharma: Buddhism beyond Asia.* Berkeley, Calif.: University of California Press, 2002.

Oida, Y., and L. Marshall. *The Invisible Actor.* London: Methuen Drama, 2002.

Peat, F. D. *The Blackwinged Night.* Cambridge, Mass.: Perseus Publishing, 2000.

Pelletier, K. "Influence of Transcendental Meditation upon Autokinetic Perception." In Shapiro, D. H., and R. N. Walsh, eds. *Meditation, Classic and Contemporary Perspectives.* New York: Aldine, 1973.

Pennington, M. B. *Centering Prayer: Renewing an Ancient Christian Prayer Tradition.* New York: Image Books, 1980.

"Physiological Effects of Weightlessness." Oracle Thinkquest. http://library.thinkquest.org/C003763/index.php?page=adapt02. Accessed September 25, 2011.

Philippot, P., C. Chapelle, and S. Blairy. "Respiratory Feedback in the Generation of Emotion." *Cognition & Emotion* 16 (2002): 605–27.

Polanyi, M. *The Tacit Dimension.* Garden City, N.Y.: Doubleday, 1966.

Prebish, C. S. *Luminous Passage: The Practice and Study of Buddhism in America.* Berkeley: University of California Press, 1999.

Prebish, C. S., and M. Baumann, eds. *Westward Dharma: Buddhism beyond Asia.* Berkeley: University of California Press, 2002.

Provine, R. R., B. C. Tate, and L. L. Gelmacher. "Yawning: No Effects of 3–5% CO_2, 100% O_2 and Exercise." *Behavioral Neural Biology* 48 (1987): 382–93.

Queen, C. S. "Engaged Buddhism: Agnosticism, Interdependence, Globalization." In Prebish, C. S., and M. Baumann, eds. *Westward Dharma: Buddhism beyond Asia.* Berkeley: University of California Press, 2002.

Ramanathan, A. S. "Contribution to 'Weather Science in Ancient India,' III—A Conceptual Model of the Rainfall Process (Vedic Period)." *Indian Journal of History of Science* 22, no. 1 (1987): 1–6.

Reibel, D. K., J. M. Greeson, G. C. Brainard, et al. "Mindfulness-based Stress Reduction and Health Related Quality of Life in a Heterogeneous Patient Population." *General Hospital Psychiatry* 23 (2001): 183–92.

Reynolds, D. K. *Plunging through the Clouds: Constructive Living Currents.* Albany: State University of New York Press, 1993.

———. *The Quiet Therapies: Japanese Pathways to Personal Growth.* Honolulu: University of Hawaii Press, 1980.

Richards, T. *At Work with Grotowski on Physical Actions.* London: Routledge, 1995.

Richardson, R. D. *William James: In the Maelstrom of American Modernism.* Boston: Houghton Mifflin, 2006.

Rinpoche, Sogyal. *The Tibetan Book of Living and Dying.* New York: HarperCollins, 1993.

Riskin, L. "The Contemplative Lawyer: On the Potential Contributions of Mindfulness Meditation to Law Students, Lawyers, and Their Clients." *Harvard Negotiation Law Review* 7, no. 1 (2002): 1–66.

Robins, C., H. Schmidt, and M. Linehan. "Dialectical Behavior Therapy: Synthesizing Radical Acceptance with Skillful Means." In Hayes, S. C., V. M. Follette, and M. M. Linehan, eds. *Mindfulness and Acceptance: Expanding the Cognitive Behavioral Tradition.* New York: Guilford, 2004.

Rohr, R. *Everything Belongs: The Gift of Contemplative Prayer.* New York: Crossroad, 1999.

Rosenzweig, S., D. Reibel, J. Greeson, et al. "Mindfulness-based Stress Reduction Lowers Psychological Distress in Medical Students." *Teaching and Learning in Medicine* 15, no. 2 (2003): 88–92.

Roszak, T. *The Making of a Counter Culture: Reflections of the Technocratic Society and Its Youthful Opposition.* New York: Doubleday, 1969.

Roth, B., and L. Calle-Mesa. "Mindfulness-based Stress Reduction with Spanish- and English-speaking Inner-city Medical Patients." In Baer, R. A., ed. *Mindfulness-based Treatment Approaches: Clinician's Guide to Evidence Base and Applications.* Boston: Elsevier Academic Press, 2006.

Safran, J. D., and Z. Segal. *Interpersonal Process in Cognitive Therapy.* New York: Basic Books, 1990.

Said, E. W. *Orientalism.* New York: Pantheon, 1978.

Salmon, P. G., S. F. Santorelli, and J. Kabat-Zinn. "Intervention Elements Promoting Adherence to Mindfulness-Based Stress Reduction Programs in the Clinical Behavioral Medicine Setting." In Shumaker, S. A., E. B. Schron, J. K. Okene, and W. L. Bee, eds. *Handbook of Health Behavior Change,* 2nd ed. New York: Springer, 1998.

Schwartz, S. *Classic Studies in Psychology.* Palo Alto, Calif.: Mayfield, 1986.

Schwartz, T. *What Really Matters: Searching for Wisdom in America.* New York: Bantam, 1995.

Scott, D. "William James and Buddhism: American Pragmatism and the Orient." *Religion* 30 (2000): 333–52.

Seager, R. H. "American Buddhism in the Making." In Prebish, C. S., and M. Baumann, eds. *Westward Dharma: Buddhism beyond Asia.* Berkeley: University of California Press, 2002.

Seeman, W., S. Nidich, and T. Banta. "Influence of Transcendental Meditation on a Measure of Self-Actualization." *Journal of Counseling Psychology* 19 (1972): 184–87.

Segal, Z. V., J. M. G. Williams, and J. D. Teasdale. *Mindfulness-based Cognitive Therapy for Depression: A New Approach to Preventing Relapse.* New York: Guilford Press, 2002.

Selver, C., and C. V. W. Brooks. *Reclaiming Vitality and Presence: Sensory Awareness as a Practice for Life.* Berkeley: North Atlantic Books, 2007.

Senju, A. "Developmental and Comparative Perspectives of Contagious Yawning." In Walusinski, O., ed. "The Mystery of Yawning in Physiology and Disease." *Frontiers of Neurological Neuroscience* 28 (2010): 113–19.

Seuntjens, W. "The Hidden Sexuality of the Yawn and Future of Chasmology." In Walusinski, O., ed. (2010). "The Mystery of Yawning in Physiology and Disease." *Frontiers of Neurological Neuroscience* 28 (2010): 55–62.

Shapiro, D. H., and R. N. Walsh. *Meditation, Classic and Contemporary Perspectives.* New York: Aldine, 1984.

Shapiro, S., L. Carlson, J. Astin, et al. "Mechanisms of Mindfulness." *Journal of Clinical Psychology* 62, no. 3 (2006): 373–86.

Shapiro, S., and L. Carlson. *The Art and Science of Mindfulness: Integrating Mindfulness into Psychology and the Helping Professions.* Washington, D.C.: APA Books, 2010.

Shea, S. A. "The Breathing Patterns of Identical Twins." *Respiration Physiology* 75, no. 2 (1989): 211.

Siegel, D. *The Mindful Therapist*. New York: W.W. Norton, 2010.

Singh, N. N., R. G. Wahler, A. D. Adkins, et al. "Soles of the Feet: A Mindfulness-based Self-control Intervention for Aggression by an Individual with Mild Mental Retardation and Mental Illness." *Research in Developmental Disabilities* 24 (2003): 158–69.

Speca, M., L. E. Carlson, E. Goodey, et al. "A Randomized, Wait-list Controlled Clinical Trial: The Effect of a Mindfulness Meditation-based Stress Reduction Program on Mood and Symptoms of Stress in Cancer Outpatients." *Psychosomatic Medicine* 62 (2000): 613–22.

Stein, J. "Just Say OM." *Time,* August 4, 2003.

"Statistics." Vestibular Disorders Association. www.vestibular.org/vestibular-disorders/statistics.php. Accessed October 2, 2011.

Stevens, W. *The Palm at the End of the Mind: Selected Poems and a Play*. New York: Knopf, 1971.

Strosahl, K. D., S. C. Hayes, K. G. Wilson, et al. "An ACT Primer: Core Therapy Processes, Intervention Strategies, and Therapist Competencies." In Hayes, S. C., and K. D. Strosahl, eds. *A Practical Guide to Acceptance and Commitment Therapy*. New York: Springer, 2004.

Suzuki, D. T. *Mysticism: Christian and Buddhist*. New York: Harper & Brothers, 1957.

Suzuki, S. *Zen Mind, Beginner's Mind*. New York: Weatherhill, 1970.

Teigen, K. H. "Is a Sigh 'Just a Sigh'? Sighs as Emotional Signals and Responses to a Difficult Task." *Scandinavian Journal of Psychology* 49 (2008): 49–57.

Thera, N. *The Heart of Buddhist Meditation*. Boston: Weiser Books, 1965.

Tolle, E. *The Power of Now: A Guide to Spiritual Enlightenment*. Novato, Calif.: New World Library, 1999.

Trousselard, M., P. A. Barraud, V. Nougier, et al. "Contribution of Tactile and Interoceptive Cues to the Perception of the Direction of Gravity." *Cognitive Brain Research* 20, no. 3 (2004): 355–62.

Trungpa, C. *Cutting through Spiritual Materialism*. Berkeley: Shambhala, 1973.

Tuan, Y. *Space and Place: The Perspective of Experience*. Minneapolis: University of Minnesota Press, 1977.

Tweed, T. A. *The American Encounter with Buddhism, 1844–1912: Victorian Culture and the Limits of Dissent*. Bloomington: Indiana University Press, 1992.

———. "An American Pioneer in the Study of Religion: Hannah Adams (1755–1831) and Her *Dictionary of All Religions*." *Journal of the American Academy of Religion* 60, no. 3 (1992): 437–64.

Vanier, J. *Befriending the Stranger.* Grand Rapids, Mich.: William B. Eerdmans, 2005.

Vergunst, J. L. "Taking a Trip and Taking Care in Everyday Life." In Ingold, T., and J. L. Vergunst, eds. *Ways of Walking: Ethnography and Practice on Foot.* Burlington, Vt.: Ashgate, 2008.

Versluis, A. *American Transcendentalism and Asian Religions.* New York: Oxford University Press, 1993.

Vlemincx, E., J. Taelman, I. Van Diest, et al. "Take a Deep Breath: The Relief Effect of Spontaneous and Instructed Sights." *Physiology and Behavior* 101, no. 1 (2010): 67–73.

Vlemincx, E., I. Van Diest, P. M. Lehrer, et al. "Respiratory Variability Preceding and Following Sighs: A Resetter Hypothesis." *Biological Psychology* 84 (2010): 82–87.

Vlemincx, E., J. Taelman, S. De Peuter, et al. "Sigh Rate and Respiratory Variability during Mental Load and Sustained Attention." *Psychophysiology* 47 (2010): 1–4.

Vlemincx, E., I. Van Diest, S. De Peuter, et al. "Why Do You Sigh? Sigh Rate during Induced Stress and Relief." *Psychophysiology* 46 (2009): 1005–13.

Wagoner, D. Collected Poems (1956–1976). Bloomington: Indiana University Press, 1976.

Wakayama, S., Y. Kawahara, C. Li, et al. "Detrimental Effects of Microgravity on Mouse Preimplantation Development In Vitro." *PLoS ONE* 4, no. 8 (2009): e6753. doi:10.1371/journal.pone.0006753.

Wallace, R. K. "Physiological Effects of Transcendental Meditation." *Science* 167 (1970): 1751–54.

Walusinski, O. "Historical Perspectives." In Walusinski, O., ed. "The Mystery of Yawning in Physiology and Disease." *Frontiers of Neurological Neuroscience* 28 (2010): 1–21.

Wangh, S. *An Acrobat of the Heart: A Physical Approach to Acting Inspired by the Work of Jerzy Grotowski.* New York: Vintage, 2000.

Wang, Y., and W. P. Morgan. "The Effect of Imagery Perspectives on the Psychophysiological Responses to Imagined Exercise." *Behavioral Brain Research* 52 (1992): 167–74.

Watson, C. G., J. R. Tuorilla, K. S. Vickers, et al. "The Efficacies of Three Relaxation Regimens in the Treatment of PTSD in Vietnam War Veterans." *Journal of Clinical Psychology* 53, no. 8 (1997): 917–23.

Watts, A. *Beat Zen, Square Zen, and Zen.* San Francisco, Calif.: City Lights, 1959.

———. *In My Own Way: An Autobiography.* New York: Vintage, 1972.

———. *Joyous Cosmology: Adventures in the Chemistry of Consciousness.* New York: Pantheon, 1962.

———. *Psychotherapy East and West.* New York: Pantheon, 1961.

————. *This Is It: And Other Essays on Zen and Spiritual Experience.* New York: Pantheon, 1960.

————. *The Wisdom of Insecurity.* New York: Pantheon, 1951.

Watts, Alan, with Al Chung-liang Huang. *Tao: The Watercourse Way.* New York: Pantheon, 1975.

Watts, A., and C. Selver. "Alan Watts on the Work of Charlotte Selver and Charlotte Selver about Herself." ca. 1961 (compact disc). Sensory Awareness Foundation. http://www.sensoryawareness.org.

Western, P. J., and J. M. Patrick. "Effects of Focusing Attention on Breathing with and without Apparatus on the Face." *Respiration Physiology* 72 (1988): 123–30.

Wilhelm, F. H., W. Trabert, and W. T. Roth. "Characteristics of Sighing in Panic Disorder." *Biological Psychiatry* 49 (2001): 606–14.

Wolfe, J. M., et al. *Sensation and Perception.* 1st and 2nd eds. Sunderland, Mass.: Sinauer Associates, 2005, 2009.

Wuthnow, R. *After Heaven: Spirituality in America since the 1950s.* Berkeley: University of California Press, 1998.

INDEX

Page numbers in *italics* refer to illustrations.